BISON
BOOKS

T0341866

Kokomo Joe

The Story of the First

Japanese American Jockey

in the United States

John Christgau

UNIVERSITY OF NEBRASKA PRESS · LINCOLN AND
LONDON

Library of Congress
Cataloging-in-Publication Data

Christgau, John.
Kokomo Joe : the story of the first Japanese
American jockey in the United States / John
Christgau.
p. cm.
Includes bibliographical references.
ISBN 978-0-8032-1897-0 (pbk. : alk. paper)
1. Kobuki, Yoshio, 1918–1997. 2. Jockeys—
United States—Biography. 3. Horse racing—
United States—History. I. Title.
SF336.K63C47 2009
798.40092—dc22
[B]
2008037839

Set in Minion by Kimberly Essman.
Designed by R. W. Boeche.

For Erick, Sally, and Jennifer

Contents

Illustrations

Acknowledgments

In March 2003, in the coffee shop among the shedrows of Pleasanton racetrack, ex-jockey Junior Nicholson told me the story of Kokomo Joe's flight from Agua Caliente racetrack in Tijuana in order to escape the roundup of Japanese by Mexican authorities on December 7, 1941. I am grateful to Junior for planting the story seed. Scores of people and institutions helped me research the rest of the story.

The origins of President Roosevelt's Executive Order 9066 can be found in the little known WWII Alien Enemy Control Program (AECP). Grace Shimizu, Stephen Fox, Lawrence DiStasi, Heidi Donald, Ursula Potter, Satsuki Ina, and Karen Ebel have all written and lectured about the AECP. I am inspired by their continued work to educate historians and the public on how broad the original WWII dragnets of suspicion and fear were. I am also indebted to Tetsuden Kashima, Arnold Krammer, and Max Friedman, who have written about various aspects of the AECP. The late Edward Ennis shared his observations with me on the AECP and the critical meeting at Attorney General Francis Biddle's house in February 1942.

My thanks to the National Japanese American Historical Society in San Francisco, especially to Rosalyn Tonai, for making their archives available to me and for their leadership on AECP issues. The Japanese American National Museum in Los Angeles, particularly Susan Fukushima and Eddie Shinfuku, provided me with important government documents and background information on Japanese American internment. Karl Matsushita of the Japanese American National Library in San Francisco also made archival material available to me.

Elsie and Jiro Kobuki helped me piece together the events of Yoshio Kobuki's early life and his life after the war. Linda Ishii, Frank Kobuki, Fred Sasaki, Anna Kobuki, and Leslie Smith also provided me with leads or information on Kokomo Joe's early life.

Stan Flewelling's book *Shirakawa* is a gold mine of information on the Japanese American community in the White River Valley. For additional information on the Kent and Auburn communities, I am grateful to the White River Valley Museum, especially to Mae Iseri Yamada, and to the Greater Kent Historical Society. Steve Jensen made old Thomas School records and news stories available to me. Evan Lee showed me the lay of the White River Valley land. The Washington State Board of Health and the Washington State Historical Society provided critical documents. The Densho organization of Seattle is an extensive archive of Japanese American history and culture. I am grateful to Alice Ito for providing leads and documents from Densho's files. Additional information on the White River Valley and sports in the Japanese American community was provided by Joseph Svinth and Brian Niiya.

Steve Drinkuth and John Laird of the Gila Bend Tourist Center supplied me with documents, maps, pictures, and impressions, as well as helping me find the old Gillespie Ranch. Glen Birchfield of the *Gila Bend Sun* put out a call on my behalf for Gillespie Ranch historians. Gary Miller answered that call and provided me with documents, pictures, and leads.

Dr. Jorge Murga helped me find and then interview Francisco "Pancho" Rodriguez, who was in the jockeys' room at Caliente on December 7, 1941. Jim Brannon and Jay Jackson shared with me their recollections of C. E. "Charley" Brown. Roy Herberger of the *Galt Herald* made copies of his newspaper available to me. Dion Dubois gave me his recollections of racing and jockeys in the Pacific Northwest in 1947. The late Don Estes shared his research and his expertise on the experiences of the Japanese American communities from San Diego and Tijuana on December 7 and 8, 1941.

The following libraries provided access to newspaper microfilm and local histories: Stanford Green Library, University of California–Davis, C. W. "Doc" Pardee Memorial Library, and the Carleton F. Burke Memorial Library. Local public libraries from the following California cities provided newspaper microfilm: San Francisco, San Mateo, San Diego, Fresno, Eureka, Stockton, Modesto, Pleasanton, Livermore, Oakland, Chula Vista, and San Ysidro. Finally, through interlibrary loan arrangements, my own local Belmont Public Library and Linda Chiochios put the resources of libraries throughout the world at my fingertips.

Aloha Smith of the National Archives and Records Administration made Yoshio Kobuki's internment records available. California horse racing steward Pete Pedersen shared memories of Oscar Otis with me. Frank "Red" Bettendorf gave me recollections of the Humboldt County Fair as vivid as any of his masterpiece watercolors. Broadcaster Sam Spear led me to Hugh Bower, who witnessed the excitement of Kobuki's streak and the breakdown of Burgoo Sal Lea. If not for the racing notebooks of Hugh's mother Mary Bower, all records of Kokomo Joe's riding at Crescent City and Eureka's Redwood Acres would be lost.

A dozen research outriders provided documents and help: Linda Eade of the Yosemite Research Library; Jay Feldman, who contributed helpful material on J. Edgar Hoover's early list keeping; Arthur Hansen and Greg Robinson, who enthusiastically provided documents on internment, especially Poston; Greg Dubois and Joe Feren, who filled in the details of Kokomo Joe's life in racetrack parking lots; David Beltran, whose history of Caliente proved fascinating; my neighbor Bob Paulus, who gave me his written reflections of life in Gardena; Ruth Okimoto, who gave me leads and background information on life at Poston; and Ann Ito, who told me again and again that the story was about much more than horse racing.

Without turf writers Oscar Otis and Abe Kemp, who reported often on little-known jockeys and inconspicuous figures in the Sport of Kings, Kokomo Joe's story would be forgotten. Officials at Bay Meadows racetrack, especially Tansy Brook, Kay Webb, and Eric Lacey, gave me access to the books, documents, and *Daily Racing Form* charts kept in the William P. Kyne Memorial Library. Dean Smith and Mac McBride at Del Mar racetrack, with the help of Gary Meads, found the promotional film footage featuring Kokomo Joe. Stuart Titus, chairman of the Humboldt County Fair Board, dug out of their archives 16MM film footage of Kokomo Joe setting riding records at Ferndale.

Debbie Bell and Jacki Rhodes provided important medical and legal documents from the Sacramento County Clerk's office. My brother Dr. Roger Christgau helped me interpret those documents. Finally, T. A. and Jan Farrell were kind enough to take me into their ranch home for an afternoon of vivid but often difficult recollections of Kokomo Joe's last days.

Kokomo Joe

The Pocket Baby

He was born a month premature and was so tiny and blue with cold that the Japanese midwives who delivered him on October 17, 1918, had to put him in an oven to give him warmth and life. But as soon as they took him out of the oven incubator, he went dead blue again. It wasn't until the fourth oven resurrection that it was clear he would survive and that he was given the name Yoshio.

"He is no bigger than a peanut," the midwives said. His father, Kotaro Kobuki, joked that he could carry him in the pocket of his suit coat.

His mother, Yoshino, was hardly back on her feet again from the birth of Yoshio when she fell ill. At first no one could tell Kotaro what was wrong with his wife. For two days she lay writhing on a crude bed in the four-room clapboard cabin outside the village of Thomas, Washington. Here, in the White River Valley east of Seattle, Kotaro was a truck farmer on five acres of leased cropland. Even in the December cold and fog of the valley, Yoshino sweated and spiked a fever. Her lips and fingertips turned blue. The magnificent roll of black hair that encircled her head began to disintegrate, and shards of wet hair lay plastered against her forehead. She developed skin blisters that popped and made her crackle like a low fire as she thrashed on the bed. What was it? The Black Death? Typhoid Fever?

"She'll be fine," the midwives told Kotaro. "It is 'the miasma,'" they insisted as putrefactions hung in the atmosphere like fog. Kotaro was advised to burn sulfur on the kitchen range. Or sprinkle the cabin with salt and vinegar and a mixture of spices. They told him to make bonfires in the fields.

None of these measures helped. Yoshino began coughing up blood and screaming in pain. She could no longer nurse her tiny baby Yoshio. Wet nurses had to be found. A doctor from the nearby town of Kent paid a visit. "It is," he said, "the Spanish Flu, an invisible but vicious virus that attacks the body in mutant swarms like pirates with grappling hooks attacking a ship."

The sickness was sweeping the world, he explained. It had begun the previous February in Kansas among soldiers recruited for the Great War and stacked close together in barracks bunks. From there it had hop-scotched across the country. Then it had jumped to Europe, South America, Asia, and finally Africa. It was highly contagious. Priests had even died while administering the sacraments to other victims.

The doctor told Kotaro to be sure that his wife drank plenty of water and gargled. "Use antiseptic sprays," the doctor instructed. "Let her breathe fresh air." The windows of the cabin should be kept open so that fresh air could circulate.

Yoshino grew worse. The midwives could not stop the bleeding from her nose. Finally, Kotaro took her to the small hospital in Kent. He was stunned to see everybody—nurses, doctors, patients—wearing white masks. How were any of *them* able to breathe fresh air?

Yoshino lay moaning and screaming in a small ward of the hospital with white sheets hung between the beds in a hopeless effort to seal off the contagion. She complained of a fire in her lungs. In an effort to breathe, she bridged herself in bed like a wrestler trying to escape a tight hold. Kotaro stood at her bedside nervously stroking his bald head, his eyes as vacant as two chunks of coal stuck in the face of a snowman.

Within ten days Yoshino Maeda Kobuki was dead, one of what would eventually be six hundred and seventy-five thousand deaths from the Spanish Flu in the United States and fifty million worldwide. She was cremated and her ashes buried on a drizzly day that December in a small cemetery in Kent, Washington. At the graveside ceremony, her five children surrounded her—her firstborn son Minoru, eleven; then sons Yoneo, nine, and Satoru, five, each wearing neat caps and thick black coats buttoned to the throat against the cold; seven-year-old daughter Matsuko also in a buttoned coat and a tiny cloche hat with a satin ribbon; and finally Yoshio, the pocket baby, wrapped in a receiving blanket and wearing a knit bonnet that fit his head as tightly as a jockey's cap, sound asleep in the crook of his father's arm.

Kotaro and Yoshino Kobuki had come to the White River Valley from the Hiroshima Prefecture in 1908. The first settlers who had come to the valley had found dense forests, thick with cedar, maple, and salmonberry bushes. Loggers had cleared the land. Then farmers planted crops between the stumps. The White River Valley became the lettuce capital of the world, a fertile crescent of wealth and prosperity. All you needed to succeed was a willingness to work hard.

Sure, America was a strange land, full of machinery and cowboys, but with the neat, snow-capped cone of Mt. Rainier in the distance, the White River Valley could just as well have been Japan. Tacoma's Mount Fuji, local residents called Rainier. And by 1915 hopeful Japanese were coming in a steady stream, mostly like Kotaro and Yoshino Kobuki from the Hiroshima Prefecture. They got five-acre land leases on which to raise lettuce, peas, blackberries, and strawberries. In the summer they worked ten-hour days in the hot sun. Their first English words were "water ... drink."

They were eager to fit in, to learn the ways of the New World. When eating soup, they were advised, don't make slurping noises. Meet the eyes of Americans. Do not bow repeatedly. When walking down the street, stop and stand at attention when the National Anthem is played.

Despite the promises of a Garden of Eden, they were not welcome. Officials protested that no alien—white, red, black, or yellow—should ever own a foot of land. The Japanese were called bandy-legged, degenerate, rotten little devils, an objectionable race. It was said that they ate food a hog wouldn't eat. They even ate thrushes and song birds. It was a moral outrage to hire them as laborers or to patronize their businesses. They were not the stuff from which American citizens were made. The white and brown races would never mix. Nor ever live side by side.

Kotaro Kobuki could not help wondering about the promise of success for his children in the New World. Their mother was dead. For the moment only Minoru was big enough and strong enough to help with the farming. The others would soon be expected to work so hard and so long they wouldn't even have time to dream. Meanwhile, a permanent wet nurse needed to be found for Yoshio.

It seemed wise to send the four younger ones back to Japan, where despite their birth on American soil, they were still considered citizens of Japan. They would be welcome there. They could have dreams there and learn the language and culture of their ancestors. Only Minoru would stay behind, to help his father in the fields of the White River Valley.

In Japan Okuma Tanaka agreed to take custody of her dead sister's children. Okuma and her husband Hiro had three children of their own. They knew the responsibilities of parenting. Further, they had a spacious home with a red tile roof on a quiet, narrow, one-lane road in the country outside Hiroshima. The home was at the end of a box canyon with pink flowers and steep forested hillsides. There was plenty of room in the house and outside for the seven children to play and roam. Meanwhile, the couple found a Japanese wet nurse for Yoshio. Kotaro regularly sent money for the support of his four children.

But it was as if the Spanish Flu was tracking the Kobuki children like a demonic killer, relentlessly picking them off in order, first Yoneo, then Matsuko, and finally Satoru. The same viral pirates with grappling hooks that had killed their mother now attacked them. They screamed and bled and gasped for air and then died. One by one, they were buried in a terraced family graveyard beside the red-tiled house, the piled tombstones so old and weathered by the wind of ages that they looked like prehistoric cairns.

Only Yoshio survived. But if good fortune had been his birthright, he gave no sign of it as he grew up in Japan. He kept to himself, disobeyed Okuma and Hiro, refused to go to school, and often ran away. Repeatedly Okuma and Hiro had to send officials to find him. When the officials finally brought him back, sometimes after days, his only explanation was that he had been walking and walking. He had slept on a beach somewhere, heavy with the smell of kelp and the racket of seagulls squawking at him. But it was no worse, he felt, than living beside the bleak graveyard that held his brothers and sister.

He became an oddity in Japan. He was supposed to be an American, from a land where everything and everybody was larger than life, a land of strutting cowboys and Paul Bunyan. But he was the smallest child in school, and the other children bullied him because he was so tiny. When teachers tried to instruct him in the Four Noble Truths of Buddhism, the endless talk of suffering and pain bored him. All the admonitions against murder and theft and lust and guile and drink—what did they have to do with him? He was an open book. He wished nobody harm. He told the truth. He only wanted to be by himself. That was when he was the happiest.

Then in 1932 the Japanese newspapers and magazines began carrying pictures of the tenth Olympic Games in Los Angeles. All Japan celebrated the success of the Japanese athletes, who ranked fifth among all countries as medal winners. But pictures of the post-Olympics ceremonies at the ballrooms of the magnificent Biltmore Hotel pictured shy Japanese athletes having to be dragged onto the dance floor. At the same time American men wearing two-toned shoes and purple suit coats danced and smiled. There were also pictures of sleek American airplanes, swift motorcars, and wooden speedboats. Americans worshipped speed. And they were daring and cocky. But they knew how to unwind. They knew how to sit in the back seat of a chauffeured motorcar and do nothing but smoke a long cigarette.

Joe admired these Americans and their ways. So what was Yoshio Kobuki doing in Japan? It was a land of stiff courtesies and strange, tedious music. He was expected to be obedient. To study long and hard. To keep a grave and quiet countenance, reflecting the silence of the box canyon. It was as if any jubilation would give offense to the sad ancestral ghosts haunting the family's graveyard.

In 1934 Hiro Satoh, the third-ranked tennis player in the world, was sent to Europe by the Japanese government to act as a tennis-playing ambassador. Satoh was a quiet, methodical player who had fallen in love with a Japanese girl. He had tried to give up international tennis in order to marry the girl, but the Japanese government had insisted on continued tours. One night in the summer of 1934, in the Straits of Malacca, on an ocean liner bound for Europe and more tennis, Satoh jumped ship in order to return to Japan and his love.

It was the kind of exciting initiative that was entirely missing from the life of young Yoshio Kobuki, and with the help of one of his cousins, he began scratching out crude letters to his father in America. "There is nothing in Japan for me," he complained. He was an American. The only thing he wanted was a chance to return to the promise and excitement of what he felt was his true native land.

He had no idea what he would do once he got there. He was only fifteen years old. His guardians had tried to make him go to junior high school in Japan, but he had stopped going to school all together. Now he could hardly read or write. And he remained small—not yet five feet tall or a hundred pounds. He was still a peanut, but he was filled with powerful desire. He was strong in his legs from all the walking. Maybe in America he could work in the fields. Or he could learn to drive a motorcar and chauffeur rich Americans with their long cigarettes. His father or his brother Minoru, who had acquired the American name of Frank and who had married and was prospering, could teach him to do *something.* Because anything was possible in America. And so in September 1934 Yoshio Kobuki packed a small cardboard suitcase with what few belongings he had and boarded a ship out of Tokyo for what he said was home.

2

Kokomo Joe

In America Yoshio remained silent and distant. If he spoke at all, it was in half English and half Japanese, and no one understood him. He was never without a broad, toothy smile that was disarming at the same time that it was baffling. If he was so happy, why wouldn't he speak except to answer yes or no? He became a solitary figure wherever he went, a loner for reasons nobody understood.

His first English words were profanities that he sprinkled in his odd language without knowing what they meant. He used them because they suggested that he at least knew *some* English. His father watched his struggle and insisted that he go to school to study English.

But where was he to go? The two nearby high schools in the White River Valley towns of Kent and Auburn offered nothing for him. There were splash parties and dance socials and oratorical contests, but he could neither swim nor dance, and his English was strange. Meanwhile, the schools were well attended by Japanese American teenagers who were among the very best students. But he could hardly read or write. His classmates would wonder what was wrong with him. He would be ridiculed and humiliated.

The only other choice was the little brick elementary schoolhouse in Thomas, Washington, which was attended mostly by the children of Japanese farmers. In an effort to capture the good will engendered by the Japanese government's planting of cherry trees in the Tidal Basin of the nation's capitol, the Japanese Association of the White River Valley had planted a dozen cherry trees beside the playground of Thomas School. The commemorative plaque for the cherry trees read, "The flowers transfer our emotion of love, appreciation, and gratitude, when words somehow fall short." *When words somehow fall short.* It was as if this phrase was commemorating Yoshio Kobuki's struggle with English.

Yoshio was not much bigger than the first graders he would be expected to sit among if he went to Thomas School. However, they had chirpy voices and played silly games, while he was almost old enough to shave regularly. His smile would not hide his humiliation, and he again refused to go to school.

He took the American name Joe with the expectation that it would make him seem to be less odd and foreign, and he began to look for a job. But the so-called American land of opportunity, which had seemed so inviting in those pictures he had seen in Japan, now offered him little. Jobs were so scarce that White River Valley newspapers were urging employers to offer a five-dollar job to the unemployed as a Christmas gift. It was the heart of the Depression, and there were few offers because there simply were no jobs to offer anybody. At night the valley was filled with the screeching, lonely whistles of freight trains passing through. It was as if even the giant locomotives were howling with hunger, and it frazzled nerves. How do we "shake the depression," the newspapers wondered, suggesting that the malaise was deeper and more tangled than simple economics.

It was especially depressing for the Japanese in the valley. White citizens had had their fill of the Japanese immigrants who had kept coming and coming. Books warned of racial pollution. In

1922 the Supreme Court ruled that Orientals couldn't become naturalized citizens. It meant permanent alienation in the land of opportunity. Then President Coolidge had signed the National Origin Acts of 1924 that prohibited Asian immigration. Finally, the Anti-Japanese League of the state of Washington had helped to pass laws prohibiting aliens from owning land. The Japanese had gotten around it by registering their American children as the property owners. But truck farming just a few acres of land permitted them to do little more than survive.

Meanwhile, what would have been Joe Kobuki's high school class graduated from Auburn High. "Many times we shall be in despair," the valedictory speaker observed at graduation. "We'll have the blues . . . then laugh it off and start anew again." Finally, as if directly addressing the onetime pocket baby Joe Kobuki, who was still not five feet tall or a hundred pounds, the speaker finished, "Success is not measured by ounces or pounds. Ah, no, not even by size."

Joe Kobuki finally found work in the valley as a lettuce crate packer for twenty cents an hour. It seemed promising work, with Lettuce Festivals and a Lettuce Queen, and even President Roosevelt invited to come and join the celebrations. But it was long hours of standing in a noisy warehouse with an endless chainline bringing lettuce heads at him, then still more hours of work on his father's little truck farm, sometimes late into the night under floodlights and with the background dirges of those passing freight trains sounding their lonely whistles while hobos dangled their feet from the boxcar doors. The hard work was hardly what he had been led to expect from those pictures he had admired of rich American men lounging in the back seat of chauffeured motorcars.

He then moved in with his brother Frank in South Park, a suburb of Seattle and found work with a wealthy family as a "houseboy," or what the Japanese called a "schoolboy," who was little more than a nanny for children only a little smaller than he was. He also had his brother Frank teach him how to drive. If he couldn't be the rich, cigarette-smoking idler in the back seat of a limousine, he could at least be the black-capped driver in leather gloves and a neat suit. And for two years he found temporary jobs around Seattle as a chauffeur. His ever-present smile and the stiff courtesies that he had been forced to learn in Japan complemented his uniform, and he earned as much as sixty dollars a month smiling broadly and driving the rich around Seattle.

But his brother Frank warned him that, until he learned English or educated himself in college, he would never be more than a menial servant.

"What good will college do?" he countered. "College graduates can't find jobs either." Still, he ought to learn to do *something* besides sit at the wheel of an automobile all day long.

Sports had always served as an entry point for young immigrants trying to assimilate quickly. Joe's tiny body was stringy and muscular, and he had strong legs and whiplike arms. His brother urged him to take up American baseball, perhaps as an infielder. Joe scoffed at the idea. It was a tedious, slow game that had no appeal for him.

Well, there was a nearby judo association he could join. But as soon as he joined, he found that all the exhilaration of sport was lost in a barrage of instruction on the spiritual components of judo. It was lessons in Buddhism all over again.

When he wasn't working as a chauffeur, he sat all day long in his brother's home in South Park, looking at magazine pictures or listening to the radio. For Frank it was hard enough feeding and caring for his own three children. Why should he have to bear the additional burden of a lazy houseguest, even if it was his own kid brother, whose habit of silence and solitude was irritating and who always wore a silly smile that seemed to border on a leer—as if he was indulging the shortcomings of Frank's family? It came to a head one afternoon.

"Why don't you finally learn English," Frank asked him. "Educate yourself. Find real work. Stop fantasizing that some day you will be a rich movie boy."

That night Joe packed the small cardboard suitcase that he had brought with him from Japan. Then he went to see his father and say goodbye, after which he hopped a train carrying lettuce to Los Angeles.

He had just turned twenty when he showed up at his cousin's home in Los Angeles in late 1938 carrying his cardboard suitcase and smelling of campfire smoke. His cousin was married, had three children, and was scratching out a living selling groceries at a little store in Gardena.

His cousin told Joe that he couldn't stay at his house without getting a job. But Joe sat around the house all day looking at magazine pictures and listening to the radio. He shared a bedroom with his cousin's son Jiro, who was just beginning high school. Joe's only talk was to brag about how independent he had been in Japan. His guardians had tried to make him go to school and to obey. So had his brother Frank. But he didn't want or need anybody pestering him with a lot of useless advice and rules. He could figure out on his own what he wanted to do and how to do it. Then one night with Jiro the talk turned into an argument and shouting. The two boys had to be separated, and his cousin ordered him to leave. "Get a job!"

The radio news was that Santa Anita Race Track had opened. Tucked up against the wall of the San Gabriel Mountains, the track seemed an inviting playground, utterly free of irritating stiff rules of conduct. Those magazines he read pictured rich gamblers wearing bowties standing alongside bathing beauties and movie actors, all of them flashing exactly the same broad smiles that had become his trademark. It was obvious that a good smile was the passkey to American success.

Carrying his small suitcase again, Joe hitchhiked across Los Angeles to Santa Anita racetrack. He made his way through a sea of pansies planted around the track to a gate at the backstretch, where a guard in a baggy suit and a police hat stopped him.

"Excuse please," he managed to stammer through his smile, but he wanted a job "guiding the horse." A group of stable hands watching broke out laughing. The guard wanted to know his name.

"Joe."

"Joe what?"

"Joe Kobuki."

"You a Jap?"

"No, I am an *American*," he said.

One of the stable hands began a scornful, singsong chant. *Kokomo Joe, Kokomo Joe, Kokomo Joe!* The others all laughed again. Joe tried to explain that he had heard on the radio that seventeen jockeys had been banned from the track. So who would they get to "guide the horse"? What he meant was that he wanted to be a jockey. He was small and strong and fearless. But the only work he could find was as a "hot walker," walking horses to cool them down after their races.

Owners and trainers let him sleep in one of the empty stalls. He was up at dawn, awakened by the smell of fresh coffee and fried bacon coming from the cook shack. Then he spent the rest of the morning mucking out stalls, watering horses, and cleaning tack. He began to smell like manure and straw. They told him that it was work he had to learn to do if he wanted to be a jockey, but after a month of standing with the railbirds and clockers watching other stable boys take horses through workouts in the morning light, he grew impatient and asked to be allowed to exercise horses. He was small but strong he insisted.

"Please, to exercise!" he pleaded.

"Can you speak English? You have to speak goddam English if you want to ride."

"I'm learning," he said. "I am getting better, day for day."

They finally let him exercise horses for fifty cents a mount in the half light of dawn, sometimes only the white of his teeth visible behind a constant smile that reflected the pleasure it gave him to be galloping horses, the wind streaming against his face and making his eyes water. During the day, while the other hot walkers and stable boys napped from the exhaustion of being up at dawn, he stood at the rail and studied every move of jockeys with names like Johnny and Jack and George and Ralph. He congratulated himself for having settled on the nickname Joe because it reflected who he really was, as American as the Johnnies and Jacks and Georges who had valets who shined their boots and lit their cigarettes.

Even if he didn't look much like Johnny Longden or George Woolf, he knew it was only *size* that mattered. Jockeys had to be tiny and compact, and he could claim that he was even *smaller* than the Johnnies and Georges. He could fold his body into a weightless feather. The horses would hardly know he was there. Yet if they became fractious or willful during a race, then they would meet *his* will, which seemed to materialize out of thin air like a tight fist.

The grooms and stable boys in the shedrows told him there had never been a Jap jockey. True, they were small enough, that was for sure. Maybe *too* small. A thousand-pound thoroughbred needed more than a peanut in the saddle to keep the horse's mind on his running business.

In spite of that, Joe saw that there were large numbers of Japanese who came to the track each afternoon and followed the races. There had even been a filly named Banzai with Japanese owners. She hadn't been much of a horse, but she proved that there was a place for the Japanese at racetracks. So however odd and quiet he was, he wasn't an alien from outer space. Trainers and grooms were all calling him Kokomo Joe now. He had no idea where Kokomo was until he looked it up on a map and saw that it was nearly the bull's-eye of North America. Even if they had laughed when they first hung the nickname on him, it was a nickname that he thought fit perfectly because it put him in the center of America.

In March 1939 there were ominous war rumblings in Europe, but it seemed to have little to do with America. Sixty-five thousand jubilant racing fans including Kokomo Joe Kobuki watched Kayak II, a stablemate of Seabiscuit, win the Santa Anita Handicap. On getaway day in mid-March, jockeys, trainers, stable boys, exercise riders, and horses began moving out of the gates of Santa Anita in a steady caravan that headed back east or north for the Bay Area, where Tanforan racetrack would open in a week and Bay Meadows in May.

For Kokomo Joe it had been a good three months, during which he had learned that he loved everything about horse racing, from the smell of the wet infield grass when he exercised horses at dawn to the sound of a radio playing music somewhere in the shedrows late at night like a taps meant to put horses and stable boys and grooms to sleep. The only thing he wanted now was the chance to be a jockey and to enjoy the episodic thrills that came with riding. No sooner was one race finished and the blood-boiling excitement over than it was time to get ready for the next race. But the meet was over. The stables were almost empty, the horses were gone, the music had stopped. So now where would he go?

He headed north, hitchhiking with his suitcase to Tanforan racetrack in San Bruno. He mucked stalls, hot-walked horses, exercised mounts in the morning, and pleaded with trainers and owners in his fractured English to give him a chance to "guide" their horses in races. "To win, please!" he assured them with a smile. "To bring the first place!" But they said he was too small and stringy or too stupid in English to follow directions. The best he could ever hope to be was an exercise boy.

That fall Hitler attacked Poland and the prospect of a world war involving America seemed closer than ever. But it had little to do with Kokomo Joe, who moved to Bay Meadows racetrack where he continued to plead his case with trainers. Then one day in 1940 a sympathetic trainer told him that the place for him to break in as a rider was at the Fairgrounds in Phoenix, where they ran Saturday and Sunday racing and where the riders were second- and third-rate jockeys just like him trying to learn to ride. The Phoenix Fairgrounds had been the place, they told him, where many a successful jockey had broken in to racing. If his aim was truly to be a professional jockey, then the bush leagues or Phoenix were the places to start, not Bay Meadows or Hollywood Park, where the jockeys were among the best in the world. Just after New Year's Day in 1941, Joe packed his suitcase again and caught a bus heading south to Los Angeles, then up over the San Bernardino Mountains and down into Thousand Palms, past the frying pan of Thermal and into the fire of Blythe, across the Colorado River, and finally into Arizona and Phoenix.

He rode his first mount in Phoenix on January 11, 1941. It was a six-furlong race with a dozen horses and nearly as many green riders whose mounts drifted in and out during the race. Joe took his mount to the rail, then wide, finally back to the rail again, but he could not find a clear path "to bring the first place," and he finished in the middle of the pack. The following Saturday he did no better in a race in which half the riders were apprentices. On the backstretch he found himself bunched in a clot of horses from which there was no exit, and this time he loped home dead last.

In the third week turf writers noted that he was the "only representative of the Japanese race to venture atop" a thoroughbred. They made it sound as if he were a pioneering mountain climber instead of a jockey. Then, in order to avoid a backstretch clot of horses like the one that had frustrated him the previous week, he sprinted to the lead and was racing along all by himself, smiling broadly at the triumph of his strategy, when his horse, suddenly exhausted by the breakneck pace, slowed to a near walk while the field raced by him.

Either as a jockey or a pioneer, Joe was having his troubles. Over the month of January he had piloted three horses to poor finishes. It had been a disappointing start as a jockey. And at the close of the Fairground meet at the end of January, he knew that he had done nothing to distinguish himself from the dozens of other apprentices who, like him, had gone there to break into racing. Who would want his services now? Where could he go next?

The answer came from a stranger with a perfectly round face, chubby cheeks, and a perpetual smile as broad as Kokomo Joe's. He said his name was C. E. "Charley" Brown Jr. He owned and trained horses, he explained, and he had noticed Kokomo Joe in the Phoenix races.

"I've never seen a jockey quite so small and compact," he said. "Why aren't there *other* Japanese jockeys?" he wanted to know.

Joe shook his head. He had no idea why there weren't.

Well, it didn't matter. What mattered was that at this point, Kokomo Joe wasn't much of a rider. Joe nodded.

"Who taught you how to ride?" Joe shrugged. *Nobody* had taught him.

"Well, it shows," Charley Brown told him. "Oh, you have courage enough," Brown conceded. It was the only reason Joe had gotten mounts in the first place. Trainers were eager to find jockeys for young horses that were so fractious and unschooled only a greenhorn desperate for mounts would agree to ride them. If he went on riding that way, he'd kill himself. Joe's smile disappeared.

"Are you willing to *learn* to be a jockey?"

"Sure, sure," Joe said. He smiled again. "Study! Learn to be!"

"You will have to learn *pace*. Do you even know what pace is?"

Joe shook his head.

"You have to learn how to *rate* a horse," Brown explained. "However, you sit as tight as any jockey I have ever seen. Where did you learn that?"

Joe smiled and shrugged again. Brown nodded. OK, he would pay Kokomo Joe forty dollars a month plus room and board. But Joe would also be expected to do chores on the ranch.

"Ranch? Where?"

"The Gillespie Land and Irrigation Company in Gila Bend, Arizona." Joe shook his head. He didn't know where that was.

"It is in the middle of the Sonoran Desert," Brown explained. "There is nothing out there except cactus and sage and rattlesnakes. But they had all the water they wanted." Water? Sure. Water was OK. Charley Brown laughed and then shook Kokomo Joe's hand to seal their agreement. The next morning, with his suitcase alongside him in the back of a pickup truck pulling a van of race horses and trailing a rope of dust, Kokomo Joe headed into the Sonoran Desert.

3

Mister Charley

It was the largest and hottest desert in North America, a bone-dry wasteland of creosote bush and bursage, described as a place "on the road to somewhere else." But if it led anywhere, it was straight to hell, and the only inhabitants for centuries had been sun-baked Indians who lived in mud huts. It would have been a flaming hell in *this world* if the waters of the Gila River hadn't flowed through the heart of the Sonoran Desert. There were cottonwoods along the banks of the river, and the huge saguaro cactus seemed to be lifting their arms to heaven as a thank-you for the cool blessings of the river.

As a young man Bernard Gillespie had played college football, had his nose hammered flat in boxing, gone to sea as a whale harpooner, learned to fly airplanes, become an expert trap shooter, and prospected for gold. In the 1920s Gillespie dammed the Gila River and built a network of canals that formed the Gillespie Land and Irrigation Company, the world's largest private irrigation system. He laid out an eighty thousand–acre ranch in the middle of nowhere. He built an adobe mansion, put in an airstrip, ran cattle, and planted a neat row of palm trees. Only the dark, sawtooth line of the distant mountains broke the manmade, boxy order of the dirt roads, canals, and fence lines of the huge ranch.

Gillespie eventually bought a string of thoroughbreds from a friend who had been thrown out of Mexico for fixing races. Gillespie cleared the creosote bushes and carved out a training track with banked turns and wood rails where the ranch hands—Mexicans, Pima Indians, gringos, gypsy grooms, rich Eastern dandies looking for adventure, and Depression Oakies who jumped off passing freight trains and then begged for jobs—sat on the fence rails like crows and watched the workouts and the mock races and cheered for their favorite horses.

Even Hollywood got wind of Gillespie's desert kingdom and shortly before Kokomo Joe Kobuki arrived, they filmed *The Gentleman from Arizona* on the ranch. It was a sappy story that melded race horses and romance and featured a wild horse named Sky Rex, whose improbable victory in the Arizona Derby saves the ranch and its owner from bankruptcy.

No one took special notice of Kokomo Joe Kobuki when he arrived at the ranch in the company of Charley Brown. He was just another itinerant ranch hand who had blown into the desert colony like a tumbleweed. He was quiet and polite and kept to himself. He was expected to fit in as he worked side by side with all the other drifters who found a place to sleep on the straw in an empty horse stall.

"Mister Charley," Kokomo Joe took to calling Charley Brown. It was a nickname that captured the incongruous mix of sternness and good humor that was the mark of Brown's character. He had been born in Kansas in 1905, the son of a horseman and veterinarian who taught him to love horses if not school, which he quickly quit. He was a promising jockey until he got too husky and fat to ride. Then he began traveling county fairs as a squat rodeo clown who wore a peppermint suit and a painted smile. His legs were so bowed that they said he could have carried a basketball between them. His act included a trained mule and a Brahma bull that jumped cars. "The mule can do anything," he bragged, "except cash a mutuel ticket." He learned how to make people laugh, and that painted, oversized smile stayed with him after the makeup was gone and he began training horses. As a trainer, Brown expected obedience and hard work beginning at dawn, and if he caught a groom or a jockey he was training asleep in the shedrows, he would chase them with a pitchfork or throw ice water on them.

Somewhere along the way, his path crossed with the magnetic Bernard Gillespie, and they formed a partnership. Brown and Gillespie Stables, they called themselves, but as soon as the racing enterprise was in full swing, with red, white, and blue silks and stables for the growing string of horses, Bernard Gillespie took off on another new adventure and left the racing stables in the hands of Charley Brown.

Mister Charley felt that the big racetracks, like Hollywood Park and Santa Anita, were nothing but tinsel and gloss. County fairs, he said, were like home to him, and he preferred to take his string of race horses to bush league or county fair racetracks, where the purses were small but there were no pretenses or affectations and where people laughed.

Money did not seem to be an issue with him. In 1940 he had only ten victories and not even five thousand dollars in purse money. But he remained confident and cheerful and went right on smiling, despite his infrequent victories. When race officials came through the stable areas desperate to find any horses to fill races with small fields, Mister Charley was always ready to accommodate them.

"But is your horse ready to run? Can he win?"

"The horse is *ready*," he answered. "He can win. I'll give my 'Oklahoma Guarantee' on it."

"An 'Oklahoma Guarantee'? What's that?"

"I can't say for sure," he answered through his broad smile. "Because my horses *always* win, and I have never had to make good on the guarantee."

Mister Charley delivered jokes and praise wherever he went. For a time, he felt that jockeys, many of whom were orphans or runty runaways who had already been pummeled enough by life, were especially deserving of pats on the back. Besides, what sense did it make to heap more abuse on jockeys who were busy mucking out stalls, exercising horses at dawn for pennies, and suffering terrifying spills?

Then late in 1939 Mister Charley made a special trip to Tanforan racetrack to purchase the contract of a new, seventeen-year-old promising jockey from Idaho named Ellis Gray. Mister Charley praised Gray and boasted to other owners that under his training young Gray would soon be a world-class jockey. But not long after Brown bought Gray's contract, the news broke: six jockeys, including Gray, had been part of a jockeys' ring that southern California gamblers had recruited to fix races. Gray was suspended pending a trial.

Mister Charley was led to reexamine his premises concerning how to judge and train jockeys. Maybe flattery and praise had only served to spoil them, he felt. Or worse, corrupt them. Telling them again and again how good they were—maybe it all went to their heads, and they wound up thinking they didn't have to follow the rules.

With Joe Mister Charley secretly told the other ranch hands that he had had a chance to watch "the new Japanese boy" ride in Phoenix. Joe was so tiny that he would *never* have to worry about making weight. There would never be Pluto Water or other disgusting emetics in his life. He would never be so weak from starving himself that he couldn't even be booted up on a horse. The boy had good hands. He had strong legs, too. And he kept a good seat on a horse. Other trainers in Phoenix liked his courage.

But Mister Charley said he didn't intend to spoil the new boy like he'd spoiled the others. His plan now was to tell Kokomo Joe how bad he was. Brown would insist to Joe that he couldn't ride, that he'd *never* be any good, that he was too headstrong, and that he'd have to learn how to follow simple directions. "And don't pester me about when you're ready to ride in races again," he told Kokomo Joe. "I'll *tell* you when you're ready!"

At first Mister Charley only gave Joe menial jobs on the ranch, like teaching the hounds to hunt coons and desert wildcats. Once a ranch visitor showed up with a flat tire, and Mister Charley barked at Joe to fix it. However, the dull chores failed to discourage Kokomo Joe or to stop his smile, and when the tire was fixed, he wanted Mister Charley to tell him what to fix next.

The nearby town of Gila Bend had been established where the Gila River looped south. It had been described as an "oasis in the desert . . . where weary travelers stopped to rest." When the two went into Gila Bend for supplies, Kokomo Joe drove the pickup while Mister Charley delivered a steady string of orders and advice. Once they got into town, Brown splashed ice-cold water in Kokomo Joe's face. It wasn't just meant to keep him awake at the wheel in the suffocating afternoon heat. It was also meant to rid him of all smugness and to be as humiliating as a pie in the face. But the brickbats and the cold water failed to disguise Mister Charley's good nature, which was as irrepressible as his smile, and Kokomo Joe smiled right back through it all and insisted, "The cold water feels fine, Mister Charley, just fine. It is exactly what I need to stay awake."

It was months of mucking stalls and training dogs to hunt coons before Mister Charley let Joe get on a racehorse. The hardest thing for Kokomo Joe to learn was pace. Again and again, Mister Charley sat on the training track rail with a huge stopwatch on a string bob and told Joe to take his mount around one lap in exactly one minute. Or fifty seconds. Or a minute and thirteen seconds.

"For the best jockeys," Mister Charley told him, "time ticks off in their heads during a race like a grandfather clock in an empty house." Joe had to learn to judge his horse's speed by the rate at which the rail posts flashed past at the edge of his vision. When they finally got to the fairground tracks, Mister Charley assured him, he'd be able to see those white posts go flashing by and regulate his horse's speed accordingly.

But his first attempts to complete a lap in exactly the time Mister Charley called for weren't even close. Mister Charley scowled. "Can't you even count?"

"Yes, I can count."

"In English? Or Japanese!"

"Both."

Mister Charley ordered Joe to go again. This time, fifty-seven ticks. But when Joe finished the lap, Mister Charley stuck out the big stopwatch and said Joe was way off. "Way off! A damn vulture can tell time better. Go again!" It was weeks before he could complete a lap in precisely the number of seconds that Charley Brown dictated.

"Well, all right," Mister Charley said, trying to hide his pleasure behind a grumpy surface. "It's about time!" Then he laughed because it *was* all about time.

In early April 1941 grooms loaded the vans, piled into Charley Brown's pickup, and headed for Agua Caliente racetrack in Tijuana, Mexico. They formed a caravan of horses and grooms and stable boys winding their way out of the desert, leaving the Gillespie Land and Irrigation Company behind them. The oasis in the desert of weary travelers and drifters of every kind hadn't been the real world. With its plentiful water, it hadn't even been the real world of the desert. But who cared? The real world beyond the distant edges of the Sonoran Desert was a world of cities and trinkets, with people laminated by wealth and fame and color into layers as separate and distinct as those in a cake.

Kokomo Joe drove while Charley Brown sat with a map on his lap and barked directions and wisdom. Caliente would be the perfect place for Kokomo Joe to start over, he said, this time with more than just the reckless courage he had displayed in Phoenix. He had brand-new white silks with a bright red "Sky" on the back in honor of the fictional Sky Rex who had saved the ranch from bankruptcy in *The Gentleman from Arizona*.

They drove through Yuma and Calexico, crossed the border at Tecate, then snaked their way across Baja and into Tijuana, down a street with music blaring and gaudy whores blowing kisses. At the entrance to the Agua Caliente backstretch and shedrows, a gate sentinel with a pistol stopped then. The Oakies and the gypsy grooms, the Pima Indians, the Mexicans riding back in the horse trailers, and especially affable Charley Brown—they were all OK.

"But where does the little Jap think *he* is going?"

4

Brilliant Queen

The guard's reaction should not have caught Mister Charley by surprise. He knew horse racing's taboos as well as anybody. It was as if all the weighty realities of the shedrows needed buoyant superstitions to keep the sport from sinking into its own dung heap: jockeys should never touch a straw broom before a race; the last horse brought to the shedrows for a meet would never win; brown silks were unlucky; big grays couldn't run distance races; and never be sitting down at the track when the clock strikes post time.

The trouble was that horse racing's superstitions and taboos kept changing. That was especially true in discussions about who made the best jockeys. It wasn't just size that mattered. For some in the sport a jockey's bloodlines mattered as much as a horse's. Was he English? French? A Cajun from the Louisiana Bayous? Did he have any Indian blood in him? Because most Indians had been *born* on horseback, they made the best and most fearless riders.

When the discussion turned to blacks, it got confusing. Blacks had learned to ride as plantation slaves and become the greatest riders in the South, even if they rode for plantation owners who didn't know their names. All that mattered was that they *were* black—they had huge hands, strong muscles, and no fear of death because their lives were worthless to begin with. With the end of slavery, their reputation as skilled riders spread, and they were soon considered the best jockeys in the country. In the Kentucky Derby of 1875 thirteen of fifteen riders were black, including the winner.

By the turn of the century the successes of black riders were so widespread that they dared to be cocky, dress impeccably, and enjoy among other newfound freedoms the opportunity to wear flashy diamonds and get drunk. Envious and bigoted white jockeys began ganging up on them, and some races were described as race wars. The white jockeys boxed black riders on the rail or rode them straight into it. They bumped them repeatedly and then slashed them with their whips.

When the black jockeys lost, the bigots said it was because "that Nigger was drunk again." It should have been clear all along, the bigots argued, that Negroes were too prone to laziness and dissipation to last as good riders. Racing associations throughout the country adopted new rules denying black riders licenses. Much later, writers and historians would coin the term "Jockey Syndrome" to describe the process by which the rules were changed to fit the need—which in racing was the need to maintain white supremacy. By 1910 blacks had disappeared from racing.

"Japs" and "Chinks" were also taboo. They were believed to be too delicate, too fragile for the rough and tumble world of horse racing. If they were fit for any sport, it was only baseball because they didn't have to slam their bamboo bodies into anybody.

Charley Brown had to explain again and again to the owners, trainers, racing officials, and turf writers who gathered each weekend at Caliente that his Japanese chauffeur was in fact his new rider. A Jap who could ride? Nobody could remember ever having seen one.

"The boy can ride," Brown assured them. "He sits so tight you have to look twice to make sure he hasn't been thrown." Brown claimed that his new rider was the closest thing he'd ever seen to Tod Sloan, who had introduced the "monkey style" of riding.

"Tod Sloan? The *legendary* Tod Sloan?"

"That's correct."

"So where has the Jap boy ridden?"

"Well, nowhere yet," Brown lied, conveniently skipping over those three races Kokomo Joe had ridden in Phoenix. Phoenix had been a false start. He had tried to begin his riding career with nothing but his own reckless bravery. It was inevitable that he had failed.

"So what is this new boy's name?"

"Kokomo Joe. Kokomo Joe Kobuki."

They'd never heard of him.

"Well, you'll hear plenty about him before too long," Brown insisted.

The open arches, the white stucco bell towers, and the marble colonnades of Agua Caliente's clubhouse seemed to invite prayer instead of gambling. It was in obedience to that mood that on Sunday, April 13, 1941, in the racetrack's saddling paddock, Charley Brown quietly took Kokomo Joe aside before the third race and gave him solemn instructions for his first race of the meet. His mount would be Brilliant Queen, a nine-year-old mare. She had won just one race in 1939, then been injured and laid up all of 1940. It had been over a year since Brown had entered her in a race, and now he had to remind himself as much as Kokomo Joe of what to expect.

The race was a mile and a sixteenth, probably too much distance for Brilliant Queen to cover—at least yet. She'd need a few races under her saddle to prepare her. "Besides, she's a 'stopper,'" Brown explained. "She has a history of going out fast, then just quitting. Not because she is exhausted. She just appears to lose interest. The long layoff has been as much to cure her of her bad habits as to heal her injuries."

Kokomo Joe was to try to keep her mind on her business. But Mister Charley said he wasn't making any Oklahoma Guarantees.

On the pari-mutuel board on the infield, Brilliant Queen was eight to one. Bettors obviously weren't expecting much of her either.

The field was crowded, Mister Charley continued, with twelve entries. The favorite was a horse named Miss Contrary, another aging nine-year-old. But Miss Contrary was a sturdy game mare. Out of the gate, it would be like the Charge of the Light Brigade to get racing room into the first turn. Kokomo Joe was to break alertly, try to be well placed, then just let Brilliant Queen run.

"With luck," Brown said, "the long layoffs and the desert training has cured her of her bad habit of quitting."

Then Mister Charley laid his hand on the bright red Sky on the back of Joe's silks. "You aren't riding now for some two-bit gypsy trainer. Or to kill yourself on a fractious colt that other jockeys are too smart to get on. You are riding for the Gillespie Land and Irrigation Company, the oasis in the desert. You are part of a desert trust. Do you understand what that all means?"

"Yes, sir, I do."

"But no matter what happens, you aren't to start thinking you are any good."

"No, sir, I won't."

"You are too reckless, too frail, and too green to be any good. You need plenty of seasoning still."

"Yes, sir. OK."

Mister Charley patted Kokomo Joe once on the back then legged him up onto Brilliant Queen.

Brilliant Queen broke quickly and raced just off the lead before the first turn. Isolated and piercing whoops from the long-shot betters who had picked Brilliant Queen rose sharply out of the steady clamor of the rest of the crowd. Twice down the backstretch her path seemed blocked, and she drifted back, only to regain her position just off the lead again. Each time she drifted back, Charley Brown nodded as if his worst fears were being confirmed—Brilliant Queen was an incurable stopper! But into the far turn his voice joined the other long-shot bettors as Brilliant Queen caught up to the leaders and then raced evenly with them toward the finish line.

She finished third by less than a length, and Mister Charley was smiling from ear to ear when he met Kokomo Joe on the track in front of the judges' stand as the jockey prepared to dismount Brilliant Queen. Kokomo Joe seemed on the edge of tears.

"I am sorry, I am sorry," he said.

"Sorry? What are you sorry for? Brilliant Queen just missed winning."

"I am sorry for *losing*," Joe said.

The smile disappeared from Brown's face immediately. Maybe he had taken his new method of disapproval too far. Now look what he had created: a jockey stripped of all self-confidence. Either the steady criticism had backfired, or worse, behind Kokomo Joe's ever-present smile there lurked a dismal disposition. Mister Charley tried to reassure Kokomo Joe that he had done all right.

"No," Joe repeated, "I *lost*."

Brown reminded him that he had finished a close third on a horse who was a stopper. Kokomo Joe shook his head. Maybe Mister Charley was saying that only to make him feel good.

"No, no, not at all."

"Maybe Mister Charley just wants to make me happy."

Brown's smile returned. No, Kokomo Joe had somehow coaxed a great race out of Brilliant Queen. He had done a good job. She had just been a little "short," that was all. Joe dismounted, stepped back, and swept his eyes along Brilliant Queen's configuration, from her head to her tail. "She looks long enough to me," he said.

Mister Charley was still laughing about Kokomo Joe's misunderstanding the next morning when turf writer Oscar Otis—"The Double O," his column byline read—recounted the episode. Otis had sold newspapers on San Diego street corners as a kid, and then become a copy runner for Caliente turf writers as a teenager. Finally, he was hired as a turf writer and handicapper by the *San Francisco Chronicle*. Over his years as the so-called dean of Western turf writers, Otis had viewed and analyzed twenty thousand races. He could recall almost every race he had ever seen, and when he wasn't rerunning races in his head, he was reciting long passages from Shakespeare, whose works he loved to spend nights reading and interpreting.

Otis could read jockeys and analyze their riding as well as he could assess King Lear or Hamlet. And despite the comic tone of the Double O's story on Kokomo Joe's confusion over English, it was clear that Otis thought he had spotted another great jockey in the making. Charley Brown's new Japanese jockey, Otis wrote, crouched like a monkey and was the "acme of politeness." Despite his inexperience, he was "better than a green hand with a horse." He had handled Brilliant Queen brilliantly. The deeper truth that Joe still couldn't read English and understood only half of Mister Charley's directions lay buried deep beneath Otis's suggestion that another great riding star was being made among the whiskey smells and grit of Tijuana.

Two weeks later, on April 27, another noisy, hot Sunday afternoon in Tijuana, Kokomo Joe stood in the paddock studying his mount, a six-year-old named Fencing Song, who was seldom in the money. The horse's habit of leaping sideways during a race prompted jockeys to complain that he was a dangerous "jumper" who shouldn't be entered in flat races. Nobody else would ride Fencing Song, but Kokomo Joe had accepted the mount eagerly. Charley Brown's expectations for the horse were so low he hadn't even stayed around to watch the race, and a groom had legged Kokomo Joe up into the saddle.

Fencing Song went off at eleven to one. Several jockeys gathered on the balcony of the jockeys' room overlooking the clubhouse turn to witness what they thought would be a riding disaster. Fencing Song broke slowly and went down the backstretch at little more than a canter, as if waiting to leap a steeplechase hedge. On the far turn he drifted far to the outside and crossed in and out of the grandstand shadows on the track. For a moment it seemed certain that if the horse didn't begin leaping shadows, he would be spooked by the sight of railbirds signaling wildly with their arms. But neither occurred, and Kokomo Joe kept Fencing Song on a straight course in the sprint to the wire and won the race.

The victory officially marked the start of the one-year period of Kokomo Joe's apprenticeship. He became the object of attention and curiosity at Caliente from both the press and railbirds because he was the smiling Japanese "bug boy" who couldn't speak English and was no bigger, they said, than a peanut.

Then on the first day in June Joe had his second long-shot victory, this time on a four year old named Thames who went off at sixty to one. It was a maiden race, and Thames had not only never won a race, he'd never even been close. During the race the field of twelve horses had run in a tight pack that bolted this way and that like spooked mustangs in the desert. It was the same racing mayhem and danger that had frustrated Kokomo Joe back in his first races in Phoenix. But this time he waited and waited and waited on Thames until the entire tiring field bolted wide in the stretch, and then he shot along the rail into the lead and never looked back.

The long-shot bettors collected $126.80 on the Thames victory, and they all gathered at the rail to whoop and cheer Joe when he weighed out and then walked to the jockeys' room. He smiled broadly but looked straight ahead as if bringing home impossible long shots was all in a day's work. Then, to prove that it hadn't been a fluke, in the eighth race later that afternoon, he brought

Brilliant Queen home a winner when she was again the pick only
of long-shot bettors.

Mister Charley offered no explanation for how it was that his
new Japanese bug boy was able to get mediocre if not downright
sorry horses to run so well. It didn't seem to have anything to do
with the pacing skills that Mister Charley had patiently taught him
so that he now had that grandfather clock ticking off seconds in
his head like the anvil strikes of a blacksmith. It also didn't seem
to have anything to do with Kokomo Joe's courage. Sure, he had
initially been reckless. But Mister Charley's criticism had tamed
him a bit. He was still braver than was probably good for him,
but what good jockey wasn't?

For Oscar Otis the explanation for Kokomo Joe's success was
simple. "He clucks to the horses in Japanese," Otis wrote. And
he would soon be brought north to ride at Bay Meadows, Otis
predicted.

Kokomo Joe's talents had been obvious at Caliente, even if you
didn't analyze jockeys as if they were Hamlet. He had had four
wins, all of them on horses who were given little or no chance at
victory. But he had also been in the money again and again on
horses who were not favorites. Was it because the betting bigots
wouldn't concede that a Jap could ride and they refused to bet
on him? Or were the long-shot successes a clear case of what Oscar Otis had written as a half joke that Kokomo Joe was a Japanese version of the horse whisperer?

Whatever it was, Kokomo Joe deserved more than just occasional mounts every Sunday at Caliente. He was "ready for bigger game on the California major circuit," Otis went on. Bay
Area fans, he wrote, "would like to see the tiny laddie from Nippon in action."

But Charley Brown wasn't ready for the tinsel and glamour of
the big tracks, at least not yet. County fairs were still his home,
the places where he felt most comfortable. Besides, the last thing

he wanted to do was bring Kokomo Joe along too fast. Because as often as not, those jockeys who found sudden fame at Caliente quickly disappeared. The most recent case had been a sixteen-year-old baby-faced jockey named Robert Rousseau, who in the summer of 1939 had arrived like a comet at Caliente and won his first two races. Turf writers called him a "riding sensation" and owners were reported to be "hot on his trail." Even Hollywood producers were making "substantial offers," as much for a cinematic career, it was implied, as for his talents as a jockey. It wasn't long before Rousseau's name had been all but forgotten.

As Joe Kobuki brought home long shots that spring at Caliente, there were sensational newspaper accounts of the race fix trial in Los Angeles that involved testimony from the same Ellis Gray whom Charley Brown had once recruited. Yes, Gray admitted on the witness stand, he had pulled horses and fixed races. It was testimony that would not let Charley forget how he had misread Gray's character. In a sport where the faster you went, the better you were, Charley Brown had to remind himself to "go slow, go slow."

"Don't pester me about when you're ready for the big-time tracks!" Mister Charley told Kokomo Joe, who hadn't even dared pester him. "I'll tell you when you're ready!"

Kokomo Joe still had plenty to learn, Mister Charley insisted, and he could learn it just as well at county fairs as anywhere else. And as June of 1941 came to a close, Kokomo Joe packed his suitcase, took the wheel of the pickup, and he and Mister Charley headed north for Pleasanton racetrack and the Alameda County Fair.

5

The Yankee Doodle Boys

The little town of Pleasanton in the Livermore Valley east of San Francisco boasted that it was the site of the oldest racetrack in America. It was *Our Town* with elm-lined streets and old two-story houses from which neighbors called to each other from porches and open windows. It was a town with tales of ghosts who peeked out from behind the purple drapes of Main Street hotels as if they were dead souls longing for the excitement of the county fair and horse racing.

In preparation for the fair's opening, the grandstand at the track had been painted so that it was now "as spic and span as a Dutch housewife's kitchen." There were new jockeys' quarters and paddock. The tomato vines, whose runners grew in the infield like snakes, had been cleared out. The fans who came for a day at the fair and the races may have been hicks who wore mail-order suits from Chicago, but there wasn't another track in the country that could offer as much history or excitement. "The joint will jump," the newspapers said, not just because the great jazz piano player Fats Waller would be there on July 4th to *play* "This Joint Is Jumpin'." Half of nobby San Francisco would also be there, eager to shed their sophistication and join the hicks for a bit of the excitement of "The Kerosene Circuit," with prize pumpkins and peach preserves in mason jars.

Kokomo Joe and Mister Charley took a high-ceilinged room in the historic Pleasanton Hotel, which quickly filled up with fair visitors who didn't mind the inconvenience of bathrooms with claw-foot bathtubs down the hall. "Japanese Will Ride at Pleasanton," a *San Francisco Chronicle* headline reported. It sounded as ominous as news reports that the Japanese army was about to invade Singapore. On newspaper maps Japan's army was a red smudge enveloping the Far East. So who was this Jap jockey who had invaded Pleasanton?

But Yoshio Kobuki had plenty of reason to be in high spirits. The grit of Agua Caliente was behind him. Riding only once a week there had made it difficult for him to put what he was learning into practice. Now Charley Brown had shipped a large string of thoroughbreds to Pleasanton, and they were ready for the races. Kobuki would be riding several mounts daily. No sooner would one race be over than he'd be breaking out of the starting gate again with a list of strategies still fresh in his head.

On Tuesday, July 2, 1941, Joe Kobuki won his very first race on opening day at Pleasanton. The horse was a six-year-old gelding named My Mint, who was a heavy favorite in the five-and-a-half furlong race. My Mint broke alertly from his post position in the middle of the gate. But the rest of the field was hardly out of the gate when one of the riders on the outside of My Mint cut so sharply across the track that he lost his cap. Meanwhile, the riders inside of Kokomo Joe squeezed toward the center of the track. The effect was the sudden formation of a flying wedge, inside of which My Mint was trapped, and Kokomo Joe had to take up sharply. By the time he had My Mint back in stride again, he was dead last and they were already in the far turn.

Still, in the stretch he came back steadily on the rail and caught the leaders just at the wire. It was described as a "sparkling ride," and the Bay Area newspapers refused to speculate on the possibility that the other jockeys at the start of the race had tried to trap Ko-buki in a flying wedge as if he *were* an invading Japanese soldier. Instead, they wrote only that the tiny Japanese rider had a strange name that nobody could pronounce, so he answered with an infectious smile to the nickname of Kokomo Joe. They said that he was the son of a Seattle vegetable merchant, suggesting that his widowed father was an agricultural tycoon instead of a dirt poor truck farmer. For the railbirds who were already puzzling over their bets for the next day, the advice from the turf writers was clear: "Don't forget Kobuki!"

The Fourth of July was proclaimed Army and Navy Day at the Pleasanton Fair. Red, white, and blue bunting hung from the grandstand. Men in uniform were admitted free for the patriotic exercises, which included salvos of bombs and rockets that could be heard for miles and that signaled that America was ready for war whenever it came. That night the northern lights lit up the Livermore Valley like celestial flares, and it was as if the entire cosmos had joined the patriotic fervor. The next day, the temperature soared to 103 degrees in Pleasanton. The heat blew out the tires of parked bicycles, but Joe Kobuki felt as if he were back in the familiar setting of the Sonoran Desert, and he won again on My Mint, the sturdy gelding who had needed only one day's rest.

The *San Francisco Chronicle* took note of the "only Japanese jockey in the United States," who was making a name for himself at Pleasanton. "That boy hasn't a nerve in his body," the Pleasanton starter claimed. "He's no trouble at the gate at all. Temperamentally, he has what it takes. He never gets mad, never gets excited." If he kept it up, the reports finished, in the fall he'd be ready to leave the fair circuit and head for the big time at Tanforan or Santa Anita.

For the other jockeys at Pleasanton, the praise for Joe Kobuki would have been a clarion call to war even if he hadn't been Japanese. Those other jockeys went by names like Hank and Ben and Don and Chew Tobacco Griffin, who was as "Irish as sham-rock." They could have passed for members of a tobacco-chew-ing all-American baseball team who dressed in the same locker room and enjoyed the camaraderie of teammates, except that once the gates opened for a race they were mortal enemies. The suggestion that they now had a Japanese invader in their midst only made them more warlike.

It was left to one of the veteran jockeys to make the general dec-laration of war. The jockey's name was Jimmy Baxter, a thirty-six-year-old grizzled veteran of two decades of bush league riding whose career had been "buried in weeds and obscurity." Baxter spoke behind the authority of a smart suit, steel-rimmed glasses, and iron-gray hair that made him look more like a banker than a jockey. Under the guise of merely offering his own riding creed, he said he didn't expect help from other jockeys and never looked for it. "I take care of myself," he said. "Let the other fellows take care of themselves."

This statement stood as a stark warning to Ben and Don and Hank to be careful. It was also a warning to the tiny Japanese jockey who had invaded Pleasanton that, no matter how steely his nerves were, he had better watch out for himself.

Kokomo Joe gave no indication that he heard the warnings, much less understood them, and on July 7 he booted home two winners. The next day, he remained in his groove and brought three more home to victory for Mister Charley. In the course of the third win, aboard Brilliant Queen again, jockey Bill Sherlock zigzagged in the stretch in what looked like an effort to block Bril-liant Queen. Kobuki had managed to shoot through Sherlock's clumsy roadblock and win the race, but the stewards still fined Sherlock fifteen dollars, noting only in their official explanation that he had failed to keep his mount straight in the stretch.

"Japanese boy scores!" the headline read the next day after his three victories. He might even have had an astonishing fourth winner if one of his mounts hadn't stumbled at the start and then lost in a photo finish. Kobuki's riding was described as sensational. Sure, the stories concluded, two of his winners had been favorites. But the speed and quality of his horses weren't the *only* explanations for his victories. It was an oblique indictment of jockeys like Bill and Hank and Jim for failing to know how to *maneuver* their horses to victory.

Kobuki with five winners in two days was pressing Donald Schunk, a young rider from Toledo, for riding honors at Pleasanton. In the every-man-for-himself creed of jockeys, too much friendliness invited vulnerability and defeat. But even in the guarded world of the Pleasanton jockeys' room, Kobuki stood out now as a special enemy. He was the invader who had established a beachhead among the others. Meanwhile, he seldom spoke and wore a silly smile constantly as if to apologize for being so reclusive. Finally, he made no effort to join the card games or small talk that helped pass the time between races.

News reports of his phenomenal success and the growing list of fans from "among his own race" only made matters worse. Those Japanese fans bet on him regardless of his chances. All they needed to see was the name Kobuki in the program. For the other jockeys at Pleasanton, it made his separation from them complete. No matter that he answered only to the name Joe. No matter that his smile never disappeared. No matter even that he managed to spit out to reporters in his fractured English that he preferred spaghetti to rice. He was from an alien tribe.

Turf writers called him Willie the Mouse, and he was a northern California racetrack legend—small and stooped and gnarled. Early in the morning of July 9 he sat high up in the Pleasanton grandstand reading the *San Francisco Chronicle*, which for weeks had been carrying stories of Japanese threats in the Pacific.

A friend spotted Willie the Mouse and climbed the bleachers to sit with him. "What do the papers mean," the friend said and began rapping Willie the Mouse on his chest, "by a Japanese menace in the Pacific?" Was war coming?

Willie said he didn't know.

"Well, that boy Kobuki, riding for Charley Brown—he's a racing threat right here in our front yard."

The friend went on to observe that the Japanese jockey had had five winners in just two days. He had five more mounts that day. "He's going to make it tough for the Yankee Doodle boys."

It was America against Japan. To drive home the point that Kobuki was the real menace, an *Oakland Tribune* headline reported, "Japanese Jockey Threat for Fair Riding Honors." It struck another ominous note, and throughout the afternoon there was a special unease in the jockeys' room. Schunk won two early races and seemed to be leaving Kobuki behind. But Kokomo Joe quickly came back with a win and seemed to be closing the gap again. Then in the eighth race, a mile and a sixteenth, Kokomo Joe was on a ten-to-one shot named Bonnie Joe, a three-year-old filly who the previous year had failed to finish in the money. Schunk rode a heavy favorite and promised to widen his lead over Kobuki. But as the horses approached the finish line, Bonnie Joe began to shoot toward the lead as Kobuki hammered at her hindquarters with his whip.

Suddenly, Kobuki found himself pinched between Schunk on his left and Chew Tobacco Griffin on his right, both of them refusing to give an inch. It was a classic mousetrap, but Kobuki went right on hammering at Bonnie Joe's hindquarters as if the filly were a splitting wedge. Schunk and Griffin refused to yield. Finally, Kobuki drifted back a half length, swerved sharply toward the rail, and came back on again before Schunk could cut him off. The three horses hit the finish line together. It was ten minutes before the photo-finish picture established that Kobuki had won.

The mousetrap had been obvious and clumsy, but it had failed to stop Kokomo Joe. He was the Japanese invader with more guts than was good for him, and the unease that had been mounting in the jockeys' room that afternoon erupted into a jockeys' room clash, and one of the jockeys took a swing at Kokomo Joe.

The next day, none of the principals would admit to the press the details of what had happened. And if Kobuki was talking, no one understood him. All that was made clear was that one of them had punched Kobuki. What had happened next was left to the readers to imagine from what little anybody knew about Kobuki in the first place. After the punch he had probably staggered. Maybe the rest of the Yankee Doodle boys had then circled his attacker and him, ready to watch a good fight. Some were surely eager to join in against the lone Japanese invader. There was even the chance that it had turned into a free-for-all, exactly the every-man-for-himself slugfest that jockey Jimmy Baxter had warned of.

But the likelihood was that, after taking the punch, Kobuki had only flashed his broad smile. His reaction had been so disarming and guileless—maybe even so pathetic—that that had been the end of the matter. One punch and it was over. Well, so what? Jockeys were high-strung bantam roosters. Fights were inevitable. It wasn't anything to be taken seriously. Furthermore, what went on in jockeys' rooms was nobody else's business. The jockeys' room was the *sanctum sanctorum* of any racetrack. It was a private hideaway in which jockeys could be free to throw up to make weight or to confess that they were stuck on a hopeless horse.

The next day, the stewards fined Kokomo Joe for failing to keep Bonnie Jo straight in the crucial race. They seemed to be faulting him for finding room on the rail to take the filly to victory. The action of the stewards suggested that the punch he had suffered in the locker room was well deserved. His only defenders were Japanese American newspapers, who said he had been slugged because the other jockeys were jealous of his wins. The other jockeys were also angry at him, the same papers said, because he hugged the rail too much. His riding rivals seemed to be inviting him to come out to the middle of the track where he could be bumped or mouse trapped or blocked by a flying wedge of horses.

Saturday, July 12, was closing day at Pleasanton. Donald Schunk and Joe Kobuki started the day tied with ten victories each. The talk for days among the railbirds, the stewards, the turf writers, and the fans like Willie the Mouse had been who would win the jockeys' title, Schunk or Kobuki? Would the invading Japanese jockey, whose fame was spreading, leave the rail and mix it up with the other riders and horses? Would he come out and fight, or would he hide in his corner like a cowardly boxer? There were also rumors that the Pleasanton jockeys, still angry over Kobuki's victories and the threat he posed, had formed a conspiracy to keep him out of the winner's circle that final day.

Among the ten thousand fans who showed up to watch the Schunk-Kobuki battle was "Mr. Big." Mr. Big wasn't the infamous and criminal figure of film fame, but Jerry Giesler, the chairman of the California Horse Racing Board, who was being credited with exposing the conspiracy in 1939 and 1940 of southern California jockeys and fixers who had nearly ruined horse racing. If there were any criminal conspiracies against Kobuki at Pleasanton, they would have to operate under his watchful eyes.

On that final day at Pleasanton Charley Brown did his best to get Kobuki the riding title, and he scrounged up mounts for his Japanese rider in nearly every race. Some of the horses were so sore or worn out from repeated races that they hardly had a chance. The effort reflected Mister Charley's agreeable nature, the same one racing officials counted on when they came to him and asked for his help in filling short race fields. But Brown also had selfish motives for getting Kobuki as many mounts as possible. If Kokomo Joe could pick up one or two victories and win the

Pleasanton riding championship, it would reflect not just on Kobuki's riding brilliance but would also be a testimony to Charley
Brown's genius for having signed him to a contract.

On Kokomo Joe's first mounts that last day, he found himself
blocked, cut off, bumped, stymied, and mouse trapped, or else
pounding a tiring horse inside a flying wedge. The best he could
do through the first seven races was finish third aboard a horse
named Michaelmas, who was running for the third time in two
weeks. At the same time, Donald Schunk booted home one winner and moved into the lead for jockey honors.

The only chance for Kokomo Joe to tie Schunk came in the last
race. The race was a mile and three-quarters. In the very early
days of horse racing two-, three-, or even four-mile races, with
horses loping and cantering along, were not uncommon. They
were an effort to relive and glorify the stamina called for by Pony
Express or United States Cavalry mounts that could be ridden at
a good clip for hours at a time. But marathon races were as long
gone from racetracks as the history they reflected.

In the modern day tracks periodically carded races of a mile
and a quarter because they were an extraordinary test of stamina, and there was always time for jockeys to overcome such bad
racing luck as a poor start or being stuck outside on a turn. Mile-
and-a-half races, however, were uncommon because there were so
few thoroughbreds who could last without breaking down. And a
race of a mile and three-quarters was rare, and it favored horses
bred for distance but who were also fit and fresh.

In Charley Brown's barn the *least* likely candidate for a mile-
and-three-quarters race was a nine-year-old gelding named Clyde,
who was as sturdy as his name but who had run four times in
two weeks and who was coming right back for his second race
in as many days. He had run well just the day before in a mile-
and-a-sixteenth race. Clyde was the best horse that Brown could
find in his tired, sore, and overworked barn. But he was giving

no Oklahoma Guarantees that Clyde would run well without even a day's rest.

At 6:30 in the evening, with grandstand shadows leaking across the track like ink, Mister Charley legged Kokomo Joe up on Clyde in the paddock for the eighth race. Nobody had gone home, not even the sore losers who were usually broke by the fifth race and stalked out of the grandstand, ripping up tickets and complaining about bad rides or crooked trainers or that their lives were jinxed. By post time for the eighth race the grandstand was still packed with ten thousand fans who wanted to see how the jockey battle would end.

The seven-horse field broke cleanly from the gate. Gambling that the rest of the small field were just as worn out as Clyde, Charley Brown had instructed Kokomo Joe to take Clyde right to the front. If he could stay close to the rail, avoid going wide on the turns, and set a slow pace, it might just turn out that Clyde would be the *least* exhausted horse as they all began a weak sprint for the finish line.

Passing the grandstand for the first time, Kokomo Joe still had Clyde on the lead and going comfortably. Down the backstretch a second time, two minutes into the long race, Kokomo Joe marked his slow pace by the steady ticking of the rail posts at the edge of his vision, exactly as Charley Brown had taught him to do. Clyde held the lead with the entire field stretched out behind him in a long file that suggested a troop of cavalry mounts missing only the guidon bearer.

Into the far turn the long file began to tighten, and a roar began rising steadily from the crowd. At the head of the stretch the field was bunched, and Kokomo Joe lifted his whip arm high in the air and then held it there for what seemed like ages before he began swinging it down along Clyde's flank. It was a series of gentle brushes and strokes more than slaps. There was simply nothing left in Clyde to bring out of him by aggressive handling.

Clyde finished fifth, too tired to even lope around to the back-stretch for the characteristic ride-out after a race. Despite the defeat, Charley Brown went right on smiling. Thanks to his Japanese bug boy, he was the winningest trainer at the meet. He publicly celebrated Kobuki's performance, and he rejected offers from other owners and trainers who pestered him about buying Kobuki's contract. The press would describe Kokomo Joe as a brilliant rider. His incredible victories proved that he was headed for greatness.

From the jockeys' room there were protests of innocence with respect to the rumors that they had conspired to keep Kobuki out of the winner's circle. Kokomo Joe had sprinted into the lead and was never behind until the end, they insisted. How *could* they have blocked him or otherwise intercepted his path to victory?

It was an explanation that was true only for that final race. And the best, most observant of the ten thousand fans, tracking each race down the back side with binoculars, had been able to pick him out in the middle of a jam of horses, his whip flashing and yanking and jerking as he repeatedly tried to find racing room or get his tired horses moving.

The conspiracy had escaped the watchful eye of Mr. Big. Still, the conclusion was obvious. Joe Kobuki, who had been just a pocket baby and then shipped to Japan to walk the beaches, was an irritating loner who had invaded the Yankee Doodle world of racing. His loss of the riding title at Pleasanton was no accident.

Despite the loss, Kokomo Joe also went right on smiling. There was no more guilt or regret because he hadn't "made the win." His numerous places and shows at Pleasanton had been impressive. If the other jockeys didn't like him because he was Japanese, that was too bad. He had learned to ride in the Sonoran Desert, where he had been almost inconspicuous working side by side with Mexicans and Indians and gaunt drifters. And when somebody suggested that members of the Japanese race had no business trying to be jockeys, he had a ready answer, in as complete a sentence as he had ever uttered and with a coherence that reflected how deeply he felt it: "The horses don't seem to mind who I am." But the real world did, and the American drumbeat of fear over invasions and spies and the prospect of war, especially with the Japanese, was growing louder and more persistent with each passing day.

6

Joltin' Joe

Fear of foreigners and invasion went all the way back to Yankee Doodle himself, who in pre-Revolutionary America had stuck a feather in his cap to scorn the threatening English. Then the fear grew, right along with the muscles of the new republic, into anxieties about the French, the "rampant enemy within," and in 1798 Congress passed the Alien and Sedition Acts. The Acts included the Alien Enemies Act, which granted the president the right to expel foreigners he considered dangerous.

After the Civil War, when strange and threatening-looking Chinese began pouring into the country, they were prohibited citizenship. At the turn of the century Japanese like Yoshio Kobuki's parents began coming in such numbers that the newspapers reported a Japanese invasion to be "the problem of the hour."

During World War I the focus of the fear was the iron fist of Germany. Germans were threatening America from coast to coast. They had organized a spy ring of diplomat-saboteurs in the nation's capital. They were burning American flags in Iowa. They were underground in secret honeycombs in Seattle. There were calls to treat every German or Austrian in the United States as a spy. Continuing the traditions of watchfulness established by the old Alien Enemies Act, President Wilson created a new government agency called the General Intelligence Division and put a young bug-eyed lawyer named J. Edgar Hoover in charge. Hoover and his new agency began keeping index cards of potential traitors and saboteurs. Over half a million Germans eventually had their freedoms restricted, and 2,300 were interned. If there were voices raised against the fear, they were hardly listened to. Some even argued that fear should be bred in the civilian population as an element of self-preservation in a hostile world.

By the 1920s it was again the dangerous and repulsive Japanese who were to be feared. "They live like beasts," a California assemblyman proclaimed at a rally against them. They existed like "the yellowed, smoldering discarded butts in an overfilled ash tray." They reproduced like rabbits and were warlike and tribalistic. They could *not* be assimilated into American culture. Even if their American birth granted them citizenship—as was the case with Kokomo Joe Kobuki—the Japanese government still claimed them as citizens if they were born before 1925. That dual citizenship made them especially dangerous. So what if President Herbert Hoover was also a dual citizen. He was white!

On the morning of August 24, 1936, that bug-eyed Washington lawyer who had begun his investigative career keeping index cards of dangerous citizens and aliens met with President Roosevelt at the White House. Hoover, now director of the Federal Bureau of Investigation, briefed the president on what he considered subversive and troubling activities within the United States. The president expressed his desire to have Hoover and his FBI conduct a broad investigation of subversive activities within the United States in order to gather "general intelligence information." But FDR wanted no leakable *written* orders to that effect, and the next day he brought Secretary of State Cordell Hull and Hoover together in the privacy of the Oval Office so that Hull could *orally* direct Hoover and the FBI to begin investigations.

Within two years, relying on confidential informants, rumor, hearsay, gossip, newspaper subscription lists, and membership lists from cultural and ethnic organizations, Hoover had carefully prepared lists of what he considered dangerous citizens and aliens, especially Germans, Italians, and Japanese. He called the lists his Custodial Detention Index, harkening back to his index card days.

In the fall of 1939 the Justice Department created a new agency to evaluate Hoover's lists. It was called the Special Defense Unit, and its members were charged with determining the degree of subversive risk—A, B, or C—that each subject on Hoover's so-called ABC lists presented. Leadership in a cultural organization or donations to a national cultural society were among those activities sufficient to warrant categorization as an A risk. Under the authority of the original Alien Enemies Act, A risks were subject to immediate arrest and imprisonment in the event of war.

Elsewhere, fears were escalating. There were arguments in Congress over the creation of detention centers in the United States. During the debate a congresswoman who bitterly opposed the idea observed that she could only imagine with what satisfaction Hitler would receive the news that America was considering peacetime concentration camps. The first of these centers came when the German liner the *Columbus* was scuttled off Cape May, New Jersey, in May of 1939. The ship's crew was interned on Angel Island in the San Francisco Bay. When anxious San Franciscans began to protest that German spies were wandering around the city, the government built a permanent internment camp for the German sailors in the mountainous wilds of New Mexico, once the hideout country of Billy the Kid. The Immigration and Nationalization Service (INS), relying on Border Patrol guards, took on the responsibility of running the camp. Within months the INS and the Border Patrol opened additional camps in North

Dakota and Montana for German and Italian sailors who had been stranded in New York.

On May 16, 1940, President Roosevelt went before Congress to alert the country to the threat from Germany, Italy, and Japan. A month later, Congress passed the Alien Registration Act, which required that five million aliens register their whereabouts and their political beliefs. They represented only a tiny percentage of the overall population, but they were the focus of alarm. Only Japanese American newspapers were offended: "It seems to be the fate of aliens," they wrote, "to become 'scapegoats' and 'whipping boys' as soon as the nation gets the jitters."

In November 1940 Heinrich Peter Fassbender sat in the spotlight at hearings held by the House Un-American Activities Committee, chaired by Martin Dies, a Texas congressman. Fassbender admitted that he had come to the United States in August 1938 as a paid but reluctant Gestapo agent who "kept stringing the Germans along" only because he needed money. Hoover's FBI index cards on Fassbender indicated that he was an unreliable showboater, but his testimony on espionage plots, spy rings, and saboteurs was subsequently cited as proof that aliens were dangerous. Around the same time, a confidential newsletter titled *The Hour* began publishing sensational reports of German and Japanese espionage in the Americas. Bracing itself for what seemed inevitable, the War Department and the Justice Department struggled to clarify what their respective roles would be in the event of a roundup of aliens and Fifth Columnists. Meanwhile, those detention camps in Montana, North Dakota, and New Mexico were in operation and ready to receive alien prisoners.

On November 17, 1940, Lewis Geiger and Gene Hunt, two young workers at the Mare Island Naval Shipyard in northern California, crawled under the cover of darkness to the site of one of the shipyard's high voltage cable towers and began carving their initials in the cement base. The two young men were caught by FBI agents and subsequently pled guilty to malicious mischief. But the FBI agent in charge in San Francisco warned the nation that there was now a real danger of sabotage in America. The power of suggestion took hold. Plane crashes, train wrecks in which the "piercing terrible screams of the injured" could be heard across the country, harbor fires, and factory explosions were all suspected to be the work of saboteurs. And what had begun as a two-man prank at Mare Island became cause for the wild suspicion that the shipyard was crawling with saboteurs.

Even President Roosevelt, who only a few years earlier had counseled the nation against rampant fear, felt the need to be extravigilant. He said that it was the purpose of the nation to quickly build factories to manufacture defense material in the event of war. Defending those factories from sabotage and espionage was critical, and in early February 1941 a Washington conference of governors and state attorneys general drew up the Model Sabotage Prevention Act. Roosevelt's critics claimed that the act was "the heaven-sent instrument for local tinpot Hitlers," but it was "thrown into every state legislative hopper" in the nation and became law in some states. At the same time, Roosevelt employed his own private Sam Spade to gather intelligence reports on Japanese spies and Nazi saboteurs. Convinced that aliens presented the most immediate threat, the FBI began interviewing German, Japanese, and Italian aliens to determine the level of risk they posed.

In mid-May 1941 "Joltin' Joe" DiMaggio, whose alien Italian father was among those facing restrictions and suspicions by the FBI, stepped to the plate against the Chicago White Sox in the first inning and stroked a clean single to center field. DiMaggio had been in a terrible batting slump for weeks, and the hit suggested only that he had perhaps finally broken out of the slump. There was no indication that the hit was the start of an historic streak that would last for two months. Writers who subsequently tried to explain DiMaggio's talent and the streak it produced noted that his only flaw seemed to be his crippling heel spurs. Those spurs suggested that he was as godlike as Achilles, whose mother had dipped him by his heel into the River Styx to make him immortal. But no one would have guessed, after that sharp single in Chicago, how legendary and immortal DiMaggio's activities over the next two months would make him.

Also in mid-May, unnoticed by all but government officials and signal intelligence eavesdroppers, German and Japanese spies met secretly in New York restaurants to share the products of their espionage. One of their joint efforts was directed at organizing America's "negroes for the purpose of retarding National Defense efforts and to commit sabotage."

Finally, in an effort to hasten America's entry into the war in Europe, a secret organization called British Security Coordination collaborated with he FBI to plant rumors—sometimes pure invention and sometimes half-truths—of espionage and sabotage in forty-five different American newspapers, including the *New York Times*, the *New York Herald Tribune*, the *San Francisco Chronicle*, and the *Baltimore Sun*. News headlines throughout the country reflected the rumor campaign: "U.S. Seeks Evidence of Sabotage in Blast"; "Sabotage Hint in Plane Crash"; and "Attempts to Block Great Lakes Harbor Laid to Sabotage."

Meanwhile, William Randolph Hearst wrote in his newspaper chain that America was being overrun with "little Japs" preparing to take over the country. The *New York World Telegram* quoted sources who said the attack would come soon. Additional news stories argued that espionage fears by naval intelligence and the FBI stood as proof that the Japanese were a serious threat to national security. In April Congressman Dies announced plans to bring his investigating committee to California, where the threat of Japanese sabotage and invasion seemed particularly menacing.

On May 22, 1941, in a rain-interrupted game against Detroit at Yankees Stadium, Joe DiMaggio stroked a clean single in the seventh inning. It extended his hitting streak to eight straight games, although nobody was counting yet. On the same afternoon in a midtown Manhattan Japanese restaurant only a few miles from Yankee Stadium, a German agent met with a Japanese naval officer to discuss the delivery of "confidential data" for secret transmittal via Japan back to Germany. The two events were an interesting contrast. The former began to focus all of America's capacity for hero worship onto the fleet-footed image of one man, who rounded the bases with the grace and speed of Achilles. The latter set off clumsy alarms and secret excursions reminiscent of the Keystone Cops.

The first of those excursions occurred on Memorial Day weekend. After receiving reports that "something is going to happen," Los Angeles police threw a cordon of officers around Los Angeles Harbor to guard against threats of sabotage. Exactly what the specific threats were no one explained, and the weekend came and went with rising fears but without incident. A week later, as American invasion fears continued to rise, the INS station in San Francisco announced plans for a special unit with seventy-five agents to investigate alien espionage and subversion.

On June 11 DiMaggio's streak stood at twenty-five games. While he and the Yankees enjoyed a day of rest because of a rainout, the FBI and Naval officials announced that Itaru Tatibana and Toraichi Kono, two Japanese nationals arrested by the FBI, would face indictment on espionage charges. As widespread as the threat of espionage and sabotage seemed to be, there was a measure of comfort in the news that the FBI was on guard. It cleared the minds of baseball fans everywhere who were beginning to follow what was now an incredible streak of hitting by their baseball god.

On Sunday, June 29, in sweltering heat and after hits in both ends of a doubleheader against the Washington Senators, Joe DiMaggio broke George Sisler's consecutive game hitting streak. The streak now stood at an incredible forty-two straight games, and a "rafter shattering roar" arose from the crowd at Griffith Stadium. It was noise that helped drown out the announcement that the two Japanese spies, Tatibana and Kono, had been released with the confusing explanation by U.S. attorneys that a jury would never have convicted them.

DiMaggio's streak also stood as heroic counterpoint to the shocking headline news the next day that two spy rings of unheroic Nazis, operating brazenly in Times Square and out of the Empire State Building, had been smashed and some forty spies had been arrested. One of the ring leaders had even acquired the code name Joe, to make himself seem as trusty and American as Joltin' Joe.

The entire world was being Hitlerized some papers reported after the arrests. Three thousand well-trained Nazi spies disguised as tourists were hard at work in America. Even more were on their way. Provisions were made to tighten our southern borders. Finally, after fighting for months over the eventual control of enemy aliens, the army and the Justice Department agreed to cooperate on the issue of what safeguards to put in place.

On July 5 much of the nation listened with rapt admiration to radio bulletins as DiMaggio's streak hit forty-six games after a towering home run against Philadelphia at Yankee Stadium. That same day, Congressman Dies and his committee began conducting what he described as a "searching inquiry" into the activities of Japanese spies on the West Coast. The committee reported that a huge fleet of innocuous looking Japanese fishing boats was ready to dynamite and bomb on orders from Japan. Thousands of Japanese Americans, Dies said, were under the direct domination of Japan.

Japanese American newspapers reported that self-appointed espionage detectives were snooping everywhere. Those same papers wrote that it would be understandable but wrong for Japanese people to withdraw because they were under suspicion. The only thing to do was to stay put, not withdraw, and take whatever was coming.

Kokomo Joe had no intention of withdrawing, no matter how suspicious and fearful the country became. How could he withdraw? How could he be any more insular and quiet than he already was? Moreover, look what he had done at Pleasanton. He had come close to winning the riding championship. Wherever Mister Charley decided to go next, he'd win the championship outright, no matter what suspicions anybody had or who threw punches at him in the jockeys' room. The latter hadn't stopped him. So what could stop him now? He'd go right on smiling back and winning races.

Smiling Charley Brown had no intention of withdrawing either, Japanese jockey in his employ or no. In two weeks the Sonoma County Fair would open in Santa Rosa. Joe and he would drive up through the Valley of the Moon, one of the most bucolic settings in the world—with its rolling hills, vineyards, and smell of grapes in the air as heavy as fire smoke. For Charley Brown it would be a chance to continue the successes of Pleasanton, in exactly the small town, countrified atmosphere he loved. He would move his string of thoroughbreds to the barns on the Sonoma County Fairgrounds at the head of the Valley of the Moon. There, he could rest his sore and tired horses. Then when the fair opened in the first week of August, he'd be ready to resume his winning ways.

On Wednesday, July 16, Joe DiMaggio went three for five against the Cleveland Indians and extended his hitting streak to an unbelievable fifty-six straight games. The streak had captured the attention of nearly the entire nation. Reporters and cameramen surrounded him at ballparks. Fans jumped out of the bleachers to steal his bat or cap. Other fans ran down the thieves to retrieve the sacred memorabilia. Small town fans were unable to wait for the delivery of the evening paper and pestered local newspaper offices for early news on DiMaggio's streak. "Did he get one yesterday?" they asked anxiously.

It was a streak that had given the country exactly two months of heroic cheering and daily wonder. Even Philip Marlowe, the fictional and cynical detective created by writer Raymond Chandler, would draw on DiMaggio's streak for light in his dark world. But how much longer could it go on? How high could DiMaggio's fame rise? What *were* man's limits after all? Pictures of DiMaggio rounding the bases made him look as swift and graceful and heroic as the Achilles some said he was.

But no ballplayer was god, and the streak had to end sooner or later. The cabbie who drove DiMaggio to Cleveland's Municipal Stadium on Thursday, July 17, said he thought the streak would end that afternoon. Despite two sharply cracked line drives down the third base line, DiMaggio went hitless and the streak was over. The next day, with no heroic baseball news to stand as counterpoint to the dark stories and growing fears of spying and espionage and the prospect of world war, Kokomo Joe and Mister Charley headed for the Valley of the Moon.

7

The Railbird Witch

It was a valley of such quiet lambent beauty that the Miwok Indians believed it was the cradle for the moon. On Saturday, August 2, at the opening of the weeklong Sonoma County Fair in the Valley of the Moon, Joe Kobuki broke that quiet by winning the sixth race aboard Brilliant Queen, the mare who had raced herself into tip-top condition. The following Monday he had two more victories. For the picture of him in the winner's circle aboard Michaelmas, an undersized but sturdy six-year-old coal-black horse who was the racing pride of Charley Brown's barn, Kokomo Joe had to tilt the short bill of his jockey's cap down as he squinted into the late afternoon sun. It was as if he were trying to make out what kind of conspiracy against him might have already been forming up because of those quick wins.

Two days later, on Wednesday, August 6, he had two more victories for a total of five wins and a comfortable lead in the jockey's race. He could have had a third win that Wednesday if he hadn't forgotten all of Mister Charley's instruction about pace. But eager to be free and clear of the threat of those conspiracies to box him in, he had raced to an early eight-length lead and was congratulating himself on his strategy when his horse suddenly went up in smoke. Afterwards, an angry Charley Brown had to remind him to listen, to *really listen*, to that clock ticking in his head.

That night one of the Santa Rosa jockeys told him, "Some day you're gonna get it," and it fed his suspicion that even more foul conspiracies were afoot. He spent a worried, sleepless night haunted by a sense of foreboding. In the morning he told Charley Brown it was going to be his "unlucky" day. "Unlucky *how*?" Charley Brown wanted to know. "What do you mean?" Joe couldn't explain. It was just a shadowy *feeling* he had. "Nonsense," Charley Brown insisted. "Just go out there and ride."

During the third race that afternoon the shadowy feeling suddenly became as palpable as track dirt and saddle leather. It was a six-furlong race with an eight horse field that did not seem to offer the other jockeys an opportunity to block him in a jam-up of horses. But the pace was painfully slow down the backstretch. Scotch Straight had the lead, and Servant Maid ran closely behind him. The rest of the field loped along in two ranks, three across the track.

Joe's mount was My Mint, an indefatigable and sturdy horse who was running comfortably in the middle of the second rank. This time, Joe heard that clock ticking clearly in his head. Either the rest of the field was already tired out, he decided, or worse, the other jockeys were misjudging the pace.

Halfway down the backstretch, the jockey on El Gorgorito, immediately in front of My Mint, also decided that the pace was way too slow, and he began moving quickly to overtake the leaders. It was just the opening that Joe also needed to move forward, and he spanked My Mint once with his whip. My Mint shot ahead. But before Kobuki could avoid it, My Mint clipped the rear heels of El Gorgorito. El Gorgorito swerved. Then his front legs buckled. It seemed the prelude to a spectacular fall that would mean jockeys bouncing and a pileup of horses twisting and rolling across the track. But El Gorgorito quickly righted himself. The stumble had been hardly more than a hiccup that briefly slowed him, and he began moving steadily ahead again.

My Mint, however, still at full speed, could not avoid a second collision. Again, Kobuki's horse clipped El Gorgorito's heels. This time My Mint stumbled and his knees buckled, exactly as El Gorgorito had done. But My Mint could not right himself. He turned his head to avoid digging his nose into the track like a spade. As he slid into the dirt, his trunk pivoted suddenly around his head. It whipped Kobuki into the air as if he had been slingshot out of the saddle. His red, white, and blue silks seemed to trace a rainbow arc as he flew into the center of the track, clear of oncoming horses.

Kobuki bounced to his feet. For a second time, disaster had been avoided. But then King Cargo, with jockey Bill Sherlock in the saddle, stumbled over My Mint, who was sliding sideways down the track. King Cargo went down also and slid along beside My Mint. The fall slammed Sherlock to the ground. The trailing horses pounded over his body and flipped it down the track as if they were dribbling it with their brittle legs. Finally, Sherlock lay splayed in the dirt, motionless. He still hadn't moved by the time the track ambulance got to him.

In the haste to load him into the ambulance and rush him to Sonoma County Hospital, no one noticed that Joe Kobuki hadn't moved from the spot where he had popped to his feet. Eventually one of the pony boys saw that Kobuki was frozen in place, his silks quivering as if he was bucking a fierce wind. Track officials took him to the jockeys' room and laid him out on a massage board.

"What happened?" Charley Brown asked him.

Joe's English, still crude and halting, was made even worse by his inability to stop shaking. "I had a bad time," he answered.

Brown told him that it could have been worse, a *lot* worse.

"Got away from the gate good," Joe went on. "But then, something happened."

"What?"

Joe answered that he didn't know. All he remembered was getting out of the gate cleanly. "Next thing, I'm standing on my feet on the track." He struggled against a new spasm of shaking. "How come?" he finally muttered.

He seemed to be asking about the mysteries of fate, not the details of exactly what had happened on the track. But there was no room for spooky fixations on doom in Charley Brown's secure little world of bullring race tracks. "You had an *accident*," Brown said.

Kobuki finally sat up. His head was clearing. "I told you it was going to happen," he reminded Brown. "So how *can* it have been an accident?"

Bill Sherlock didn't regain consciousness until that night in the hospital. He was released the next day with nothing more than a cut across his right eye. It had been a spectacular collision. But what had been the most spectacular aspect was that no horses had had to be destroyed on the track and that no jockeys had been killed. There had even been something odd and comic in the picture of Joe Kobuki left standing all alone in the middle of the track, as if he had been frozen into a colorful pillar of salt for daring to look at the evil pileup of horses and Bill Sherlock's lying in the dirt.

The episode might have set Joe to brooding again about conspiracies, but he had only himself to blame for riding up on the heels of the horse in front of him. There were no conspiracies, at least not in this instance. There had only been his own rashness. There had only been the same foolhardy impatience of which Charley Brown had tried to cure him without castrating him as a rider.

Joe had escaped the mishap without serious damage. And for the time being at least, he was only afflicted with "tremors of fright" over how close he had come to being killed. The question of whether it was fate he was up against or an earthly jockeys' conspiracy that might one day kill him remained unresolved.

In the fourth race the next day at Santa Rosa, a six-furlong sprint for fillies and mares, Joe won easily on a five-to-one shot named Sarajevo Miss. It was his sixth victory of the one-week meet, and the *Santa Rosa Independent* celebrated him as a leading rider at Santa Rosa and the only Japanese jockey on American tracks. The competitive spirit of jockeys and the every-man-for-himself creed that the grizzled veteran Jimmy Baxter had expressed at Pleasanton were enough to make *any* leading rider a target. But each news story identifying Kobuki as a Japanese "stirrup boy" stood as a reminder that he was also an invader. It made him a special target.

In the fifth race he was aboard Michaelmas, the sturdy little six year old who was going for his third consecutive victory for the meet. The field broke cleanly from the gate. Kobuki and Michaelmas, stuck on the outside post position, raced for the lead, but the rest of the field sprinted with them and kept the horses spread wide down the backstretch.

Kobuki decided not to waste Michaelmas in a protracted struggle for the lead, and he dropped back and tried to move to the rail. Immediately, the field collapsed around him and left him caught in a gaggle of horses. Twice he made sharp moves to extricate himself from the trap, and both times the gaggle flowed around him like a gelatinous blob determined to envelop him.

There was nothing to do but wait because as Kobuki knew for all jockeys the imperative of victory eventually trumped whatever other foul motives they harbored during a race. Those jockeys intent on trapping him would soon begin whipping their mounts in a sprint for the wire. When they did, the glob would dissolve and become a looser field from which escape was possible.

Joe had to wait until he was only two hundred yards from the wire before the knot dissolved. Three, four, five whacks to Michaelmas's flanks, and the runty horse exploded along the rail. He won easily going away but not without turf writers noticing that he had been blocked twice during the race. The next day the *San Francisco Examiner* even ran a huge head-on picture of the gate break, starkly illustrating that Kokomo Joe had had a "tough time finding racing room." Still, Kobuki had expertly guided Michaelmas through on the rail in the stretch. He was, the turf writers noted again, "a Japanese sensation."

With seven victories under his belt on the final day, Joe seemed a cinch to win the riding championship. And it would have been foolish now to try to stop him. It might even have caught the eye of those turf writers who seemed to be looking for blocking conspiracies. As it was, Kobuki was already getting plenty of admiring press. Turning him into an innocent victim would only have gotten him more.

On Saturday, the final day of racing at Santa Rosa, Jimmy Baxter, the dog-eat-dog grizzled veteran, had three wins in the early races. Suddenly, he had a chance to tie Kobuki, and it came down to the last race. But neither Baxter nor Kobuki could coax a good run out of their mounts, and Kobuki had the championship all to himself.

What Joe had been deprived of at Pleasanton was now his all alone. He was exactly the rising star that Oscar Otis had noticed at Caliente. He could ride, and he could win. But there was no chance to celebrate. As he walked back to the jockeys' room after that last race, he noticed an old lady glaring at him from behind the rails. She had been following the horses on the fair circuit that summer, and now she began screeching at him. "You gave that horse a bad ride! You gave that horse a bad ride!" Her voice was as scratchy and angry as if she were a railbird witch.

He turned to walk on, but she followed him along the rail. "You gave that horse a bad ride!" she kept on screeching at him. Then the next morning, as if it were an even more menacing railbird witch in his life, the headline news was that Japan was preparing for war against America.

8

The Oriental Invaders

After the close of the fair in Santa Rosa, Charley Brown considered where to go next. The Humboldt County Fair, with only four days of racing, opened that Thursday in the remote northwest corner of California near Eureka. Going there would mean a long drive up the perilous Redwood Highway through dark woods to the village of Ferndale, with a half-mile bullring track and a crude grandstand that drew only small crowds of dairymen and lumberjacks. Conversely, the San Joaquin County Fair opened on Friday in Stockton and promised a newly laid track surface, huge crowds, a brass band on the roof of the grandstand, vaudeville acts in the infield, and "chimps on bikes." A stewards' provision that all foreign jockeys had to be able to speak English seemed directed straight at Yoshio Kobuki, but Mister Charley was confident that Kokomo Joe's fractured speech would be good enough to get by. So the choice of where to head next was simple: Stockton, and the San Joaquin County Fair.

For three days Brown negotiated with racing officials over the fees for stall space at the Stockton fairgrounds. Even if he didn't need to, Brown had always lived frugally. It was a habit he had acquired at Caliente and on the bush league racing circuit where extravagances and luxuries were rare. But the likely appeal of brass bands and chimps on bikes had convinced the Stockton officials that they could charge owners and trainers a premium for shedrow stall space, and Brown balked. Then the jockeys and trainers who had already arrived at Stockton began complaining about the new track, which was described as dangerous and "cuppy." The horsemen threatened to strike. That was enough for Charley Brown. Late Wednesday night he told his stable boys and Kokomo Joe, "Riders up!" There was no time to waste. They were heading for the four days of racing at the Humboldt County Fair in remote Ferndale.

They drove up the Redwood Highway toward Humboldt County and Ferndale in a caravan of trucks and horse vans carrying seven of Charley Brown's best horses. Kokomo Joe and Mister Charley were in the lead with Joe driving and Charley chattering all through the night to make sure that he didn't have to splash ice water on his jockey-chauffeur to keep him awake as they moved steadily north.

It was just after sunset when they passed the entrance to Ridgewood Ranch just south of Willits, where the owner Charles Howard had finally brought the great Seabiscuit to pasture in the hills of his huge ranch. As they passed the ranch, Brown looked up at those moonlit hills, where Seabiscuit roamed as free as a winged horse. Brown thought of stopping, perhaps to catch a glimpse of the great horse and his owner. But Charles Howard and Seabiscuit were the swells of the world of horse racing, rich and famous and celebrated. So celebrated that Hollywood stars drove to Ridgewood to enjoy the privacy and beauty of Howard's sprawling ranch. When they complained that the long, tortuous drive from San Francisco was exhausting, Howard dammed one of the ranch's creeks and created a lake for seaplanes. It was a life of glamour and pigeon-wing hats and sunglasses and poolside cocktails that Charley Brown would never know. Or ever *care* to know. His heart was in the bush leagues and the fair circuit, in bullring tracks and gypsy grooms and towing a string of sturdy horses who could run and run and run. Neither he nor his string of ordinary but iron horses would ever be as famous as Charles Howard or Seabiscuit. No matter. It was the prospect of more bullring adventures in tiny Ferndale that excited Brown, and they drove on without stopping.

The caravan entered thick forests so impenetrable they would not even admit the moonlight. On each sharp turn their headlights punched into the murk like drill bits and illuminated the smoke from tourist campfires hanging in the trees like cobwebs. They pushed steadily north toward Ferndale, along a two-lane twisting route that took four days to travel at the turn of the century and wasn't even paved until the 1930s. It was a dangerous road with hairpin turns that bent the caravan right back onto itself so that it seemed to be swallowing its own headlights.

They passed motor villas and auto camps and tourist courts with diners whose message—"Good Eats, Visitors Welcome"—was lit by a single bare light bulb. They stopped and ate in the middle of the night and then walked the horses. On the road again they passed the Singing Trees Inn and the Garber Auto Court as they moved deeper and deeper into forests of the oldest living things on earth, giant redwoods that the roadway swerved around as if they were slalom gates. Then they crept over passes cut into the hillsides above the Eel River with only huge logs laid along the shoulder like pinball rails to keep them from dropping off a sheer cliff two hundred feet into the river.

The sun was just rising through the fog over the low mountains of the Six Rivers National Forest when they crossed the Eel on an old bridge with cement pylons and moved across the estuary into Ferndale. It was the opening day of the Humboldt County Fair, the oldest continuous fair in California. There were horses on the track exercising. The strange echoes of roosters welcoming the dawn seemed only feet away in the fog. Roustabouts tinkered with the machinery of the Tilt-a-Whirl and Loop-the-Loop rides. The smell in the air of shedrow coffee, even of Midway popcorn and caramel, was already as thick as the fog.

They unloaded the horses and found stalls for them, and then Kokomo Joe and Mister Charley headed into Eureka for breakfast. What they learned over breakfast stunned them. Twenty-five hundred soldiers headed for Washington state would soon be camped in pup tents in Sequoia Park in Eureka. They were coming up the very same Redwood Highway that Mister Charley and Kokomo Joe had just spent the long night traveling. Headlines in the Eureka newspapers made it clear why they were coming: "Troops Speed North to Meet 'Invader.'"

The rest of the story indicated that invasion and world war had finally come. A huge armada of "oriental origins hovering in the fog bank" off the coast of Oregon and Washington had launched a surprise attack on the United States. The attack had begun the previous Monday at 2:00 a.m. The enemy had come in waves of dive bombers. Smoke rose in black columns from the rubble of what had been the shipyards of Seattle. McCord Air Force Base lay in ruins, half its planes destroyed. Ft. Lewis had also been destroyed. Urgent army dispatches from the front reported that enemy troops were pouring ashore at Puget Sound. Fort Worden, at the entrance to the Sound, had been captured in sixteen minutes. Enemy paratroopers had seized Olympia, Washington, and established a line of defense running from Olympia to Centralia. Half a dozen other Washington cities had been captured. The Oregon and Washington defenders were praying for a speedy arrival of California troops.

Intercepted enemy communiqués indicated that it was only the first strike of what was an expected invasion of the entire West Coast, from Seattle to San Diego. Antiaircraft batteries manned by volunteer spotters prepared to pick off enemy fighters caught in searchlights that slashed across the night sky like sabers. Army officials said that low visibility along coastal waters prevented aerial reconnaissance. So they could *not* identify for an anxious public where they thought additional enemy landings would be made. The attacks could come *anywhere*, they warned.

It should have given rise to coastal panic. But the army seemed to know exactly what to do. Responding to prayers from Oregon and Washington defenders for the speedy arrival of California troops, an advance column of infantry was already on the way. These were the same soldiers who would arrive in Eureka shortly and make camp in Sequoia Park. Their mission was to clear the roads and stand guard against the possible ambush of subsequent troop columns racing to the front. Four regiments of infantry from Ft. Ord in California were headed up Highways 101 and 99 for the Washington battlefields. They dragged artillery caissons with 75MM French guns. Twenty-two thousand California National Guardsmen from San Luis Obispo were also on their way. Eventually, a force of one hundred thousand infantry would move north by long troop trains and throw the invaders back into the sea. Meanwhile, General DeWitt, commander of the West Coast's Fourth Army, was already on the battlefield in Washington. He would soon be joined by army chief of staff Gen. George Marshall and Secretary of War Henry Stimson.

It was expected that the battle with the oriental invaders, who were supported by "innumerable battleships" and "hordes of dive bombers" lying offshore on aircraft carriers, would be joined at the mouth of the Columbia River. In California a gala sendoff party was held at the Ft. Ord outdoor theater for infantry headed to the front. The party featured dancers, acrobats, ventriloquists, singers, three swing bands, and the comedian Señor Wences. But the mood of the troops was described as tense as they awaited battle and possible death at the hands of the enemy invader.

Only three years earlier, the actor Orson Welles had presented a convincing sixty-minute radio broadcast with official-sounding bulletins reporting a Martian invasion. It was of course only a radio drama, but the broadcast on Halloween evening in 1938 had spooked much of the nation.

Now vivid news bulletins from the Pacific Northwest that appeared in newspapers up and down the Coast, and especially in Eureka, described what was, in fact, *not* a real West Coast attack by "oriental invaders." Nor was it the start of World War II. It was instead the biggest war *game* in the history of Western civilization. Those bulletins describing the hypothetical attack didn't frighten the nation in the same way that Orson Welles had, but all the vivid details served to make the threat of invasion, whether by an alien force from outer space or oriental invaders lying offshore in the fog, seem more frightening and real, especially to Kokomo Joe.

All that summer there had been war news from remote places like Egypt and Singapore. The news had nothing to do with Kobuki, who was just a Japanese gnome and whose first images of America had been pictures of wealthy men smoking cigarettes in fancy motor cars. Out of that beginning had come a hunger for fame and a desire to one day be a great jockey. "You'll never be any good!" Charley Brown had told him again and again. It was transparent goading that Kokomo Joe had seen right through, and he had ironically nourished his hunger in the sagebrush deprivations of the Sonoran Desert. His failures at the Fairgrounds in Phoenix had only increased the hunger.

The first sweet taste of success had come at Caliente on Fencing Song. Then the fact that he had almost won the riding title at Pleasanton made him still hungrier. Finally, Santa Rosa had proved that he could survive the rancor of competitive jockeys, whether motivated by racism or simply the dog-eat-dog ruthlessness of the sport, and still win races. But that rancor had been confined to the tight enclosures of a bullring. Now, suddenly, it had been set loose and seemed everywhere in the world, and those soldiers headed for Eureka seemed to be intent upon targeting *him* as one of the "oriental invaders," even if he had done nothing wrong, even if the only thing he wanted was to be famous.

Kokomo Joe Kobuki wasn't the only one to feel a noose of suspicion tightening around his neck. Those so-called enemy aliens were again a worrisome presence in the country's midst. And one of the first to feel the noose tightening was as innocent and unlikely an enemy as Kobuki.

His name was Edward Heims, and he was a wealthy German Jew who in 1937 had come to Marin County in California seeking freedom. He bought a thousand-acre dairy ranch on the headlands near Point Reyes. But it wasn't long before vicious rumors began to circulate among his neighbors: the flat headlands of his ranch would be the perfect airstrip on which invaders could land their fighters and dive bombers; he had secret gun emplacements and artillery arsenals on his land; he had a radio transmitter and receiver; and finally, there was every indication that he was a Nazi agent.

On the very Thursday that racing began at Ferndale, Edward Heims decided that he had had enough, and he took out an ad in the Marin County papers protesting his innocence and calling for help "to end a malicious whispering campaign against me." He had no gun emplacements on his land, he insisted. No weapons arsenal. No radio transmitter. And he was *not* a Nazi. He was a Jew who had come to America seeking freedom. He had bought his ranch in an effort to become a "constructive American citizen." Now he was awaiting his citizenship. "I hope only to live here in peace," he said.

The same newspapers that published his call for help in identifying the rumormongers described his plea as "touching." But that didn't end the rumors, and he became the object of secret surveillance by the San Francisco FBI. If he had had anything to hide, he might have fled, but he did just the opposite and invited the FBI agents to come onto his land and search every square foot and every building. They declined, preferring instead to add the name of Edward Heims to the list of dangerous enemy aliens they were watching closely.

Meanwhile, there were more fires and factory explosions and derailments that were suspected to be the work of Nazi saboteurs softening up America for the attack. In the event of war news-papers predicted that as many as five million dangerous aliens could wind up interned.

But it wasn't just characters like Edward Heims, suspected of being Nazi, who were to be feared. They were in league with the "oriental invaders," in this case, Japan, which was preparing for war. Japan was described as arrogant, brooding, paranoid, and envious of more powerful nations. It had spies everywhere on the coast. Those rumormongers had it as a fact that an association of Los Angeles Japanese gardeners was a cover for an espionage ring. Their long garden hoses concealed short wave radio equip-ment used to send messages to Japan. The point was that world war was inevitable. And Kokomo Joe Kobuki seemed trapped on the battlefield in Humboldt County.

It hadn't been that long ago that Japanese merchants who had tried to open businesses in Eureka had fled after their stores were dynamited. The violence had been considered "sufficient to keep these people out of Humboldt County" except as tourists. Now the same county would soon be headquarters for an army ready to throw the oriental invaders back into the sea. It was the last place in the world where Yoshio Kobuki expected to make a per-manent mark in the world of horse racing.

The four days of racing, with five races daily, began on Ferndale's half-mile bullring track on Thursday afternoon with the raising of the flag at 1:30, a bugle call, and the playing of the "Star-Spangled

Banner." The wooden grandstand had been draped with rosettes of red, white, and blue bunting. Admission was free for soldiers in Sequoia Park or elsewhere if they showed up in uniform. Nearly a dozen jockeys were on hand. Even if none of the lumberjacks and dairymen in Humboldt County had ever heard of them, the jockeys were described as "well-known" riders who would bring plenty of racing excitement to quiet Ferndale. The local papers presented a primer on track slang so that the lumberjacks and dairymen could eavesdrop on "ginney boys" in order to learn which horses looked good, how fast they had been "clocked" in workouts, and which jockeys were "kings of the bullring."

Bullring! It was the proper term for a half-mile track that was more ring than oval. During bullring races jockeys were hardly out of one tight turn before they were into another. For longer races it meant twice around the track and twice as many tight turns. The riding could be dangerous with the field bunched and inexperienced jockeys making sudden moves that led to accidents. Additionally, the stretch runs were much shorter than the long sprints of major tracks like Churchill Downs, where the stretch was over twelve hundred feet and gave jockeys plenty of time to find racing room in the sprint to the wire. The stretch at Ferndale was less than half that length, and no sooner did jockeys come out of the final turn than the finish line lay just ahead.

Certain jockeys—those kings of the bullring—had a gift for anticipating the tight turns and positioning their horses properly at the head of the stretch. But Joe Kobuki had never been on a track quite like Ferndale, and it took the opening race on Thursday for him to get comfortable with the turns. At the end of the race he was closing fast on the lead horse, but the best he could finish was second.

The second race of five furlongs featured a small field of just six horses. Kokomo Joe rode Kriegsman, one of Mister Charley's untested three year olds. Donald Schunk, the young jockey from Toledo who had won the title the last day at Pleasanton, rode another three year old named Goole. The two horses went off as the cofavorites in the race. They battled it out the entire race, first one and then the other leading. Through the brief stretch run, they were side by side until just at the wire when Kobuki poked Kriegsman's head in front.

In the third race Schunk and Kobuki again battled it out, but this time in the stretch Kobuki faded to third and Schunk prevailed. Kokomo Joe had no mount in the fourth race, and it gave him an opportunity to wonder if the rivalries and conspiracies that had led to fisticuffs at Pleasanton were back in his life. Was it going to be Kobuki versus Schunk *again*? Many of the same jockeys who had watched him get punched at Pleasanton were now at Ferndale. It suggested not just a continuation of the dog-eat-dog, Kobuki-Schunk rivalry but the possibility for more conspiracies in his life, this time concealed behind accidents that were considered the price jockeys had to pay for the natural dangers of bullring riding.

It was four o'clock and the sun was still high in the sky when the fifth and final race went off. It was a small field of only five horses going seven furlongs, and Kobuki rode Michaelmas, the coal-black runt who was still the star of Charley Brown's barn. Donald Schunk was on Cerro, a nine year old who raced frequently and was regularly in the money. But whatever rivalry there might have been between Schunk and Kobuki failed to materialize. Kobuki broke Michaelmas cleanly out of the gate and took him straight to the lead, which he never gave up. He crossed the finish line all alone.

In the winner's circle, hardly bigger than a crib floored with sawdust, Michaelmas, Charley Brown, and two stable boys from Brown's barn had to crowd together to fit into the tight confines for a picture. Just as the flashbulb cracked like a bolt of heat lightning, the track announcer let it be known that Michaelmas had broken the Ferndale track record for a seven-furlong race. It prompted Mister Charley to deliver an affectionate slap on the rump of his prize horse before Kobuki dismounted and the stable boys took Michaelmas back to the shedrows.

9

Lumberjacks and Truckers

Friday was payday in Humboldt County. The bars in Eureka and off the plaza in Arcata were open and already crowded at noon. If Kokomo Joe had a premonition concerning events that were about to unfold that second day of racing at Ferndale, he kept it to himself. Maybe a premonition, especially a dark one, like the one he'd had at Santa Rosa, maybe it was realized only when he expressed it. Maybe if you refused to recognize premonitions, they went away.

By 1:30, post time for the first race, logging trucks, their cribs empty and their drivers nowhere in sight, were parked on the huge dirt fields surrounding the fairgrounds. Six horses broke in a wide phalanx from the gate in the first race and then swung through the first turn still stacked six wide as if they were playground kids playing crack the whip. Halfway through the first turn, the outside three horses dropped off and drifted back. That left three horses still stacked across the track in close formation as they pounded down the short backstretch.

Kokomo Joe rode the favorite Cariel, who held the middle between Briar Mint on the inside and Gold Blossom on the outside. The three horses stayed in formation through the rest of the race and then came down the stretch stride for stride, head bob for head bob. As they approached the finish line, only the sight of whips jabbing irregularly in the air indicated that they weren't a single horse plunging ahead in perfect synchrony. Squeezed in the middle, Kokomo Joe seemed in danger of being popped from the saddle like a cork, then dropped beneath pounding hooves that would leave him mangled on the track. But he held his place during a nerve-wracking finish that brought the fans to their feet and kept them cheering and whooping for nearly fifteen minutes until the photo-finish camera revealed that Kobuki had managed to get Cariel's nose in front at the wire.

The fans had hardly sat back down from the excitement when the second race went off. Six horses were immediately strung out in a dull race, Kobuki on the lead, the others trailing in an order that never changed during the race. Approaching the wire, Kokomo Joe kept looking back unable to believe that none of the field could mount a charge against him. Meanwhile, still exhausted from the excitement of the first race and too bored by the dullness of the second, the crowd delivered only a weak cheer for Kobuki when he crossed the finish line.

While Kokomo Joe, Mister Charley, and the two grooms again crowded into the winner's circle, a small brass band from the nearby logging town of Scotia made a brief appearance. Their music was ragged but homegrown, and in the cheering and whistling for their performance, little notice was taken of the fact that Yoshio Kobuki had his second victory of the day.

The third race was seven furlongs, nearly twice around the track. It was an uneven gate break, and the crowd gasped as the horses collided and swerved going down the backstretch. Then the crowd began cheering, as much in relief for the narrow escape from disaster as for their picks in the race. But as the field came out of the final turn the second time and entered the stretch, the scramble for position brought *more* collisions and swerving, and this time a four-year-old mare named Burgoo Sal-Lea went down directly in front of the grandstand, snapping her front legs like toothpicks.

As the rest of the field sprinted toward the finish line, all eyes were on Burgoo Sal-Lea's jockey as he slid down the middle of the track, his face plowing a furrow in the dirt before he finally came to a stop. He lay lifeless on the track while a squad of stable boys rushed to his side, surrounded him, and, like pall bearers, carried him away.

Burgoo Sal-Lea thrashed and heaved herself back to her feet. But once standing, she began frantically biting one of her legs at the ankle where it flopped loosely because of the break. Her owner hurried onto the track and grabbed her reins in an effort to steady her. But she continued to thrash and pitch. Suddenly, the owner pulled a pistol from his belt and gripped her halter. Then he put the pistol directly to her head. The sound of the pistol shot echoed in the bleachers. The crowd, which had been winding itself up with cheers, immediately fell silent.

In the silence and horror nobody appeared to notice or care that Yoshio Kobuki had managed to keep an eleven-year-old relic named Clear on his feet throughout the two laps of bumping and swerving and win the race. For Kobuki it was three straight racing victories! Or four, if you counted the last race from Thursday. It was a streak in the making, and it would have begun to draw interest and chatter in the grandstand in the same way DiMaggio's remarkable hitting streak had slowly gained an audience if a horse hadn't just been shot on the track and what appeared to be a dead jockey carried off. What difference did it make who had won what and for how many times? Even after the track announcer reported that the jockey in question wasn't dead after all but only bruised and shaken and excused from his mounts for the rest of the day, even then nobody in the grandstand was in a mood to appreciate the fact that remarkable racing history was being made before their very eyes.

For the fourth race, a five-furlong sprint, Kobuki rode Cold Wave, a twelve-year-old horse who had shown nothing in the hands of a different jockey just the day before. Racing particularly durable horses every third day or every other day was common practice in the bush leagues where the horses were so cheap to begin with that little was lost if they broke down. But racing a horse over successive days was an invitation to the same kind of broken-leg disaster that had just horrified the crowd, and thus few bettors expected aging Cold Wave to win. But Kobuki kept the old horse on the rail and just off the pace through the entire race, and Cold Wave still had enough run in him for the sprint to the wire to win easily.

The mild cheering for Kobuki's fourth straight win did not reflect the importance of what was at stake. Those hardworking lumberjacks and dairymen in the stands had little appreciation for the finer points of sports, especially horse racing, which they saw only once a year. What was a streak after all? Maybe it was just the work of those same mysterious laws that controlled coin flips and card games. It was all luck. That streaks were breakable, that they were human events fraught with the dangers of failure or injury or foul conspiracies, that was not taken into account. Not even the news, delivered by the track announcer with appropriate gravity, that Yoshio "Kokomo Joe" Kobuki had now won four straight races and might be on the verge of setting a record—the announcer didn't explain *what* record—caused a stir in the crowd.

In the saddling paddock at the end of the grandstand, Mister Charley gave Kokomo Joe his instructions for the fifth and last race of the day. The race was a mile and a sixteenth, in the course of which the runners would pass in front of the grandstand and across the finish line twice before the final sprint. It was a common jockey mistake, in the longer races, to lose track of where they were in a bullring race as they circled like figures on a dizzying merry-go-round. To keep track, some jockeys kept marbles in their cheeks and spit one out at each lap. When they had "lost all their marbles," the joke was, the race was over. Kokomo Joe was to *stay awake*, Mister Charley emphasized. Don't misjudge the finish line!

The field itself was small, just five horses. Kobuki's horse, a nine-year-old gelding named Beginner's Bait, had been lightly raced but was very fit. He was the odds-on favorite in the race. His only real competition would come from Donald Schunk on Goole, the same horse that Kobuki had beaten in the fierce wire-to-wire battle the day before. Brown was betting now that without even a day's rest Goole would not be able to last. "For once," he told Kokomo Joe, "you can forget about pace, you can forget about listening to a grandfather clock ticking in an empty house. You are to go straight to the front and *stay there*."

The race went exactly as Brown directed. Kobuki took Beginner's Bait to the front, kept leads of two, three, even four lengths as the horses continued to circle. On the last turn Donald Schunk was in second place, and his whip cracked and slapped as he jackknifed his body in an effort to coax some sprint life out of Goole. But Brown had been right. Goole would not respond and finished a distant second. Kokomo Joe stood straight up in the saddle and lifted both arms as he crossed the finish line in record time for his fifth straight victory.

Yoshio "Kokomo Joe" Kobuki had swept the entire Ferndale card. Newspapers in Arcata, Eureka, Sacramento, Stockton, and even faraway San Francisco took notice. Two winners in one day lifted a jockey's spirits. Three was cause for special celebration. Four winners in a single day were rare. The previous year, among the thousands of jockeys who rode in tens of thousands of races, only a handful could claim four victories in one day. Sweeping an entire card of five or more races was unheard of, and nobody at

Ferndale—none of the grooms or stable boys or owners or track officials—could recall ever having seen it done.

In fact, it had been done only twice in American thoroughbred racing. A black jockey named James Lee, bent on proving he could ride better than the white jockeys who tried to shut him out, had swept an entire card of six races in 1907 at Churchill Downs. Ten years later, an apprentice jockey named Herman Phillips swept the full card of six races at a tiny track in Reno, Nevada. Now Kokomo Joe had swept an entire card of five races, and even if it was Ferndale and even if it was a merry-go-round track in backwater America, it put him in select company. And more records were in sight. Over two days he had won six straight races. Nobody at Ferndale could remember any jockey ever having done that either. It was a remarkable feat, perhaps another one for the record books. And with Saturday's racing still ahead and with his streak still alive, he wasn't done yet.

Fireworks that lifted into the dark sky above the midway Friday night seemed as much in celebration of Kobuki's feat as it was the carnival atmosphere of the fair. News that Kobuki had swept the card spread, and on Saturday the largest crowd ever to attend Humboldt County racing packed the grandstand and stood at the rail to see if he could continue his streak.

But the rumor was everywhere in the huge crowd that Kokomo Joe had been beaten up Friday night because he had won *all* the races. The speculation was that the beating had been administered by jealous jockeys. Others insisted that lumberjacks and tough truckers had cornered him in one of the local Ferndale bars.

Whatever had happened, the rumors of violence against Kokomo Joe were in keeping with those stories of the Japanese merchant in Eureka who had once had his store dynamited. And Saturday morning, before the first race, the saddling paddock was jammed with spectators who wanted to see if Kobuki had been beaten so badly he wouldn't be able to accept his mounts. But there he was in the saddling paddock, flashing his characteristic broad smile. If he *had* been beaten up, he showed no sign of it.

Charley Brown legged Joe up on a six-to-one long shot named Crystal Lover, who would have been even longer if the "pint-sized Japanese rider" hadn't by then earned a band of loyal followers who would have bet Kobuki if he had been on a mule. Their confidence was rewarded after Kobuki and Schunk, aboard the favorite, battled it out in the stretch, Schunk's horse bumping Kobuki's repeatedly. At each separation Kobuki quickly fixed himself back against Schunk's horse as if he had a strong magnet in his saddle cloth.

Despite the repeated bumping, Kobuki won the race, his seventh straight. While the fans roared, all memory of the previous day's horrifying accident gone, the stewards, who had up to that point not punished aggressive riding, disqualified Schunk for the bumping. It reminded Kobuki that despite his victories—perhaps *because* of them—he could still be the object of conspiracies and plots.

The streak ended with the next race. Aboard Zeluso for the second time in three days, Kobuki could not get any run out of the exhausted horse, and he finished dead last. But after the defeat, the significance of what he had done finally set in, and he was too excited to ride the next race. The stewards excused him from his mount, and he sat all by himself in the jockeys' room whipsawed by the exhilaration of the streak and disappointment because it had ended. An hour later, in the final race on Saturday, despite what was described as a "blazing home stretch challenge," he had to settle for a second-place finish.

By Sunday the pup tent army was in place in Sequoia Park. There were only four races that day, with no betting permitted because it was Sunday. However, in the grandstands there was heavy betting between fans and especially among the soldiers who showed up. Much of the betting was on Kokomo Joe because it was clear he was hot. Still, his only victory on Sunday came in the third race.

That Sunday night, while the soldiers camped in Sequoia Park prepared to hurry north to defend against the mock invasion of Washington and Oregon, Joe had time to take stock of what he had done at Ferndale. Over four days of racing he had had sixteen mounts and won nine races. He had come second five times and third once. He had been out of the money only once, on a horse that had no more chance than a mule. On Saturday he had swept the card and made racing history. Beyond that, over three days, without declining a single mount because he might have felt the horse had no chance, he had won seven races in a row.

Sunday night in the Ferndale barns, a few grooms who insisted they knew a little racing history assured him that there might have been some jockey somewhere who had won more races in a row. But that accomplishment had been in Australia or Timbuktu or someplace else remote, where they probably *did* ride mules. What Kobuki had done, the grooms insisted, *had* to be an American record.

Driving back down the Redwood Highway, Kokomo Joe could hardly contain his excitement or his newfound confidence. What did it matter that there was ominous news about the Japanese preparing to attack Russia or America? Who was General DeWitt anyway? And what did it matter that somewhere in Washington beleaguered troops were praying to be saved from oriental invaders? What did it matter that the FBI was preparing to move against suspicious characters like Edward Heims? What did it matter even that other jockeys might already be moving against *him* on the racetrack? His remarkable performance at the Humboldt County Fair proved that he could swat them away like flies.

Now Joe and Mister Charley were headed for Stockton, where Brown had finally come to terms with Stockton officials over the price of stall space. Kobuki would be hailed in Stockton as an emerging star. After Stockton there would be more glories in Sacramento at the state fair. In late September and October they would head for Fresno, where he could continue to expand his reputation. Finally, when the fair circuit ended and the year closed, he and Charley Brown could go back to Caliente, where he could sharpen his riding talents while he waited for Santa Anita to open on the last day of the year. Santa Anita, where only a year earlier Seabiscuit had made racing history. Santa Anita, where famous riders like George Wolff and Red Pollard and Jack Westrope set records. Santa Anita, where just three years earlier they had laughed at him and hung the sing-song name "Kokomo Joe" on him and only let him clean the stables. How could they laugh at him now? How could they hold him back now?

10

Joe Btfsplk

Before the meet at Stockton had even opened, headlines in the *Stockton Record* announced, "Kubuki Will Ride." The story of his anticipated arrival was accompanied by a huge picture in the sports section of Kobuki aboard Michaelmas in the winner's circle at Santa Rosa. He was heralded as the outstanding Japanese jockey whose sensational riding had excited racing fans at Pleasanton, Santa Rosa, and Ferndale. It was as if a figure as celebrated as Joe DiMaggio was coming to Stockton, except that this Joe was Japanese, the only such jockey on American tracks. It would be the Yankee Doodle boys versus the Japanese again, and Kobuki would be the one to beat.

But because of Charley Brown's decision to head to Ferndale, Kobuki didn't arrive in Stockton until Thursday, August 21. By that time there were only three days of racing left at Stockton. Fans who had been expecting to see a battle between America and Japan were disappointed. So where the hell had Kobuki been? Laying satchel charges at some power plant or shipyard?

Sabotage! Espionage! Enemy invasions! The subjects continued to frighten the entire country. Only a few days before Kobuki's arrival in Stockton, the news was of a huge fire back east in Brooklyn Harbor. It was the greatest waterfront fire in years and *possibly* the result of a saboteur's torch. Just weeks earlier, the *San Francisco Chronicle* had reported that the Mare Island Naval Shipyard was home for four hundred suspected saboteurs. In Seattle a Nazi spy and his blond consort, who had been charming secrets out of hitchhiking soldiers, were captured trying to flee the country. Additionally, there were fears that the Japanese in Hawaii would "cause trouble" in the event of a war in the Pacific.

So who was it who had finally arrived in Stockton? A Japanese troublemaker or a record-setting jockey? Whoever he was, the fans who were looking forward to a racing battle between a Yankee Doodle boy and Kobuki got their wishes immediately. In his first ride on Thursday on a three-year-old filly named Timber Girl, Kobuki hugged the rail the entire five-and-a-half furlong race. At the head of the stretch, without even going to the whip and steadily working his arms as if he were pumping a railroad handcar, he moved Timber Girl into a two-length lead and appeared the easy winner. Then jockey Harry Kilgore on a long shot, a three-year-old filly named Scotch Straight, came flying through the stretch so far on the outside that Kobuki didn't see the threat until he heard the sudden roar exploding from the crowd. By then it was too late to get Timber Girl back in full stride, and Scotch Straight laid her nose on the wire with Timber Girl.

While stewards waited patiently for the photo-finish picture, the fans had an opportunity to appreciate the America-versus-Japan match up. The thrilling finish featured a jockey named Harry Kilgore, who sounded as all-American as one of Tom Sawyer's gang or a character out of *Our Town*, versus a real oriental invader named Yoshio Kobuki. After weeks of Japanese assaults and victories in Malay and Singapore, a good ol' Yankee Doodle boy had a chance finally to even the score.

A whoop went up from the long-shot bettors when Kilgore was eventually declared the winner. In the jockeys' room Kobuki blamed himself for the loss. He said he should have seen the horse that came "flewing" by him on the extreme outside. Charley Brown was one of the few who had a good laugh at Kokomo Joe's fractured English. For everybody else Kobuki's clumsy English was proof of how un-American he was.

On Saturday, getaway day at Stockton, not even Brown could find anything to laugh about in the front-page headlines, "Japanese Mother Kills Babe!" The details in the story were gruesome. The mother had prepared a concoction of orange juice and poison and let her baby suck from a bottle of the deadly mixture. Then the woman had tried to kill herself. She explained that her husband was deep in debt, and she had sought to take the baby and herself "off his hands so that he could more easily pay his obligations."

It was a shocking tale of personal desperation, but in the context of invasion fears and Japanese military conquests, her story stood as proof to some readers that the Japanese people were so heartless that they poisoned their own babies. It darkened the cloud of suspicion and strangeness that hung over Yoshio Kobuki's head like the rain cloud that would soon follow the poor comic book character Joe Btfsplk wherever he went in 'Lil Abner. When the races closed Saturday afternoon at Stockton, Kobuki could not get out of town and head for Sacramento fast enough.

The California State Fair in Sacramento was considered the greatest state fair in the nation, offering color and celebration and romance. Despite the promises of a carnival atmosphere, the theme in 1941 was national defense, with fireworks and the red glare of rockets and military marching bands and a solid sea of people singing the National Anthem. Even the Sacramento Fair's golf tournament was made to fit the military theme as one more way for the less active citizenry to remain battle ready in the event of war.

Joe Kobuki had five mounts but only a single victory on a prohibitive favorite on the opening day of racing. He could not even get

Michaelmas, the little powerhouse pride of Charley Brown's barn, on the board. The cannon fire and the rockets and the patriotic rattle of snare drums—none of it seemed to be meant for Kokomo Joe or the horses he rode. And in the racetrack battle between the United States and Japan, it was clear who was winning.

The battle lines weren't just being drawn on the racetrack. The steady din of war news created worldwide divisions as sharp as those that separated two old armies marching into the smoke of each other's cannons. In Seattle the Japanese American Citizens League wanted to make it clear whose side they were on. "It is our prime duty," the league urged their members, "to make of ourselves first loyal and substantial citizens." It added, "America is worth dying for."

Nobody in the nation seemed to be listening. Meanwhile, the question remained: who did Joe Kobuki think he was trying to win races against good American boys? And despite seven mounts on Saturday, the sensational, record-setting jockey who was supposed to be the next Tod Sloan again only had one winner. In stretch run after stretch run, he found himself boxed in or trapped on the rail or having to take up because another jockey suddenly cut in front of him. Even turf writers took note of the strange zigzag riding through the stretch, but the stewards dismissed the erratic riding as innocent efforts by jockeys to find a softer track surface.

Over a hundred thousand fans jammed the Sacramento fairgrounds on Labor Day. They came to laugh at Abbott and Costello, to dance to Gene Krupa's swing band, and to tremble at the sight of Orson Welles, who was still enjoying the "scare me! scare me!" popularity of his radio broadcast three years earlier of a Martian invasion. They also came to see the Japanese jockey Kokomo Joe Kobuki, who did "some of his best riding" and had two victories.

The two victories came because he had finally figured out how to avoid the troublesome zigzaggers. But when turf writers asked him to explain his Labor Day success, he told them only, "I yell at the horses in *English*." It was his awkward way of making sure that everyone understood where his loyalties lay. He was an American. And he was *proud* of his American heritage.

"*Kobuki*?" they asked and wondered. "*Yoshio Kobuki*? Isn't that Japanese?"

"I am *American*," he repeated. "Born in America!"

"But don't you *speak* Japanese?"

"Of course, I speak a little Japanese."

"So how come you don't whisper to the horses in Japanese?"

He flashed his toothy smile. "Very few horses understand Japanese."

That night the newspapers described him as a "smiling package of Nipponese dynamite." It sounded as if they were characterizing a clever saboteur instead of a jockey. For the next three days that smiling package of Nipponese dynamite looked anything but explosive. On Tuesday, September 2, riding the only mount on which he had a chance, he went wide on the far turn to avoid the zigzaggers and lost all chances for a victory. On Wednesday none of his four mounts responded to him no matter what language he whispered or shouted. On Thursday he was out of the money on five straight races. It was as if, having set a record at Ferndale for straight victories, he was trying now to set a record for straight failures.

The leading jockey at Sacramento was a twenty-one-year-old rider from Dodge City, Kansas, named Isaac Bassett. Bassett, whose one-year apprenticeship had ended the previous June, had quickly shed his reputation as an inexperienced bug boy. With two victories on Thursday and a total of eight wins, he was running away with the Sacramento meet. If anybody could catch him on the last two days of racing, it certainly wouldn't be Joe Kobuki, who was fighting not just dead horses but ever more distressing news of Japanese imperialism.

Despicable Japanese militarists were reported to be behind the Far East opium trade. Their ships had been "slinking" out of Iranian ports bearing opium, the "soul destroying narcotic" that was meant to turn China into a nation of sleepy lotus eater who would be powerless to resist Japanese invasion. Closer to home, cryptanalysts had cracked the Japanese diplomatic code. Pieces of the subsequent intelligence about espionage plots and the efforts of Japanese diplomats to recruit spies appeared in the *Los Angeles Times*. The troubling reports contributed to rising fears about coastal Japanese and subversion.

The more reports there were of international Japanese treachery, the more Kokomo Joe was determined to prove that he was a promising and recognized *American* jockey, not one of those secret agents the newspapers kept warning about. On Friday, in his first race, Kobuki sprinted to an easy six-length victory. Then in the third race he put his mount Alma Mae on the lead immediately and never looked back for his second victory of the day. Finally, in the sixth race in a ride that was described as sensational, he came "fairly flying down the outside" and missed a third victory by a nose. Still, the day's victories put him just two wins behind Bassett. The meet championship, which only a few days earlier had seemed all Bassett's, now was within striking distance for Kobuki.

The possibility promised a Saturday duel between Bassett and Kobuki for Sacramento riding honors. But Saturday morning the stewards suspended Bassett for lazy riding the day before. So those who came to the track Saturday afternoon expecting a Japan-versus-United States duel were disappointed, even angry. Who did the stewards think they were, meddling in what amounted to a global standoff between Bassett and Kobuki? It wouldn't be a fair fight if Bassett couldn't even defend himself.

Still, Kobuki was determined to win riding honors at Sacramento, whether it was a fair fight or not. He had almost won the championship at Pleasanton. He had won at Santa Rosa and had set what they said was a modern American record at Ferndale. It had brought him notoriety and celebration. It hadn't been accompanied by the mighty roar that got raised at Hollywood Park or Santa Anita for those all-American riders who came into the stretch battling for the lead. But the small bit of fame he had enjoyed on the fair circuit had been intoxicating. Now he had a chance to be back in the limelight again, and he intended to do all he could to make sure that he had at least two wins, which would be enough, he hoped, to at least tie Bassett.

Saturday, September 6, 1941, was Veterans Day. Ceremonies at the Sacramento fairgrounds included drill teams marching with rifles and fixed bayonets, drum-and-bugle corps, and solemn reminders of the country's need for soldiers and patriots in the event of war. Meanwhile, Kokomo Joe's start was not promising. In the second race his mount My Mint finished far behind the leaders. In the third race he finished dead last. He battled four other riders in the fourth race to narrowly avoid finishing dead last again. In the fifth race his horse Jocktell quit shortly out of the gate, and there was no avoiding the fate of dead last for the second time.

His first victory of the day came in the sixth race aboard an unremarkable six-year-old mare named Hilda May, who seemed overmatched against stronger colts and horses. But halfway through the race she moved to the front with little urging, and she won easily. It put Kobuki one victory behind Bassett, and with two races to go, his chances of tying or beating Bassett were more than just a hope.

But in the seventh race Kokomo Joe finished dead last for the third time that afternoon. Those fans who had been deprived of the horse-to-horse combat between Bassett and Kobuki could at least celebrate Kobuki's repeated dismal finishes. Three dead lasts on one card, with a chance for a fourth, were as ignominious as his seven straight victories at Ferndale had been glorious.

Charley Brown knew perfectly well what was at stake in the eighth and final race of the day, and he was emphatic in his directions to Kokomo Joe in the saddling paddock. Kobuki would be aboard Brilliant Queen, the nine-year-old mare he had first ridden so well in Caliente. Brown reminded Kobuki that she was no longer a stopper. She was a durable, tough old lady. On Monday she had romped to an easy victory in a mile-and-a-sixteenth race. That race had been the perfect stepping stone for today's mile-and-a-half marathon, and bettors had made her the favorite to win the race.

With a crowded ten horse field Kobuki was to hustle Brilliant Queen out of the gate quickly from her outside post position. He was to get down to the rail as soon as he could and then take the lead and hold it. The only other horse in the field who would have a chance to catch him would be a four-year-old bay gelding named Wound Stripe. He was to keep track of where Wound Stripe was the whole way. *"Don't fall asleep!"* Brown emphasized. It was as stark a warning as if Mister Charley were splashing ice water on Kobuki's face on the streets of Gila Bend. Charley continued, *"Don't get caught!"* Not the way he had gotten caught earlier in the meet by Scotch Straight, who had come "flewing" by him on the outside.

Brilliant Queen began the race as if she had been catapulted from the gate. By the first turn Kobuki had the old mare in second place and was closing fast on the leader. Moving into the backstretch, Brilliant Queen took a one-length lead, and the rest of the field was strung out behind her in a long file of horses. Kobuki repeatedly checked behind him and had no trouble picking out Wound Stripe far back, still coming out of the first turn.

Down the backstretch the only horse closing on Kobuki and Brilliant Queen was Wound Stripe—from seventh to sixth, fifth, swallowing the lengthy gaps between horses, fourth, third, and then eating up five lengths to pass the second horse at the head of the stretch, leaving only Brilliant Queen still to catch.

Wound Stripe caught Brilliant Queen halfway through the stretch and took a half-length lead. As the two horses flew at the wire, a roar rose from the crowd of thirty thousand fans that was just as mighty as the pandemonium of Hollywood Park or Santa Anita. Brilliant Queen came on again and put her neck back in front. Then it was Wound Stripe's turn to take the lead once more, this time by just a head. But Brilliant Queen came back a second time, and the two horses were nose to nose as they caught the wire.

Once again, the wait for the photo-finish results gave the exhausted fans a chance to appreciate what was a stake. Never mind the distant battlefields of Malay and Singapore or the fate of the poor lotus-eating Chinese. This was jockey war on the home front, right on Main Street with elm trees and Ferris wheels and American swing bands. In just the previous race Kobuki had seemed defeated, the world's record holder for consecutive dead lasts. Now with a victory aboard Brilliant Queen he could tie Isaac Bassett for the riding championship at Sacramento.

"No, no, Wound Stripe came back again and put her head in front."

"But Brilliant Queen and Kobuki refused to give up."

"Well, yes. It was close, *close*. Too close to even call."

"What the hell is taking so long?"

"Maybe they're 'doctoring' the film."

It was twenty minutes before the decision came down from the stewards: *dead heat*! That night, Kobuki celebrated his tie for the riding championship by walking the Midway and throwing baseballs at lead milk bottles.

1. Kotaro Kobuki, Kokomo Joe's father, age sixty-two. From Yoshio Kobuki's scrapbook, courtesy of Elsie and Jiro Kobuki.

2. Yoshino Kobuki, Kokomo Joe's mother, age twenty-six. From Yoshio Kobuki's scrapbook, courtesy of Elsie and Jiro Kobuki.

3. Home in Hiroshima Prefecture in Japan where Kokomo Joe was raised. View of family graveyard where Joe's brothers and sister were buried. From Yoshio Kobuki's scrapbook, courtesy of Elsie and Jiro Kobuki.

4. Gillespie Ranch—single horse with an unidentified rider outside the shed-rows, circa 1947. Courtesy of Gary Miller.

5. Cover of *Turf and Sport Digest* for August 1960 showing Ko-buki as an outrider for Royal Orbit in the Kentucky Derby. Photo by H. Harold Davis.

6. Kokomo Joe beside his camper-pickup, Santa Anita, 1960s. From Yoshio Kobuki's scrapbook, courtesy of Elsie and Jiro Kobuki.

7. Kokomo Joe on duty in his parking lot captain's uniform, Hollywood Park, 1970s. From Yoshio Kobuki's scrapbook, courtesy of Elsie and Jiro Kobuki.

8. Kokomo Joe in the bleachers at the Sacramento County Fair, 1985. *Sacramento Bee*/Randy Pench.

9. Kokomo Joe at the home of his brother Frank, 1980s. From Yoshio Kobuki's scrapbook, courtesy of Elsie and Jiro Kobuki.

11

Miserable Saboteurs

It was Thursday, September 18, 1941, and it hadn't rained in Yosemite National Park for nearly a month. Bridal Veil Falls was a trickle that misted and then disappeared. In the park's high country the bright yellow leaves of the aspen trembled and sparkled. The oaks on the valley floor were also beginning to turn golden. In the crisp dry fall atmosphere United States Attorney General Francis Biddle's voice seemed especially sharp and clear.

Biddle stood at the podium in the dining room of the magnificent Ahwahnee Lodge in Yosemite Valley. The occasion of his speech was the annual meeting of the California State Bar. Biddle had beady eyes, a perpetually clenched jaw, and a pencil mustache. On the street he could have been easily mistaken for a bookmaker or a swindler. But he was the nation's chief law enforcement officer, and his subject "The Power of Democracy" was being broadcast nationwide on radio. The dining room had massive windows and a high ceiling with sugar pine beams that gave the room a woodsy, expansive smell. The effect of the openness was to reinforce Biddle's intent to speak not just to a room packed with seven hundred attorneys but to the entire country.

Biddle's neat vest was opened at the top button so that he could gesture freely as he spoke; he made a thumbs-up fist that he pumped to drive home his points. It was his first public speech since his Senate confirmation as attorney general the previous June. One headline after another that spring and summer had warned of sabotage and espionage. So what did the new attorney general intend to do to safeguard America? A half moon of microphones was arranged in front of him to make sure that eager listeners throughout the country heard what his plans were.

The government must "deal firmly, yet fairly, with miserable saboteurs," Biddle emphasized. No one need fear that democracy would disappear just because the national emergency required strength. It was reassurances that had been prompted by critics who said that fear and anxiety had caused some administrative agencies to run "hog wild." There had been alarming reports of new and secret intelligence agencies to fight espionage. It had been reported that U.S. census data from 1940 was being used to identify suspicious persons of "enemy ancestry." In addition, the Alien Registration Act had ordered millions of aliens to register with the government. Finally, J. Edgar Hoover's lists of dangerous immigrants were increasingly worrisome. Who was on the lists? On what basis were they deemed "dangerous"? And which of the freedoms that they had come to America in search of would they have to give up? It made no constitutional sense, the critics protested, for *anybody* to give up their freedoms in the very fight to protect them.

Biddle spoke directly now to those objectors. It was utter nonsense, he said and pumped his fist, to claim that during the national emergency freedoms would be forever lost. Those who made that claim were "timid souls" who doubted democracy could be made to work whenever disaster or war threatened. Broad grants of power to the president were neither a new nor a dangerous thing, he went on. "The magnitude of the threatened disaster" was what determined the extent of the president's powers and what steps needed to be taken to prevent espionage.

But there *had* to be limits, the civil libertarians had insisted. Where were the boundaries? Was the president's authority absolute? Was nothing constitutional and sacred and beyond the reach of presidential power?

Biddle proceeded as if he had anticipated the need for specifics. "Freedom from searches and seizures . . . and trial by jury," he said, were part of our heritage. They would *never* be lost in a democracy. Wiretapping would be done but only under the strictest limitations.

That was as specific as Biddle would get, and he returned to lofty assurances. If war should come, he said, his voice rising and his fist pumping again, "individual liberties in America will be safeguarded." Some in the crowd leaped to their feet to applaud, and Biddle had to pause. "All subversive activities must be curbed," he finished, "but civil rights will remain." More of the crowd stood to applaud. Biddle's voice soared now. "We should do everything in our power to hold our precious liberties in peace and at war. The cruel stupidities of vigilantes must not take over," Biddle finished. The cheering carried outside the Ahwahnee and then rose from the valley floor like the roar in a football stadium.

The very need for the attorney general of the United States to speak to the entire nation about its personal liberties was proof of how anxious the country had become. And Biddle's speech did much to reassure constitutional watchdogs as well as the lawyers gathered in the bucolic setting of Yosemite. But headlines the next morning reported that Biddle had given "carte blanche" to the president. However, to do exactly what if war came was not explained.

It was all troubling, especially to a group calling itself the Northern California Committee on Fair Play for Citizens and Aliens of Japanese Ancestry. Just days after Biddle finished his speech, the committee issued a statement: "Popular resentment against

Japan may find expression in mounting discrimination or even physical violence." Kokomo Joe knew exactly what they were talking about. "Such animus would be un-American," the committee went on, "a menace to public welfare and the good name of the state." If there were suspicions of espionage, the committee urged, they should be reported to the FBI. Otherwise, leave the Germans and Italians and especially the poor, beleaguered Japanese alone.

On the day Francis Biddle spoke to the lawyers in Yosemite, Kokomo Joe and Mister Charley left Sacramento and headed back into the lumberjack country of northern California, this time to the four-day Del Norte County Fair. Despite his success at the Sacramento Fair, Kokomo Joe had cause to worry now about the noose of war that seemed to be tightening around his neck, and as he and Mister Charley drove steadily north, he had time to take stock of what all of his racing successes had brought him. In less than three months he had won over sixty races. If he kept up that winning pace for an entire year, it would put him among the leading jockeys in the country. Yet his name did not even appear among the names of the leading riders listed in the *Daily Racing Form*'s monthly chart books. So each of his victories as a Japanese jockey seemed to connect him less to the world of racing heroics than to a warlike Japanese nation that was gobbling up the Far East. What had been a small cabal of competitive and perhaps bigoted jockeys at Pleasanton had become a state and a nation harboring anxiety and suspicion about the Japanese. It had prompted the attorney general to acknowledge that there were American vigilantes out there ready to execute their "cruel stupidities." So what was Kokomo Joe doing heading for the little coastal town of Crescent City? If there was any place in America that had cause to be anxious about things Japanese, it was Crescent City, which was located on lowland that made it especially vulnerable to being swamped by a Japanese tsunami.

But it was Kokomo Joe who swamped the competition at Crescent City and won the meet with eight wins over four days of racing. Heading south again, the caravan stopped at the Redwood Acres racetrack in Eureka. The soldiers and pup tents were long gone from Sequoia Park, and whatever menace Kokomo Joe had felt by their presence in August was long gone also. Over four days of racing he went to the winner's circle so many times—fourteen in all—that he won his fifth straight fair meet that summer.

After the Eureka meet Kobuki and Brown headed for Fresno, California, with a string of thirteen horses. Despite the grim war news from Europe and the Far East and despite the anti-Japanese fever that was rising steadily on the West Coast, Kokomo Joe and Mister Charley could not help feeling confident that their successes would continue.

The Fresno County Fair with five days of racing opened on Tuesday, September 30. Kokomo Joe was greeted in the press as the sensational Japanese rider who had had seven consecutive victories earlier in the summer at Ferndale. But as Kokomo Joe found himself increasingly in the uncomfortable spotlight of California's anti-Japanese mood, it was difficult for him to focus on racing, and he did little to distinguish himself at Fresno, which was turning out to be nothing more than a temporary stop for him on the way south to Agua Caliente.

He began to hope that, once back in the carnival atmosphere of Tijuana and among the same nomads and footloose adventurers who had peopled the desert democracy of the Gillespie Ranch, he could go unnoticed. He would also remain out of the reach of whatever activities the U.S. government decided to officially undertake in response to calls to restrict the movement of aliens or to lock them up, especially the Japanese. He could spend the rest of the fall in Mexico waiting for the 1942 racing season to begin at Santa Anita. In the intervening weeks and months perhaps the world and the nation, and especially California, would settle down. The Nazi tank columns thundering across Europe and the Japanese jungle fighters laying waste to the Far East would come to their senses. The crisis would pass.

On Saturday, October 4, the last day of racing in Fresno, Joe Kobuki's hope of taking refuge in Mexico was nearly lost. It happened in the fifth race in front of a huge horrified crowd. Kobuki was on Clyde, whose running habits he knew so well it might have been the aging gelding he had in mind when he said he spoke to the horses in English. The longer the race for Clyde—and the more often—the better he seemed to like it, often loping along far off the pace and taking his own sweet time in the marathons. But at a mile and a sixteenth today, Charley Brown told Kobuki to stay close to the leaders and then be ready for a vigorous stretch sprint.

A small field of six horses broke cleanly from the gate in front of the grandstand, then went into the first turn in a tight bunch fighting for the lead. Because of the shuffling for position on the turn, few fans noticed the drama unfolding back at the starting gate directly in front of the grandstand.

As soon as the horses were gone, a tractor had begun pulling the gate off the track through a rail opening. But the chain cable snapped with a clang and the tractor bucked forward before it backfired and fell silent. Efforts to restart the tractor produced more backfires. A member of the gate crew picked up the two loose ends of the snapped chain and then just stared at them. Meanwhile, grooms, starter's assistants, pony boys, hot walkers, and a few railbirds who leaped onto the track put their shoulders to the gate and began to try to push it off the track. In the soft, freshly plowed track dirt, the gate would not budge.

By then the horses, still tightly bunched, were coming out of the backstretch and moving into the far turn. Kobuki's position was in the rear of the pack but strategically placed on the rail with room to move forward. He had been through four days of unremarkable riding, despite having been hailed upon arrival in Fresno as a "sensational apprentice" and an "outstanding" rider. But on Tuesday, as the Fresno Fig Queen looked on, he had done nothing outstanding and had given what the turf writers said were "dull performances under weak handling." On Thursday the turf writers had faulted him for going wide and ruining his chances. On Friday it had been even worse, and his mounts had lacked speed or had to be steadied or were simply "done early."

The Fresno meet was the first meet all summer in which Kobuki hadn't been pressing the leading rider or the leader himself. Now with only a handful of victories over the previous four days, there was no hope for Joe Kobuki to catch the leading rider. All that was left for him to do was to give a strong, determined ride on Clyde, and he went to the whip as soon as he came out of the final turn.

On the rail Clyde responded and began to slide slowly past horses. The rest of the field moved suddenly to the outside, as if to give him room to continue making his move.

The absence of flying wedges or efforts to trap him on the rail surprised Joe, and he glanced repeatedly over his left shoulder. The race was his to win he was certain, and he didn't intend to be caught this time by a horse coming *inside* him.

Joe had only the lead horse named Chiana to catch when he finally focused down the track. One of the gate crew, waving an arm and throwing dirt, was running straight at him and the leader Chiana.

It was then that Kobuki spotted the stuck gate behind the oncoming, frantic runner. He had only a second or two to decide what to do. There would be no sailing over the high gate as if it were a hedge in a steeplechase race. He could hold his course and try to thread Clyde through the needle of one of the gate's open post positions. He could give up any chance of victory and brake Clyde suddenly like a saddle horse during calf roping. Or he could keep moving forward as the rest of the field was doing, and if need be he could stiff arm the gate like a scatback as he shot around it.

Ahead of him Chiana swerved sharply just short of the gate and threw up clods of dirt. Before Kobuki could decide what to do, Clyde swerved even more sharply than Chiana and jackknifed suddenly. Like a bull rider, Kobuki threw one arm out for balance and tried to hang on with the other. But his momentum slipped him sideways off Clyde's shoulder like a trick rider. He managed to keep one leg hooked over the saddle to avoid falling. Then he reached for Clyde's mane, grabbed a handful of hair, and yanked himself upright just in time to watch the field he had been about to beat as it curled around the gate and passed him.

In the confusion a horse named Cinar came from dead last to win the race. Chiana managed to recover enough to finish second. But Clyde yawed and bucked as he trotted warily around the gate. He crossed the finish line fourth, still full of ornery bucking.

Fans who only moments earlier had been horrified by the possibility of a bloody spectacle quickly recovered themselves and stormed the judges stand at trackside. "Refund the entire mutuel pool!" they screamed. "Run the race over!"

But the judges held firm. Once the horses break out of the gate, it was a race! And the results could not be undone. One of the judges took pains to relive a track horror he had once seen back east when one of Charles Howard's horses had crashed at full speed into a stuck gate and been crushed into a bloody slaughterhouse mess. It was only by a stroke of good luck and expert riding that a similar disaster had been avoided at Fresno.

Joe Kobuki sat shaking uncontrollably in the jockeys' room after the near disaster. From fractious, unpredictable horses to cutthroat jockeys to a world of jackboots and bayonets for which others seemed to blame him, there were already enough perils in his life. A starting gate left in the middle of the stretch like an impossible steeplechase hurdle to be jumped was an additional terror he didn't need.

It wasn't until Charley Brown and his caravan were on the road again for Mexico that Kokomo Joe finally stopped shaking. He had narrowly escaped a bloody disaster at Fresno. Mexico and Agua Caliente would be different. There would be no soldiers in pup tents defending against mock invasions. Agua Caliente would be an easy carnival of racing and Hollywood stars in their two-toned shoes and purple smoking jackets. Even if he had been able to read the papers, his sense of relief over the prospect of temporary refuge in carefree Mexico was so great he would not have paid attention to the alarming news. Because of the gathering war clouds, all Germans and Italians and Japanese were being advised to get out of Mexico.

12

Nipponese Dynamite

Mexican taxis carried tourists along dusty back roads and short-cuts into "T.J." to buy trinkets or to have their pictures taken beside the painted Zebra on the Avenida de la Revolucion. Music from juke boxes and mariachi bands floated out of Avenida bars serving a fiery tequila that some said went down your throat like a torchlight parade.

It was noon on Sunday, December 7, 1941, and Kokomo Joe had been up since dawn galloping horses and then lying alone in the room he kept in the track's dormitory for jockeys and grooms who did not want the trouble of weekly border crossings at San Ysidro. The room was small, but it was big enough for everything that Kokomo Joe needed in his nomadic life: a bed, a dresser, an armoire in which to hang a few shirts and pants, and a small bed-side table for magazines. The December 1issue of *Life* magazine lay on the table. It wasn't just the prospect of interesting pictures that had prompted him to buy the magazine for a dime at a news-stand on the Avenida. It was the fascinating cover picture with a belly view of a menacing B-17 Flying Fortress bomber in flight, its nose-turret machine guns poking forward like the fangs of a venomous snake.

Life's depiction of America's new military character was a far cry from those pictures Kokomo Joe had once admired of America's rich and smoky indolence. In the two months since he had arrived back at Agua Caliente, that transition of America from a country of peaceful limousines to squadrons of Flying Fortresses prepared for war had accelerated. In November, in what was described as an effort to improve America's bargaining power with an increasingly aggressive Japan, President Roosevelt announced that he was prepared to pull U.S. Marines out of various locations in China. The overwhelming Japanese forces in China made the marines little more than suicide battalions anyway, so Roosevelt's move was less conciliatory than it appeared. But Tokyo's top diplomat Saburo Kurusu still headed for Washington seeking a peaceful resolution to its quarrel with America. Failing that, Kurusu warned, Japan was ready to move forward "by other means."

Three days later, Secretary of the Navy Frank Knox said that America could no longer ignore Japanese actions in the Far East. Knox added that "the hour of decision" was here for America, and he called for "instant readiness" for war. Then as November came to a close, Secretary of State Cordell Hull sent an ultimatum to the Japanese government. Among its provisions were demands that Japan withdraw from China and Indochina, or else.

There was no immediate response from Tokyo to Hull's ultimatum. And on December 1, the day that *Life* pictured the Flying Fortress on its cover, the Japanese consulate in Washington began destroying its records. At noon that same day President Roosevelt cut short his vacation at Warm Springs, Georgia, and returned to the White House. Meanwhile, despite the commitment of Gen. Hideki Tojo's cabinet to continuing negotiations with America, the official Japanese news agency reported that America was trying to turn the Pacific Ocean into her own pond and the Pacific rim into her own garden. Japan's position seemed final: the United States must correct *her* attitude.

On Saturday, December 6, as Yoshio Kobuki galloped his mounts in preparation for Sunday's Agua Caliente races, Roosevelt made one last move to go around the intransigent military government of Premier Tojo. The president sent an urgent personal message to Emperor Hirohito. It was, the newspapers reported, the last step America intended to take before it broke with Japan.

War seemed imminent, but war seemed to be the last thing on the minds of the nearly thirty jockeys scheduled to ride mounts in the twelve-race card at Agua Caliente. They began gathering at midmorning in the jockeys' room, and they chattered and shouted with anticipation of the day's races.

Johnny Adams, a twenty-six-year-old jockey from tiny Iola, Kansas, had a slim lead in the battle for national riding honors. With just three weeks to go in the year, whatever victories he could pick up in Sunday racing at Caliente—he had mounts in all but one of the twelve races—would help secure the title for him.

Junior Nicholson from Imperial, Nebraska, had just turned twenty. He had been the leading rider as an apprentice that spring at Santa Anita. Despite having gone flat in the fall at Bay Meadows, he was back in form at Caliente and riding winners. He had three mounts that Sunday, and he expected to win on all three.

At just eighteen young José Martin del Campo was the dean of Latino riders in America. He had anglicized his name to Joe Martini hoping not just to separate himself from all the other Mexican Josés and Martins but to acquire the same appearance of American character that Joe Kobuki had sought. In the United States Joe Martini had ridden against and beaten the best—from George Woolf to Johnny Longden. He had only two mounts that Sunday, but one of them would be against Johnny Adams in the feature race, and Martini looked forward to the battle.

Seventeen-year-old Francisco "Poncho" Rodriguez, whose stepfather owned a small ranch adjacent to Agua Caliente, had been hanging around the track since he was old enough to walk mucking stalls, then hot walking horses, and finally galloping them.

Today, he would have his first crack at actually riding in a race. It would be, he hoped with sweaty excitement, the start of a promising career.

Finally, no one in the crowded jockeys' room was more excited than Kokomo Joe Kobuki. With his arrival at Agua Caliente in October and riding only on Sundays, he had continued his winning ways. On Sunday, October 19, he had had three winners. Then the following Sunday he had had four winners and upstaged Johnny Adams. "Japanese Pilot Steals Spotlight," the *Los Angeles Times* headline reported. It was, they said, the best riding effort of the fall. From Terminal Island to Tokyo, the *Times* said, the Japanese were celebrating Kobuki's victories with rice and tasty shrimp.

Energized by his new successes, Kokomo Joe had even begun riding with some of the daredevil spirit that Charley Brown had first spotted in Phoenix. It was an important riding quality, but Brown had had to remind Kobuki it needed to be measured and disciplined, or it was nothing but reckless abandon that would get him injured, or worse, killed. Kobuki had tried to discipline himself, but back in November he had still been called into the stewards' office at Caliente to explain his actions after he had shot from the starting gate in one of his races and then cut off the rest of the field.

"What in the world are you doing?" the stewards asked him.

"Mister Charley told me . . . cut 'em off," he said and flashed his broad smile. "Mister Charley . . . want to *win!*" he added. As if *he* didn't. As if he was just a smiling, obliging chauffeur, this time of horses. As if on that December 7 Sunday he wasn't as hell-bent and determined as all the other eager riders in the jockeys' room.

Shortly after noon that Sunday, across the border in San Diego, paper boys began rushing into the streets with an extra edition of the *San Diego Union*: the Japanese had bombed Pearl Harbor.

Rumors of the attack began circulating among the track's seven thousand fans shortly after the first race. By the time Kokomo Joe walked to the paddock for his first mount in the third race, bettors and railbirds stood in small groups discussing what they had heard. "Who attacked whom?" "Where? Oahu?" "Where the hell is that?"

The question for the moment was whether or not the border station at San Ysidro would remain open. Should all Americans head back across the border? It was one thing to spend a sunny Sunday with Hollywood stars and American playboys in the Spanish baronial setting of the Agua Caliente Turf Club. It was quite another to be stranded for days, maybe weeks, in dusty and bawdy Tijuana, when there was no weekday racing and only the pleasures of rotgut tequila.

Kokomo Joe was dismounting after a disappointing finish in the middle of the pack in the third race when the announcer made it official: the Japanese had attacked Pearl Harbor in Hawaii. But he said there was little likelihood of the border closing. The spirit of friendship that existed between the United States and Mexico was too long-standing, he explained. "There will *never* be a barrier between the two countries."

But rumors and speculation continued to fly around the track, and a "spirit of uneasiness prevailed" throughout the afternoon. It wasn't until just before the tenth race that someone brought a radio into the jockeys' room, and the riders listened to urgent radio bulletins describing the Japanese attack on Pearl Harbor.

Charley Brown had no horses in the tenth race, and Kokomo Joe had accepted a mount from a small barn called Georgia Stables. Kobuki was changing slowly into the stable's silks when several of the jockeys told him that he better leave the track. He wasn't sure if it was friendly advice or an angry order.

"How can I leave?" he asked. "I have a mount in the tenth race!"

"Georgia Stables can get a substitute rider," they told him.

"No, no." Failure to meet a riding obligation was the worst sin a jockey could commit. He'd be fined. Suspended.

The other jockeys laughed. His loyalty to the kingpins and bosses of thoroughbred racing was misplaced. To owners and trainers most jockeys were no more than tiny gladiators and just as expendable. He should leave the track immediately, they repeated.

Then Junior Nicholson delivered a warning. "The Mexican police are unpredictable," he said. "There is no telling what they might try to do in the crisis. Or actually *do!*"

Other jockeys agreed. There was still talk around the track of a black stable hand who had refused to cooperate with Tijuana police in an investigation of track corruption. The stable hand hadn't agreed to talk until police led him to a bullet-riddled stone wall in front of a firing squad and then offered him a last cigarette and a blindfold. If Kokomo Joe didn't want to be put against a stone wall and shot himself, he should get back across the border to the safety of America. *Now.*

"No, no!" What did they know about being "Nipponese dynamite" at an American racetrack alongside patriotic jockeys named Johnny and George? Kobuki insisted he was safe in Mexico, and he continued changing into his silks for the tenth race.

His mount was Precious Moon, a four-year-old gelding who went off as the third favorite in a large field of eleven horses going a mile and a sixteenth. Kobuki went straight to the front, and down the backstretch he opened up a three-length lead. Three different horses moved up to challenge him during the race, but each time they did, he stroked Precious Moon with his whip and kept the three-length lead. But at the sixteenth pole, a fourth horse, a twenty-to-one long shot named Ylee Bar, came from the middle of the field in a rush and slid easily past Precious Moon despite Kobuki's furious whipping.

After the race Kokomo Joe sat in the corner of the jockeys'

room still in his silks, nursing the disappointment of his loss. Two track stewards appeared suddenly in the room. Because of the news from Pearl Harbor, the last two races of the day had been cancelled, they explained. Then they headed for the corner where Kobuki sat. For a moment he wondered if they had come to chastise him about his aggressive ride on Precious Moon through the stretch.

But the stewards had a different message: Mexican officials were rounding up the entire Japanese population of Tijuana. They would be sent to a camp in Sonora. Or worse, a hellhole prison in Panama City, Panama. Kokomo Joe needed to leave the track immediately, they warned.

Kobuki stood up and began slowly unbuttoning his silks.

They stopped him. "You don't have time to change," they said. "You need to drive back across the border, for your safety."

"I have to talk to Mister Charley first," he insisted.

"No! There isn't time! Get going! Now!"

They began pushing him toward the door of the jockeys' room as he tried to explain that he didn't have a car. By then a small crowd of jockeys stood around Kobuki. Whatever dog-eat-dog competitiveness he had experienced at every track that summer, some of it clearly driven by bigotry, was momentarily forgotten. This was one of their own, a tiny fellow gladiator trapped in an unpredictable country by the sudden emergencies of a global war. But no one seemed to know what to do.

The answer came from a twenty-one-year-old freelance rider from Austin, Texas, named Roy "Tex" McWhorter. He was a race-track jack-of-all-trades, from stable hand to valet to exercise boy for Charles Howard's horses. He even rode an occasional race himself. But he had had no mounts that day, and now he offered to drive Kobuki quickly back to the San Ysidro border station. His car, he said, was parked outside the track.

The two men trotted out of the jockeys' room to Kobuki's room in the dormitory where he grabbed what few belongings he had and threw them in his cardboard suitcase. With Kobuki sitting inconspicuously in the back seat, McWhorter raced to the border along the back roads, passing even the Mexican taxis raising dust clouds.

At the border, Kokomo Joe jumped out of the car, thanked McWhorter for his help, then trotted toward the gateways marking the border. Mexican police with pistols and badges as big as breastplates stopped him on their side immediately. In broken English they demanded to know where he was going.

"Back to San Diego," he answered.

"From where?"

He pinched his silks. "I am a jockey. I've been riding at Agua Caliente."

"So why are you going back to San Diego?"

"I am an American," he answered, raising his voice.

"Not Japanese?"

"No, no. Not Japanese. I am American," he repeated.

The police explained that they had orders to stop any Japanese nationals trying to leave Mexico.

"I am *American*!" he repeated for a third time, pleading now.

"So what is your name?"

The police scowled as they waited for him to answer. Meanwhile, car horns blared from long lines of impatient drivers who were trying to cross back into the safety of California. The sun had set but turned the distant sky red as if it might have been Pearl Harbor burning beyond the horizon. Against the noise and rancor Kobuki had only his trademark, toothy smile, and he flashed it now.

"My name is Yoshio Kobuki," he said. "Everyone calls me Kokomo Joe," he added.

The police seemed puzzled. "*Kokomo Joe?*"

"Yes. Kokomo Joe. *Born* in America."

They smiled back now. Well, all right, he could go. But he better stay out of Mexico. The border was closed to all Japanese nationals, coming or going.

He fairly skipped around the Mexican police and might have celebrated the fact that his engaging smile had worked again and his troubles were over. But he had no sooner reached the American side of the border, manned by Border Patrol inspectors in garrison hats and Sam Browne belts, when he was stopped again.

That ill-defined invader who had been only a murky threat in the fog was now a jackbooted Nazi or a Japanese fighter pilot. World war had finally come. The threat of invasion seemed real. And nobody, especially a Japanese peanut flashing a cartoon smile and dressed in jockey's silks, was going to come waltzing into America when Pearl Harbor was ablaze just beyond the horizon.

13

Hoover's Lists

It had been building for weeks, the American-Mexican border restrictions that stopped Kokomo Joe in his tracks. American officials feared that the Baja Peninsula would be the staging point for
a Japanese invasion of the Pacific Coast. As recently as December 1 British intelligence had intercepted communications suggesting that Axis spies in Mexico were using secret microdots to
communicate with their handlers. Accordingly, American intelligence officials characterized Baja California as a "boundary
outpost" for Japanese spying. Additional American intelligence
reports were that a Japanese diplomatic officer was traveling the
West Coast from Vancouver to Tijuana, contacting spies and collecting information. Two hundred FBI agents had been stationed
in the Hotel Maria Cristina in Mexico City to help identify Axis
nationals for arrest and internment as spies in the event of war.
And by the afternoon of December 7 the Border Patrol station at
San Ysidro had tightened its crossing rules. The movement of Japanese aliens in and out of America was brought to a halt.

For the border authorities who confronted Kokomo Joe, the
issue was not just *who* the hell he was standing there with a ner-
vous smile in his colorful riding silks and carrying a small suitcase. The issue was *what* was he: Japanese or American? They took

him into a small room of the border station where an INS immigrant inspector began grilling him.

"What's your name."

"Joe. Joe Kobuki."

"Where were you born?"

"Born Thomas," he stammered.

"*Thomas?*" The inspector was confused. Was his name Joe or Tom?

"Joe. Kokomo Joe!"

"Born where?"

"Thomas," he repeated. "*Thomas.*"

"Thomas? That is the name of a *place*?"

"OK. Yes." He nodded vigorously and smiled. "A place! OK."

"Where is this place named *Thomas*?"

Joe struggled to pronounce Seattle.

"Seattle? Seattle, Washington?"

"Yes. OK."

"You were born in Seattle?"

"No, no. Thomas!"

"Thomas is *near* Seattle?"

"Yes, yes. Near Seattle."

The inspector was beginning to understand him now. "You were born in a small town named Thomas, near Seattle?"

"OK. Yes."

"When?"

"1918. October 17. *American citizen*," he added.

"Well, yes," the inspector conceded. "If what you say about your birthplace is true, you would be an American citizen. But you are also a Japanese citizen."

Joe shook his head. "No, no."

"Didn't you just say you were born in 1918?"

"Yes. 1918."

"Then you are a Japanese citizen."

The inspector was being as intractable as the Mexicans had just been, and Kokomo Joe's smile had disappeared. "No, no," he insisted. "Not Japanese."

The inspector explained it to him patiently then. Persons of Japanese ancestry born anywhere in the world before 1925 were automatically considered by the Japanese government to be Japanese citizens.

Kokomo Joe shook his head. "American citizen!"

The inspector suddenly changed the subject. "Did you ever *live* in Japan?"

"Well, yes, I did."

"For how long?"

"Sixteen years."

"And you still insist you aren't a Japanese citizen?"

"No, no. American." He had never thought of himself as anything but American.

"So what have you done to give up your Japanese citizenship?"

"I didn't know I had to do anything."

The inspector explained what he had had to do to renounce his Japanese citizenship. It was a five-step process that took months, if not years, and involved securing certified documents, writing letters, filling out various application forms, and then waiting and waiting.

When the inspector was finished, Kobuki asked why he had to do any of that? He had done nothing to acquire Japanese citizenship. So why did he have to go through such a complicated process to give up what he had never had?

It was, the inspector conceded, a complicated process. But it was nevertheless what he had had to do. Because he hadn't done it, it meant that he was a *dual* citizen, Japanese and American. But only if and when immigration authorities could confirm that his place of birth was Thomas, Washington. If they couldn't confirm

it, then he was *not* an American citizen. He was a Japanese enemy alien, subject to the mandates of the Alien Enemy Control
Program.

"What does that mean?" Joe asked.

It meant that, relying upon J. Edgar Hoover's lists of dangerous aliens, the Department of Justice and the FBI would con-
sider his case. It meant being caught in a dragnet so expansive
that it even ensnared Jewish refugees like Edward Heims, who
had had to take out ads in his local newspapers protesting his innocence. It meant that some of Kokomo Joe's belongings would
be confiscated.

"I have very little," Joe interjected. "I am a jockey who travels
with only my small suitcase. I am on the road all the time with
Mister Charley."

"You travel a lot?"

"Yes. I drive for Mister Charley. From racetrack to racetrack."
He took out his driver's license and showed it proudly.

The inspector studied the license, then explained that, if it
turned out that Kokomo Joe was an enemy alien, it meant also
that his travel would be restricted. Further, it meant the possibility of detention and internment in one of the many camps run by
the Department of Justice for dangerous enemy aliens.

"Dangerous? Why am I dangerous? I am just a jockey who rides
horses for Mister Charley."

"It is clear that you are Japanese," the inspector explained again.
"But it has not been established, at least not yet, that you are also
American. It will take immigration authorities a day or two to confirm it. Meanwhile, you have to be held in the San Diego County
jail with other Japanese aliens who are being rounded up."

"Jail? All I want to do is be a jockey. To ride horses to the victory. Why do I have to go to jail?"

They drove him to the county jail in San Diego, where he was finally permitted to change out of his riding silks. He spent the

night in a drunk tank with other Japanese who had been arrested in the San Diego area or at the border.

In the morning a female Japanese American missionary who had been arrested returning from Tijuana spotted all the worried long faces of other Japanese detainees. She exhorted them to stop feeling sorry for themselves. Their detention was only a temporary nightmare.

Despite the missionary's predictions, the nightmare did not pass. Kokomo Joe and twenty-five other Japanese detainees, many of them fishermen and farmers or leaders of judo and kendo clubs, were taken to the FBI headquarters on Sixth and Broadway in San Diego. There, FBI agents confronted him with the same accusations and suspicions that he had faced at the border: Where was he born? How could he prove he was an American citizen? Then the FBI agents were joined by interrogators from the Office of Naval Intelligence, and they also grilled him: What did he know about Japanese espionage organizations on the coast? Why had he been in Mexico? Who were his friends and associates?

Seventy enemy aliens who had been arrested at the Mexican border or in San Diego, among them eight Germans, were eventually moved to the Department of Justice detention facility for enemy aliens at Big Tujunga Canyon outside Los Angeles. From there they were sent by train to permanent internment facilities in Missoula, Montana, and Bismarck, North Dakota. Pressed by *San Diego Union* reporters for the names of the dangerous Japanese, the agent in charge of the San Diego FBI office revealed only that they were probably all aliens and that they were being held on "open charges." He conceded that none had exhibited anti-American behavior. But he said nothing to indicate that among them was a promising *American* jockey who had been riding that day at Agua Caliente.

While Kokomo Joe waited in the San Diego jail to have his citizenship verified, teams of FBI agents, joined by local police, swung into action under the authority of the Alien Enemies Act and presidential proclamations focused on enemy aliens. The first to be rounded up were suspected Axis sympathizers—German Bundists, Italian fascists, and Japanese organizational leaders, all of whom were on J. Edgar Hoover's ABC lists. The suspicions were based on investigative reports gathered by Hoover's agents. Those reports were in turn based on information that was more hearsay, rumor, and ethnic gossip than hard evidence. But it was enough to lead to the arrest of over two thousand enemy aliens in the days immediately following Pearl Harbor. Thousands more were ordered to turn in their cameras, firearms, and shortwave radios.

Once immigration authorities verified Kobuki's birth in Thomas, Washington, he was released from detention but not without several warnings. Yes, he was an American citizen, they conceded, but also Japanese. He was to be careful where he traveled. The presence of enemy aliens or suspicious looking persons—it was clear they meant anybody who looked Japanese—around shipyards, coastal gun batteries, power plants, or munitions factories would be cause for arrest. Generally he would be safe if he stayed away from the coast. If he tried to return to Mexico, he would be arrested and sent to Montana or North Dakota with the rest of the dangerous enemy aliens. Additionally, he was reminded that a lot of people were angry about what the Japanese had done at Pearl Harbor. If he insisted on being a celebrated and highly visible jockey, he was only asking for trouble, and nobody could guarantee his safety.

The sprawl of Los Angeles seemed to promise Kokomo Joe the best chance of anonymity and refuge, and he headed there by bus after his release from the San Diego County jail. But one Los Angeles resident had already written Attorney General Francis Biddle that "no Jap should be permitted to remain in America." And as soon as Kokomo Joe arrived in Los Angeles, he discovered that one of those FBI teams had swept into Terminal Island, a six-mile-long island home for the Japanese fishing and canning industry, and carted off what they considered the most dangerous Japanese enemy aliens. Elsewhere, they were continuing to pick off German and Italian enemy aliens, among them Edward Heims, the German Jew whose Marin County neighbors continued to spread the rumors, despite his newspapers protests of innocence, that he was a Nazi spy whose farmland would be a convenient airfield for invading Axis troops.

Meanwhile, the Japanese rampage in the Far East continued—the Malay Peninsula, Thailand, Hong Kong, Wake Island, Midway, the Philippines. So what was next? San Francisco? Los Angeles? It would be, newspapers warned, another sneak attack. There were reports of "unidentified planes" approaching San Francisco. Hardware stores sold out their supplies of long-handled shovels for digging citizen foxholes. Sentries shot a woman who wandered innocently onto the Golden Gate Bridge. Civil defense officials ordered blackouts. In the pitch dark anxious citizens tried to follow the progress of aerial dogfights. The public was urged to "be calm, stay home. The enemy wants you to create a panic and rush into the streets."

Despite the warnings to remain calm, at nightfall on December 10 an unusual thunderstorm struck southern California. The bolts of lightning and the deep thunder sounded like enemy ship salvos or an aerial bombardment, and the jittery citizens of southern California feared they were under attack.

At 8:00 p.m. anxious aircraft spotters charged with protecting the California coast reported that unidentified planes were circling near Los Angeles. Civil defense officials ordered all radio stations off the air. Military officials sounded lights-out sirens. From Bakersfield to San Diego and inland all the way to Las Vegas, "a great pall of darkness spread" and there was panic in the streets.

A German nanny from Beverly Hills ran into the night crying, "Mein Gott! Mein Gott! We're raided!" Hollywood cops warned pedestrians and motorists to take shelter. Citizens shot out streetlights in the frenzy to black out the city. Los Angeles motorists caught in the streets tried to work their way through snarls of traffic, blinking their dimmer lights at dark intersections. A San Diego driver who refused to dim his lights was dragged from his car and severely beaten. Los Angeles hospitals were swamped with calls for ambulances to cover traffic accidents involving panicked drivers. Three hours later, the all-clear signal sounded, and radio stations came back on the air to report that all danger had passed, but only "for the present."

The suggestion that more dangers were still to come, with more panic, led Joe Kobuki to decide quickly that Los Angeles offered no refuge from citizen panic or from authorities who had already jailed him once and were still rounding up enemy aliens. He was no longer the conspicuous Japanese jockey standing there in his riding silks, inviting attention and suspicion. But if the Justice Department's dragnet did snare him, it would again be his so-called dual citizenship that would be an issue. He decided then to head north for Seattle and his father's truck farm in the White River Valley of Washington. If there were dragnets being cast there, the officials would at least know that Thomas was not his name but the name of the little town where he was born. What better proof could he offer of his citizenship than to stand on the American dirt floor in the clapboard cabin of his father's truck farm and point to the bed where he had come into the world no bigger than a peanut.

But back in the White River Valley he found himself again under a cloud of suspicion. Alien Japanese, Germans, and Italians were being rounded up. Or they were ordered to turn in their radios, their cameras, their maps, even their kitchen knives. What few friends Yoshio Kobuki had made among the white teenagers when he worked the lettuce chainlines refused to talk to him. Elsewhere, there were calls to ship all Japanese back to Japan. It prompted Japanese American leaders to issue public reaffirmations of their loyalty. "We are Americans," they said. But few in the public were sympathetic. "This is total war," an admiral declared. "Every civilian is in it."

Well, all right then, Kokomo Joe decided. If it was total war, and they needed every civilian to be in it, then he would enlist. But at the recruitment office in Seattle, they looked him up and down.

"How tall are you?"

"*Almost* five feet," he answered and straightened himself.

"How much do you weigh?"

"*Almost* one hundred pounds!"

The recruiters politely escorted him out of the enlistment office and sent him on his way.

He had come back to the White River Valley in search of home and a refuge. But once there, things were no better than they had been in Los Angeles. One night, a passenger train lugged through the valley sounding its lonely whistle, its shades drawn, its windows barred, and loaded with Japanese enemy aliens from Seattle who were being trained to the prison in Missoula. Meanwhile, the police made spot raids on Japanese homes in the valley. They searched the truck farm cabins of enemy aliens like Kotaru Kobuki. They were looking for and confiscating contraband, which even included family radios, BB guns, and toy telegraph keys, any of which the authorities felt, might somehow have turned out to be a weapon of war. Finally, the local railroad workers threatened to strike if their Japanese colleagues weren't fired.

For days Yoshio worked on the truck farm, expecting that the grit and sweat of the work would fix him to a specific place. But he remained disconnected and pointless, no different than what the other racetrackers called bindlestiffs, who carried everything they owned in a blanket roll and wandered from racetrack to racetrack picking up odd jobs mucking stalls or hot walking horses until they had earned enough to move on.

He had been the Japanese sensation, the little package of Nipponese dynamite who was on his way to the top, where somebody would be chauffeuring *him* while he smoked long cigarettes. But he was as lonely now as he had been in Japan and as much a nomad as he had been in Pleasanton, Santa Rosa, Ferndale, Stockton, Sacramento, Crescent City, Fresno, and Caliente. In each of those places he had been able to overcome the rivalries and bigotries and the menace of passing troop convoys and eventually prevail. Now it was total war, a grinding, enveloping threat from which it seemed impossible to escape because the battleground was everywhere, even the little truck farms of the White River Valley.

So where was he to go now? The excesses and revelry of gambling seemed utterly contrary to the spirit of sacrifice necessary to win wars, and the racing seasons at various California racetracks had been cancelled. Santa Anita had been shut down. Hollywood Park was also closed and would eventually be used as a wing assembly plant for fighter planes. Thoroughbred owners were shipping their stock back east or to Caliente, where racing continued on Sundays but which would have been another, even more threatening battleground for Yoshio Kobuki.

All around him there were rumors of what might be coming for the Japanese. Yet beyond occasional poignant declarations of loyalty, no one seemed to be trying to *do* anything to stop it. Well, the rest of them could wait to be jailed or confined to their truck farms but not Kokomo Joe. He was the impetuous jockey who had been told he had more courage than was good for him. And he felt now that there was still one place where he might be safe from the turmoil of war—the Gillespie Ranch in Arizona.

Among the sagebrush and the rattlesnakes. Among the gypsy grooms and the Pima Indians and the bindlestiffs.

The New Year came. The war news was not good. American troops abandoned Manila to the Japanese. Australia passed out what it called battle kits to a militia bracing itself for a Japanese invasion. In Europe German Panzers had advanced to within sixty miles of Moscow. It was a worldwide battle for survival. In an America at war now mothers saved their kitchen fat for explosives. There were depots for collecting soup cans and the tin foil from gum wrappers. Children brought dimes to school to help make battleships and bombs. There was a sense of national purpose everywhere in America, and in Seattle they shot Roman candles into the night skies. But Yoshio Kobuki packed his cardboard suitcase, said goodbye to his father, and headed for Arizona.

14

Fibber McGee

It rained in Washington DC the morning of February 17, 1942, and some of the reporters who gathered three deep around President Roosevelt's desk in the Oval Office for the Tuesday press conference leaned on their umbrellas. "Mr. President," a young reporter asked, "there are rumors in Washington that the damage at Pearl Harbor was worse than reported."

Roosevelt stiffened. "R-O-T!" he said firmly.

The young reporter was confused. Was that an acronym for another New Deal agency? Laughter filled the Oval Office. Roosevelt smiled. His predecessor Herbert Hoover had complained that facing pesky reporters at press conferences made him feel like a "common thief." But FDR enjoyed the twice-weekly ceremony, and he waited patiently for the laughter to die before he explained, still smiling, that Washington was the worst rumor factory in the country. What the young reporter had heard about Pearl Harbor was not true, the president said.

Then the questions turned to the issue of the Japanese. Despite two days of headline news about a heroic GI who had killed 116 Japanese soldiers on the Bataan Peninsula and who was described as a "one man army," Singapore had fallen and Australia was still preparing for an invasion.

"Isn't there the possibility, Mr. President, of an enemy attack in Alaska?" the reporters asked.

"The enemy could come in and shell New York tomorrow night," the president answered.

A stunned silence followed.

"—or he could drop bombs on Detroit."

The silence continued and none of the reporters could immediately pose the next question. Roosevelt took advantage of the silence to lift a piece of paper from a stack of documents on his desk and pretend to be studying it. Eventually, the reporters filed out quietly, still stunned by the prospect of an attack on New York or Detroit.

That night, seven men from Roosevelt's administration met in the home of Attorney General Francis Biddle on the crest of the hill that ran up 31st Street in the northwest section of the city. The seven men sat in a circle in Biddle's living room. Biddle and his Department of Justice aides formed half of the circle, while Assistant Secretary of War Jack McCloy and two members of the army's staff formed the other half. Distant laughter carried up the hill from neighborhood radios tuned to the weekly broadcast of "Fibber McGee and Molly."

The subject of the meeting at Biddle's home was not what to do in the event of a Japanese attack on New York or Michigan. What if they struck California and the West Coast?

For months, under a shaky agreement, the two departments, War and Justice, had been handling the problem of enemy aliens and the threat of sabotage and invasion. War's responsibility was to map out the coastal areas that needed to be evacuated because of what it said was military necessity. Riding point for the War Department was sixty-two-year-old general John DeWitt, who had come up through the army's ranks at the end of an era of cavalry glories. He and his generals had argued for weeks that *all* enemy aliens needed to be cleared out of the areas that War was mapping out.

To Justice the idea of moving over half a million residents was a foolish idea—a throwback to cavalry troops clearing the Great Plains of Indians—and Justice had simply ignored DeWitt's proposal. Instead, Justice had focused on the removal of only what it considered "dangerous" German, Italian, and Japanese enemy aliens.

But the public pressure for large-scale evacuations of enemy aliens from the West Coast had continued to mount throughout January. There was no time to separate the sheep from the goats evacuation advocates felt. The Germans, the Italians, and the Japanese enemy aliens, they all had to be cleared out. The Japanese were especially dangerous because there were "known subversives" among them. Governor Olson of California warned that, if nothing was done, the people would take the law into their own hands. The widely read columnist Walter Lippman wrote that California was threatened by an attack from within and from without. The fact that no sabotage had yet occurred was proof that the saboteurs were *waiting* to strike. A delegation of California congressman also urged clearing out all enemy aliens and their children from DeWitt's military zones. The few military men who argued that there were no special coastal dangers were dismissed as "jackasses."

Despite the disagreements between War and Justice, or perhaps in an effort to end them, on January 29 Biddle announced that two small prohibited zones—the San Francisco waterfront and the Los Angeles airport—would be evacuated of *all* German, Italian, and Japanese enemy aliens. Additional evacuation zones would be announced shortly. The evacuation was to be *voluntary,* Biddle clarified, and the enemy aliens would have until February 24 to clear out.

The reaction from California congressmen and newspapers in early February was furious. The *San Francisco Examiner* charged that the evacuation timetable was too slow and gave the Japanese time to perfect their bombs and their sabotage plans. Biddle was no better than a "third assistant dog catcher," the *Examiner* wrote. California congressmen joined in the attack on Biddle, and they took their protests of the voluntary slow nature of the evacuation to General DeWitt, who promptly announced he was ready to take charge of the entire program.

It had all seemed to have little or nothing to do with Kokomo Joe on the Gillespie Ranch in Arizona. What did the German and Italian and Japanese enemy aliens have to do with him? He had made it clear to authorities that he was an American! For now his days were filled with the work of mucking stalls, exercising horses, and cleaning tack. Even the most skittery of citizens would have had trouble finding anything subversive in his behavior. In the middle of the desert he felt safe among the bindlestiffs and gypsy grooms working beside him.

During the first week in February, as the calls for restrictions and evacuations continued, the number of prohibited zones was expanded to include more areas around dams, power plants, airfields, harbors, military installations, and a long strip of the coast. Ten thousand German, Italian, and Japanese enemy aliens and their families were under orders to move out of the prohibited zones, but the *San Francisco Chronicle* felt that the evacuations were "necessary and proper acts of national defense, regardless of individual injustices."

On February 9 General DeWitt joined the chorus of protests against Justice and recommended that the western halves of Oregon and Washington along with all of California be declared prohibited zones and cleared of enemy aliens. Biddle protested that only War had the equipment and personnel to handle such a mass evacuation, and he again refused to act on DeWitt's proposal.

West Coast hysteria against the Japanese was now in full force. Six vigilantes—the very vigilantes that Biddle had vowed would never prevail—had shot up a Japanese asparagus camp near Sacramento. Armchair generals warned that the Japanese were capable of invading the West Coast and controlling the Pacific slope all the way to the Sierras. "The Japanese race is an enemy race," General DeWitt declared.

In the early afternoon of February 11 Secretary of War Henry Stimson had discussed the West Coast problem with the president. "Do what you think best," the president told Stimson. "Evacuation must be a military decision."

Justice's measures against enemy aliens had done little to calm West Coast fears. On Monday, February 16, the day before the meeting in Biddle's living room, the *San Francisco Chronicle* had reported a "tidal wave of demands" to clear the prohibited zones of *all* enemy aliens. The Germans and Italians were not as dangerous as the Japanese, the *Chronicle* conceded, but they were all a "menace," and they all had to go.

The meeting in Biddle's living room began with a discussion of DeWitt's prohibited zones and the "insuperable" problem as far as Justice was concerned of clearing them of *all* enemy aliens. Each time Biddle had balked about removing enemy aliens from the prohibited zones, DeWitt's response had been to recommend more and larger zones. Now Biddle sat buried in his chair, his fists in his coat pocket as he listened to the army's Jack McCloy, Colonel Bendetsen, and General Gullion repeat the demand that Justice clear the areas of all German, Italian, and Japanese enemy aliens.

Biddle pulled one fist from his pocket. He had said it before, and he would say it one more time. He lifted his thumb from his fist, as if to count the one more time. If there were to be mass evacuations, he said, "the military will have to handle it." James Rowe agreed and repeated the warning he had previously given to De-Witt: "Evacuation of enemy aliens from such large areas will create misery and hardship."

Edward Ennis sat in a straight back chair directly across from Biddle so that he could read his boss's face. If anyone knew what Justice could or could not handle, it was thirty-four-year-old Ennis, whom Biddle had put in charge of the Alien Enemy Control Program that past December. Not long after, Ennis and Rowe had tried to calm the fears of congressmen who were insisting that Japanese Americans had to be moved from the West Coast.

"No, they didn't!" Ennis and Rowe had insisted.

"Well, just suppose you and Rowe are wrong?" the committee worried.

Ennis had delivered a wry smile and told them, "Then take us out and shoot us." That mordant, feisty streak Biddle felt equipped Ennis to stand up to the army's arguments about military necessity.

"Justice is unequipped to handle mass evacuations for military necessity," Ennis said now. "And we are not going to do it!"

It was a refusal meant for the War Department's half of the circle, but Ennis stared at his boss. Biddle stared back, and Ennis wondered whether Biddle was agreeing with the hard line or shocked by Ennis's bluntness.

Colonel Bendetsen shot back, "You *have* to do it. It's military necessity."

Military necessary! There it was again. Biddle considered it a "mystic cliché" that had the power to make government officials ignore human rights.

Now Jack McCloy joined the argument. He had a ruggedly handsome face and big hands that reflected his college football toughness. "If it is a question of the safety of the country, or the Constitution, the Constitution is just a scrap of paper to me."

McCloy, Gullion, and Bendetsen each took turns offering what had become a litany of invasion fears: enemy submarine sightings, intercepted radio transmissions, supersecret spy rings, coastal bombardments from enemy ships, mysterious explosions and fires, and hints of sabotage. When they finished, Biddle only stirred slightly in his deep chair: How can I tell these fellows I know their business better than they do? he thought. But he said nothing.

Meanwhile, Rowe had listened carefully and respectfully to War's litany. "It is all pretty thin stuff," he said.

Ennis nodded. They needed to "cool" the fear.

For a moment there was silence. It was long enough to suggest, at least to Rowe and Ennis, that perhaps some compromise had been reached between Justice and War. The few enemy alien precautions that needed to be taken would continue on course. War's recommendations on critical areas would be sought by Justice and respected. But there would be no large-scale evacuations. It appeared that a paralyzing bureaucratic crisis had been averted.

But then provost marshal Gen. Alan Gullion shifted his weight, cleared his throat, and retrieved a folded paper from the pocket of his military jacket. As provost marshal, General Gullion was the army's chief of police, whose duties included control of enemy aliens. In the days immediately after Pearl Harbor, General Gullion had proposed registering *all* Americans as a security measure. It would be, Gullion argued, a good way to keep a watchful eye on the entire country. With characteristic bluntness Ennis had told him it was a lot of nonsense. "We have a war to fight!" he reminded Gullion. Ennis considered Gullion a lightweight, and the fact that the general's duties with respect to enemy alien control overlapped with Justice was irritating.

But after clearing his throat, Gullion proceeded as if he was delivering the finishing touches to the evening's discussion. He had in his hands, he said, General DeWitt's recommendations.

Ennis and Rowe screwed up their faces. "Recommendations on what? To whom?" They both looked at Biddle, whose hands were still in his pockets and who remained stone faced.

Gullion began reading from the paper he had unfolded. De-Witt recommended "that the Secretary of War receive authority from the President to designate military areas in the combat zones of the Western Theater of Operations." The request for the authority to declare most of Washington, Oregon, California, and Arizona as combat zones came as no surprise. The requests seemed the logical extension of weeks of having DeWitt expand his prohibited zones.

But then came the bombshell: "The Secretary of War may exclude from those combat zones *all* Japanese, *all* enemy aliens, and all other persons suspected for any reason . . . of being actual or potential saboteurs, espionage agents, or fifth columnists."

Rowe and Ennis were incredulous. *"All* enemy aliens? *All* Japanese?"

Gullion was angry now. "Yes, all enemy aliens! And all Japanese!" It was clear that he felt they were all like Kokomo Joe—potentially dangerous human packages of Nipponese dynamite.

But the subject of removing all Japanese hadn't even been discussed, and Ennis and Rowe broke out laughing.

Gullion glared at them both.

Rowe stopped laughing and growled, "Ridiculous!" It was a throwback to the past again, of cavalry rides and sweeping crusades against Indians on the Great Plains.

Rowe glanced at Biddle for support. But Biddle was still stone faced. The martial law procedures, declared and administered by the army that Gullion was spelling out, had been exactly what Biddle had proposed weeks earlier as the only solution to De-Witt's grand evacuation plans.

Gullion stopped reading for a moment, insulted by the laughter and Rowe's charge that what was being proposed was ridiculous.

Rowe was also angry now. "Citizens cannot be taken from their homes," he said, "without at least having individual hearings to establish some dangerousness." Ennis reminded General Gullion that the FBI was on public record as having declared that Japanese Americans presented no special national defense danger.

But Gullion returned to his reading, declaring "that all enemy aliens be evacuated and interned immediately at the time of their evacuation . . . that all Japanese Americans be offered voluntary internment." Gullion stopped and looked up. "If the Japanese refuse," he explained, "they will still be excluded and evacuated from designated military areas." Gullion finished, "Mass internment is largely a temporary expedient until selected resettlement could be achieved."

Colonel Bendetsen nodded after Gullion finished. As far as he was concerned, there was nothing shocking or controversial about what Gullion had read. It had all been decided. FDR had given them "carte blanche." There was no time to try to separate the loyal from the disloyal Japanese. And no matter how much Ennis and Rowe laughed or argued, Biddle had been aware of the final decision. Yes, he had lodged his objections. He had told War that in his judgment the present military situation did not require the removal of U.S. citizens. But then he had said no more.

Ennis and Rowe both looked at Biddle and waited for him to speak. If he wouldn't take issue once again with the army's vapid military necessity arguments, they wanted him to at least say that what Gullion had just read was unconstitutional. But Biddle still said nothing. On behalf of Justice he had already drawn what he felt was a line in the sand. He had made it clear that Justice would not interfere with citizens, whether they were Japanese or not. Now the decision had been made, not just by the half circle of War Department bureaucrats, batmen, and lightweights who sat in his living room but by the president of the United States himself, whose deep, resonant voice put Biddle in a state of respect and awe. Only that afternoon the president had acknowledged that an attack on New York or Detroit might be possible. So who was the attorney general to defy him if he said the West Coast was in danger? Citizens were going to be evacuated. If the president himself said it was a "military matter," then that was the end of it. There was no point in further opposition. From across the room Ennis stared at Biddle and recognized on his boss's usually set jaw the slack of submission.

Masses of American citizens would be rounded up and interned. Among the victims would be a harmless and tiny jockey who had sought sanctuary in the desert. It was, as Rowe had claimed, ridiculous, and the distant radio laughter provoked by the antics of *Fibber McGee and Molly* seemed to suggest that the whole country was laughing. But in Biddle's living room Edward Ennis had to struggle not to cry.

15

The Whiz Kid with the Jive Drive

He stood at the head of a long line at a row of tables set up in the Block 15 mess hall. The Japanese American woman who took down the information in neat printing looked up at him and smiled.

"What is your name?"

"Yoshio Kobuki."

"Do you have an English name?"

"Joe. Kokomo Joe."

"Kokomo Joe?" His English had improved by leaps and bounds over that summer and fall, but he would never have been able to explain how he had earned the nickname "Kokomo Joe."

"Joe," he said. "My English name is just Joe."

The interviewer wrote it down.

"Where were you born?"

"Thomas," he answered and then added "Washington" to avoid the confusion that had arisen at the San Ysidro border station. But the young clerk was still confused. What was he doing reporting to the Colorado River War Relocation Center in Arizona? If he was from Washington, how had he been swept up in the dragnet intended for all Japanese living in southern California and Arizona?

It *was* confusing to Kokomo Joe as well as the young clerk. He had been exercising horses and mucking stalls for Mister Charley in what he thought was the safety of the Gillespie Ranch near Gila Bend. But two days after the meeting in Biddle's living room, President Roosevelt had signed Executive Order 9066, a draft of which General Gullion had read over the distant laughter of *Fibber McGee and Molly*. That order gave General DeWitt and the army the authority to draw up exclusion zones based on military necessity and remove "any or all persons" from them.

Then on February 23 a Japanese submarine had surfaced off the coast of Santa Barbara and lobbed a few shells at oil tanks on shore. Despite the fact that spectators stood on the shore watching as the harmless melodrama unfolded, there were calls to put *all* Japs in concentration camps and keep them there. California especially needed to be preserved as a "white man's paradise" before the Japanese overran the state like rabbits in Australia. Others had argued that it was impossible to determine Japanese loyalty, so General DeWitt had explained that he would "probably take the Japs first, then maybe the Germans and Italians." Those Japanese who tried to assert their patriotism were told that if they *really* wanted to prove their loyalty, they should agree to being placed in concentration camps.

DeWitt's first move on March 3 had been to declare the western half of Washington, Oregon, and California, and the southern half of Arizona as restricted military areas that would be cleared of *all* Japanese, followed by German and Italian enemy aliens. Initially the moves would be voluntary just as they had been with the Department of Justice. But by late March it was clear that DeWitt's voluntary plan had flopped as dramatically as Justice's plan. Where could the relocatees move? Who would accept them? Interior states protested against becoming "dumping grounds" for dangerous spies. Others put it more bluntly: coastal states that needed to be cleared of potential spies and saboteurs should "kill their own snakes."

Throughout March and April 1942 hasty construction was begun on ten sites in six states to be run by the War Relocation Authority for the confinement of all persons of Japanese ancestry. Until such sites were completed, the relocatees would be housed in existing facilities called assembly centers—fairgrounds, racetrack shedrows, Civilian Conservation Corp camps, and army installations. On March 24 DeWitt had begun issuing a series of Exclusion Orders that provided for the evacuation of all Japanese from narrowly proscribed areas. The first such exclusion area was Bainbridge Island in Washington. Eventually there would be 108 exclusion areas, each carefully drawn to encompass a similar number of resident Japanese who would require evacuation.

Throughout March and April DeWitt had continued issuing Exclusion Orders, and the evacuations moved south from Washington, to Oregon, to northern California, then to southern California, and finally to Arizona. Wartime suspension of racing in California had led to a windfall for racing in Arizona, and the Fairgrounds racetrack in Phoenix held daily racing for four weeks in February and March. Kokomo Joe had had no mounts during the meet and had kept a low profile on the Gillespie Ranch as he watched the dragnet of exclusion close around him. But the prospect of him having to be removed seemed remote. After all, what was there for a "Nipponese package of dynamite" to blow up on the Gillespie Ranch? How could he signal enemy submarines from the middle of the Sonoran Desert?

On a light pole in tiny Gila Bend, the authorities posted the Evacuation Notice affecting nearby Japanese, and Kokomo Joe was finally trapped. That trap had been set one hundred and fifty years earlier in the Alien Enemies Act, the codification of the country's general fear of foreigners and the threat they posed to national security. Through innumerable crises and two world wars, that fear had led to dragnets that swept up dangerous enemy alien immigrants from dozens of different countries—France, Austria,

Italy, Germany, Peru, even Canada and Australia, and now the Japanese, thousands of the "little yellow men" who bred like rabbits, swarming and teeming and possibly laying satchel charges or signaling ships.

For a time Kokomo Joe had seemed safe, if not in Mexico, then as just one inconspicuous figure in the Sonoran Desert beyond the reach of such a loose and general dragnet. But all the time the bureaucracies of injustice had been developing the logistical confidence that they could round up and then isolate the enemy before he seized the Pacific slope and overwhelmed the country. What General DeWitt himself described as a "series of intermediate decisions" had led authorities to gradually tighten the dragnet from a general suspicion of five million aliens, to actions against a million German, Italian, and Japanese enemy aliens, and then to an anxious fix on eighty thousand U.S. citizens until only a peanut jockey named Kokomo Joe seemed to be standing as a lone figure on a desolate desert landscape.

Then word spread that, for a fifty dollar fee paid to FBI or Secret Service agents, Japanese farmers in the Salt River Valley around Phoenix could avoid the evacuation dragnet and stay on their farms growing produce for the army and the Red Cross. It seemed a small price to pay for freedom. But the FBI agents were in fact two swindlers—a private investigator and a Phoenix peace officer—preying on desperate Japanese. The truth for Kokomo Joe was that there was no way for him to avoid the evacuation dragnet.

On May 8, 1942, lugging his small cardboard suitcase, he reported with other Japanese from the Salt River Valley to the Mayer Assembly Center in a narrow slice of valley between low mountain ranges north of Phoenix. The group was a small enclave of less than two hundred Japanese, mainly farmers, who hardly had time to plant flowers and vegetable gardens before they were moved east to the Colorado River War Relocation Center in June.

Five thousand workers from the Del Webb construction company had worked double shifts for three weeks to throw up the center, and it became the third largest city in Arizona, holding eighteen thousand persons of Japanese ancestry from southern California as well as Phoenix, Chandler, Tempe, and that lone figure from the Gillespie Ranch. The internees called the center simply Poston after a nearby town that was no more than a grease spot along the ribbon of road running alongside the center. There were no guard towers because the surrounding desert baked everything to a crisp and offered no escape. It was, the internees joked, a Devil's Island in the desert with no bushes, no trees, and no birds.

There were three separate Poston cantonments nicknamed Roastin, Toastin, and Dustin. Each cantonment had wood-and-tarpaper barracks laid out in neat rows and then divided into blocks. And that June day when Kokomo Joe stood in line for his intake interview for Block 15, the internees said it was so hot that it was melting the cast-iron stoves in the block kitchen, so the center had put ice water and salt tablets on the table.

Still, Kokomo Joe dripped sweat in the heat as the young clerk continued her questions. "When were you born? Are you married? What is your father's name?"

"My father is dead," Joe explained.

Kotaro Kobuki had died just three weeks earlier in Washington. He had abandoned his truck farm in the White River Valley and moved in with his son Frank in Seattle. But then he and his son had been ordered to report to the Puyallup Assembly Center at the Puyallup Fairground south of Seattle. Once there, Kotaro Kobuki was overwhelmed by the dislocation and confusion. Where would they be sending him next? And what were they going to do to him? In a matter of days Kotaro Kobuki was dead of a massive stroke that dropped him onto the Puyallup Fairgrounds like a rag doll.

Yoshio had received the sad news while confined at Mayer Assembly Center. There had been no provisions for Kokomo Joe to travel to Washington for the funeral. So Kotaro Kobuki had been cremated and then buried without ceremony in the cemetery in Kent.

"What is your mother's name?"

"Yoshino Maeda Kobuki. She is also dead," he explained, adding that she had died when he was a baby. "I was raised in Japan," he said, "with my brothers and a sister. They all died too."

The clerk looked up at him, and it was a moment before she could phrase her next questions. "How long did you live in Japan? When did you come back to America? Where did you go to school? What is your profession?"

"Jockey."

"You ride horses? In horse races?"

"Yes. OK. Horse jockey."

She was confused over what to ask next. "Are jockeys free spirits, as independent as artists and poets? Or do you work *for* somebody? How much money do they pay you? Where have you raced the horses?"

It was an opportunity to take her through everything he had done since that July meet at Pleasanton. He could have told her that he would have been the leading jockey at Pleasanton if they hadn't conspired against him and then slugged him in the jockeys' room. Every single one of the eighty wins he had eventually posted in 1941—from the anvil clang of the starting gate as it opened, to the fighting for position on the turns, to the tick-tock counting in his head, and then to the stretch runs with wedges and traps and zigzagging horses—were all as clear in his head as if they were on film. He had nearly won the meet at Pleasanton. Then he had won the meet at Santa Rosa. He had won the meet at Humboldt County on the strength of seven straight victories. There had been the dead heat to win the Sacramento Fair title.

He had run away with the meets at Crescent City and Eureka. Finally, he had scored a triple and then a quadruple at Caliente. His picture had been plastered across half the sports section. And all the time Mister Charley had been telling him that he would *never* be any good, a statement that was in fact a compliment so backhanded that it might have been missed if Charley hadn't delivered it with a generous smile and if the turf writers hadn't been calling him "Kokomo Joe . . . the Japanese sensation."

But it all seemed lost now, a part of some other glorious life that wasn't even his, or why would he have been standing in a sweaty line in the sweltering heat while they grilled him like a convict? His life as a jockey seemed so separated from him now that it could just as well have been one of those pictures he had once admired of chauffeured American playboys with their cigarettes. Indeed, his fair circuit appearances, with all the excitement of colorful riding silks and dead heats and flower wreaths in the winner's circle, all could have been just something he had watched on the silver screen. So why even bring it up? He told her only that he had worked on the Gillespie Ranch.

"Have you done any other work?"

"Yes. OK. I was once a chauffeur. I have also trained hunting dogs."

"Do you wish to work in the camp?"

"Yes, I wish to work."

"Where?"

"In the block kitchen." Joe had been told that the kitchen was a good place. The head chef was demanding but very dignified. His roasts and pastries were excellent. He wished to work in the kitchen.

They measured him and weighed him and assigned him to barracks 13, one of the bachelor barracks in Block 15. Here, he worked daily as a kitchen helper, washing dishes for twelve dollars a month. For the first months he only slept and ate and washed dishes. Then in September the internees organized what they called the Yuma County Fair with folk dances and a talent show and pony rides and a queen coronation. Signs went up on the barracks walls and light poles: "All roads lead to the County Fair!" But all the festivities were inside the compound. The only road leading anywhere was outside the barbed wire fence, and it disappeared into both horizons and didn't seem to lead anywhere. It only served to remind Kokomo Joe of the lost glories of the *real* county fairs he had spent six months traveling, with their swing bands and Ferris wheels and horse racing, and so he slept right through the bugle calls and tinny voices on the camp loudspeakers that kept exhorting the internees to "Join the fair crowd! Join the fair crowd!"

Winter came and the temperatures dropped and shrunk the redwood barracks siding so that it was impossible to keep out the bitter desert cold. Spring brought a brief period of purple and yellow flowers in the block gardens, but summer returned with scorpions and howling winds and sandstorms and the sun burning as if through a magnifying glass that turned the landscape back into a campground for the dead. At night the barracks cooked anybody inside like pottery in kilns, and some internees soaked their mattresses in water in an effort to keep cool and fall asleep.

Days, weeks, and months passed, and Kokomo Joe went right on eating and sleeping and washing dishes. He was not even stirred by the news that there was another Japanese mite nicknamed Stump somewhere in Poston who was preparing himself for the possibility of jockey stardom by regularly chinning himself on the barracks rafters. But what was the point of Kokomo Joe preparing for a stardom that he had already gained and then lost, a stardom that now seemed like something out of a motion picture?

Calls came for young Japanese Americans of military age to show their patriotism by volunteering to fight. The military had already rejected Kokomo Joe once for being no more than a stump himself, so he went right on sleeping while hundreds stepped forward to take induction physicals and the bachelor barracks were almost emptied so that there were no more noisy poker games or loud music. He could now sleep without interruptions.

He slept through camp protests and a small riot against stooges in the camp, and the seasons went right on turning as if they were pinned to a wheel. Lonely bugles sounded taps for those soldiers who had gone off to fight but were already beginning to come back in military caskets. The mournful taps played over the camp loudspeakers were painful reminders that his own life seemed to have come to an abrupt end, except that there were no caskets or bugle calls; he could only lie buried alive on his barracks bunk mourning the loss of himself. Meanwhile, those who received permission to leave the camp and resettle in the interior quickly returned to Poston. They couldn't get food, they reported, or gasoline. "There was nothing to do but come back," they said.

Each day that passed for Kokomo Joe in Poston stood as another small piece of his jockey career having been irretrievably lost. The prospect that had once seemed so real of riding at Hollywood Park or Santa Anita or even the big tracks in New York or Florida seemed gone forever because the momentum of a jockey's life was like a horse's in the stretch run. If a horse has to break stride to avoid a collision or to find racing room, it hardly had time to get back in stride again before the race was over. The cryptic "Lost His Action" that appeared the next day in the *Daily Racing Form* charts read like an obituary, and that was Kokomo Joe's fate lying on his bunk in the Poston barracks. General DeWitt's dragnet had caught him, and he had "lost his action." He was dead.

It was a whiz kid with a jive drive who brought Kokomo Joe back to life. His name was Wat Misaka, and he was a sparkplug Japanese American guard for the Utah Utes in the NCAA basketball tournament of 1944. He was from Ogden, Utah, and half a foot taller than Kokomo Joe, but he was fleet and agile on a basketball court. Because General DeWitt had left Utah off his map of declared military zones, Wat Misaka had narrowly escaped DeWitt's dragnet. That the Japanese in Utah were considered harmless and left alone while those in California were considered dangerous seemed as arbitrary a separation as that white line that ran down the middle of the street in Eureka, California, on one side of which certain nationalities were dangerous but on the other side of which, ten feet away, they could shoot pool and slurp patriotic sundaes.

The "Whiz Kids with the Jive Drive," as sportswriters nicknamed the powerful Utes, had swept the NCAA regionals. Then on March 23, 1944, with barracks radios in Poston tuned to the broadcast, Wat Misaka had been not just the darling of interned Japanese sports fans because he reflected what heights of stardom the Japanese could achieve if free, but he was also the darling of fifteen thousand wild fans at Madison Square Garden as the Utes beat Dartmouth in a thrilling overtime game for the NCAA championship.

The whiz kids with the jive drive became the subjects of a Hollywood short film that highlighted their basketball heroics. It put Wat Misaka in exactly the same national spotlight Kokomo Joe would have been enjoying if he had not been on the wrong side of the line that General DeWitt drew in the sand through the Arizona desert. But Misaka's example suggested that maybe Kokomo Joe still a chance for stardom. True, he was twenty-five years old and had lost nearly three years, perhaps the best, of his riding career. Still, jockeys were durable and often ageless. If they weren't crippled or killed in racing accidents, they continued riding into their thirties, sometimes into their forties or even their fifties. Perhaps it wasn't too late for Kokomo Joe. The war couldn't go on forever. If it ended soon, he could return to racing and pick up where he left off—the Japanese sensation on his way to the Big Time.

It was one more long year of waiting before Kokomo Joe was released from Poston in late March 1945. In the Sonoran Desert the saguaro cactus were beginning to bloom early, putting out big white blossoms that suggested peace and reconciliation. But the reality was not peaceful at all. After a long fight the island of Iwo Jima had just been secured. The struggle against the Japanese on Okinawa was still raging. Three years of bloody battle in the south Pacific had only exacerbated the fear and bigotry that had helped close the government's dragnet on the Japanese: in the White River Valley residents were slapping up posters saying "Remember Pearl Harbor" and "We want no Japs here!"

Joe's father was dead. Because of the wartime suspension of racing, there were no meets for Kokomo Joe to enter in California. Even a brief Charities Day Meet at Hollywood Park had brought the ire of the legendary Grantland Rice, who claimed that the distraction of horse racing contributed to absenteeism at war plants. And Mister Charley, who had taken his string of thoroughbreds back East during the war, had disappeared from his life.

Kokomo Joe stood alone with his cardboard suitcase on that highway outside Poston that disappeared into both horizons. South only led deeper into the desert from which there was no escape. And north seemed to go nowhere. So which way should he head now to start over in racing?

16

The Canadian Mounties

Joe had no idea where he was. Or what day it was. Or week. Or month. Each time he opened his eyes, there was a haze in the room that made him wonder if he was back in the bachelor barracks during a Poston sandstorm. A blinding white light spilled from the ceiling. Was this heaven? In which case where were the angels? Or was he experiencing the perfect windless bliss of Nirvana that the Buddhists had tried to teach him about in Japan? But if that was the case, why was he experiencing episodes of pain that shot through his entire body?

It was days before he understood that he was in a hospital somewhere, his right leg fixed to pulleys and weights and a tangle of ropes that seemed to disappear into the white light. He had no immediate recollection of the accident, and he lay drifting in and out of sleep, remembering in pieces everything that had happened to him after he had gotten out of Poston.

He had stood on that disconnected piece of road that ran outside the camp trying to figure out which way to go. He had finally decided to head north, and in the spring of 1946 he had arrived at bullring tracks in the tiny towns of Waitsburg and Dayton, Washington. Here, he hoped to secure mounts as a freelance rider. But he got few good horses to ride, and he had no victories. In June he moved to Longacres outside Seattle, but his horses were all impossible long shots, and he managed only one victory.

In the White River Valley, where he had once found work on the lettuce chainlines and where the ashes of his mother and father were buried, those signs in store windows warned him, "We want no Japs here!" So he moved to Gresham Park outside Portland, but his two mounts opening day in August finished far out of the money, and he got no more rides. By the end of the year he had managed to get only sixteen mounts, mostly hopeless horses, and the lone victory served only to remind him of what was missing from his riding. None of his past riding achievements, including his sweep of the Ferndale card or his seven straight victories there in 1941, appeared in the horse racing record books. It was as if he had been expunged from racetrack memory.

In the spring of 1947 he rode again in the bush leagues of Washington. Once more he had had to settle for only a few mounts. Then one night at a bullring track in Waitsburg, the spectacle of the northern lights, described as wide shafts of "glowing fluorescence" that shot across the night sky, appeared as a reminder of Kokomo Joe's brief spectacular path through horse racing. Yet all but one of the few mounts he managed to get ran out of the money, and there was nothing luminous about his riding. Not long after, at a short meet at the bullring track in Dayton, Washington, the racing was described as a "ding dong affair," but not for Joe Kobuki, whose sorry mounts all finished out of the money.

In June Kokomo Joe had headed for Longacres racetrack again. But his luck was no better at Longacres where swarms of riders fought to be assigned mounts. The competition was so fierce and tempers so short that a huge gathering of jockeys and their families at what was supposed to be a pleasant family picnic alongside a nearby lake turned into a drunken brawl in which a hundred jockeys slugged each other in an angry scrum while their wives screamed at them to stop.

Kokomo Joe had had to flee the possibility of being jailed in Mexico after Pearl Harbor. America had been even worse, and the dragnet had finally swept him up. Now the American press carried stories of the trial of Japanese generals in Tokyo for horrific war crimes and of "Jap man eaters" on Mindanao who survived by cannibalism before finally surrendering. It reminded Kokomo Joe that American wartime hatreds had not gone away, and in search of a safe haven he had traveled to Vancouver, Canada, and bedded down in one of the shedrow stalls at Hastings Park, whose entrance resembled a familiar Japanese pagoda. But he was the first Japanese to enter the shedrows since Japanese Canadians had been sent there as the first step in the Canadian government's wartime relocation program that had rallied around the slogan "No Japs from the Rockies to the Sea." When Kokomo Joe arrived at Hastings Park in July of 1947, the Japanese Canadian relocatees still had not been permitted to return to the coast, and Vancouver newspapers described Kobuki's presence as a "bombshell."

Reporters found him in the shedrows, feeding the horses. "What the hell are you doing at Hastings Park?" they wanted to know.

"I am a jockey," he explained. "I have only come to ride."

"But aren't you uncomfortable? Don't you feel out of place?"

"The horses don't mind who I am," he said, giving his stock answer, "as long as I keep their feed boxes full."

The Canadian Mounties arrived to interrogate him before they gave him permission to ride. Despite newspaper reports that half-mile tracks were "Kobuki's meat," he got few mounts. And when he lost on a mild favorite, the track talk was, "The horse might have won but for its Japanese rider." Elsewhere, reporters wrote that Kokomo Joe Kobuki "didn't have what it takes." He was of "no help" to his horses, they said.

The fear-driven bigotries and anger that had surrounded him during World War II had proved just as bad in Canada, and in the days that followed when the jockeys' agents gathered in front of the racing secretary's office at Hastings Park, his agent could only call out, "Gentlemen! Kobuki is open!" The agent was nearly begging for someone to employ Joe as a rider. Once again, Joe was reduced to exercising an occasional horse in the morning, and a Vancouver turf writer noted, "He is at loose ends right now. But he is hoping that one day he'll be accepted by society."

On September 1, after a dismal performance on a horse named Ocean Moon in the fourth race at Hastings Park, Kokomo Joe had packed his small cardboard suitcase one more time and headed back to the Gillespie Ranch in Arizona, where he knew he could at least keep his skills sharp exercising horses, if nothing else. It had been four years since anybody at the ranch had seen him. The drifters and the gypsy grooms were all gone. And Mister Charley had settled permanently on his ranch in San Ysidro, they told him, just across the border from Tijuana, where he was racing horses every weekend. Mexico was still no place for Kokomo Joe, and he resigned himself to what work he could get on the Gillespie Ranch.

Nobody remembered who he was or cared. He was just another racing bindlestiff. But so were thousands of once-eager jockeys like him. It was the arc of a jockey's life. Many of them entered racing like starbursts, then suddenly disappeared. The few who lasted and became famous—*they* were the freaks. The rest were quietly united by their grand entrance into the world of horse racing, followed by a sudden vaporization. A few of them worked now as grooms and muckers and hot walkers at the Gillespie Ranch. They moved slowly through their ranch chores, their eyes milky with the promise of what might have been.

That spring, a Japanese American baseball player named Bill Shundo had signed with the Chicago White Sox. He was assigned to a Class C team in Bisbee, Arizona, not far from where Kokomo Joe waited for a new opportunity. But in Shundo's first game Arizona fans pelted him with pop bottles, and then the rest of the league's fans boycotted Bisbee games. "Why don't you go back to camp, you yellow Jap!" they shouted at him.

On the Gillespie Ranch the new hot rider had been an apprentice who was young and promising. So what was the point of hiring Kobuki to ride when he would only resurrect wartime anger and get him and his mounts pelted with pop bottles? Bad racing luck, a weak ride, a good horse that simply refused to run—there were already enough ways for a jockey to lose a race. Thus there was no point in contracting for Kokomo Joe's riding services, and he went to work silently alongside the other ranch hands, mucking stalls and occasionally exercising horses.

Early one morning that fall in the half light of dawn, Joe had gone to the shedrows to saddle and exercise a horse whose name he didn't even know. In the predawn quiet an occasional hoof thudded against a stall. Grooms cursed and grunted. Radio music played somewhere, and the smell of coffee brewing in the shedrows followed him as he walked the horse to the training track.

He crossed one of the crude wood bridges across an irrigation ditch, an open sluice gate gushing with running water. He entered the track and stood for a moment at the edge. To the east a nibble of soft red light appeared just over Gila Bend, and he could make out the shadowy figures now of other horses approaching at a gallop as they circled the track. He swung himself into the small exercise saddle and urged the horse into an easy gallop along the rail. There was still a night chill in the desert air, and he stood almost erect in the irons to let his face feel the cool breeze.

He had been galloping along the backside of the exercise track when he heard the sound of a horse approaching at full speed. He moved off the rail, to let what was obviously a horse in full sprint shoot through inside him along the rail. But instead the horse approached as a shadowy figure *outside* him, then slowed to his pace and began to force him steadily toward the rail.

Spontaneous challenges between two exercise boys eager to test themselves or their horses, if only for short sprints in the course of a workout, were not uncommon. But this was more than just a challenge, and Kokomo Joe had to struggle to keep himself and his mount on course. Yet the determined force of the horse and jockey outside him was too strong to overcome, and in a matter of seconds, Kokomo Joe found himself fighting to keep his horse from skidding against the rail. Then his mount hit the rail and bounced into the outside horse. He careened back against the rail again, this time even harder, and the force flipped Kokomo Joe out of the saddle. His legs scissored apart in the air and the rail caught the inside of his right thigh and the bone broke with the snap of a dry stick.

It took almost three hours to get him to the hospital in Phoenix. His right thigh had fractured cleanly as it whipped against the rail and left the bone ends sticking out through a rip in his riding pants like a broken broomstick. In the first light of dawn they had strapped on a traction splint at the training track, but because of the long ride to the Phoenix hospital, the traction hadn't been enough to keep his strong thigh muscles from convulsing and contracting until the bone fragments overlapped.

In Phoenix they surgically widened the break site along the outside of his thigh to nearly a foot, forced the bone ends apart, sawed off just the tips, which had been plunged into the track dirt, and then screwed a metal plate to the bones to rejoin the two ends. When Joe had hit the rail, his kneecap had shattered like a light bulb, and he had also broken his hip, and he lay in the hospital in a morphine haze for weeks in a body cast from his chest to his ankles.

He wound up hospitalized for almost a year. It brought a strange silence to his life. It was as if Kokomo Joe had a volume knob that somebody had been turning down, deadening his life, from the happy cacophony of county fairs with midway barkers and race calls, to the low howling of sandstorms in Poston, and to the near silence now of his hospital room with only the rubbery screech of a nurse's shoes or an occasional yelp of pain somewhere or a lone radio breaking the silence with news of a Joe Louis prize fight or Mahatma Gandhi's assassination.

The news was also that Wat Misaka, whose NCAA basketball exploits had been so encouraging, had signed a contract with the New York Knicks for the 1947–48 season. Misaka was described as a "ball hawk" and "a sensational defensive player," but his signing made only a small impression in a sports world still fascinated by the presence of Jackie Robinson in baseball. Then within weeks of Misaka's signing, he was cut from the Knicks, and the whiz kid with the jive drive soon found himself settling for what competition he could find in bowling leagues in Salt Lake City.

For Kokomo Joe it was just one more piece of discouraging news as he lay in his hospital bed and watched the New Year's celebrations of 1948 come and go. He could hear firecrackers somewhere and snake whistles, but the New Year seemed to hold nothing for him except the prospect of continued hospitalization and more long months of lying flat on his back, immobilized like a tiny Gulliver by ropes and pulleys and weights.

There were no reports in the news of the accident. He had few visitors. One or two of the gypsy grooms from the Gillespie Ranch came and stood at his bedside. They cleared their throats and fiddled nervously with their cowboy hats and told jokes they had heard on Milton Berle's radio program. There were few other visitors, and if anybody asked what had happened to him, he would say only, "They rode me into the rail." Who "they" might have been was left unexplained.

When the doctors sawed off his cast and got him walking again, his knee had frozen and he walked with a stiff leg. Further, weeks of morphine and months of lying in the blind glare of white lights left him with a sense of vagueness and uncertainty, and when the hospital finally let him leave, it was as if he were standing on that Poston road again trying to figure out which way to go.

17

Chester from *Gunsmoke*

Kokomo Joe wore a black fedora with a broad white hatband and sat high up in the bleachers of the Sacramento State Fair on opening day of racing in late August 1985. His oversized glasses made him look especially studious as he held up the racing program and posed for the photographer who circled him, the camera's rapid shutter clicking like a castanet.

The reporter asked him to spell his name.

"K-O-B," he recited slowly, "U-K-I." "Kokomo Joe," he added with a smile.

"Kokomo Joe?"

"It was a nickname," he explained. "They gave it to me when I was riding way back in the forties."

"Is it true that you were the first Japanese American jockey in the United States?"

"As far as I know, yes."

"And how old are you now?"

"Sixty-six."

The reporter flipped the pages of his spiral notepad and looked at his list of questions. That previous January Congressman Norman Mineta, who had been interned as a ten year old, had introduced the Civil Liberties Act that called for a national apology

to the Japanese community and a twenty thousand dollar repa-
rations payment to those who were interned. They had not been
"foreign spies carrying briefcases bulging with secrets," Mineta argued. "The whole nation was, and *still is*," he emphasized,
shamed by what had happened to the U.S. Japanese.

"So what happened to you during the war?" the reporter
asked.

It had been decades since he had been the subject of a news story,
and now nearly forty years of horse racing glory, along with bitter
memories, came in a steady but awkward stream. "I was riding in
Tijuana," he said, "and I had to get out of Mexico in a hurry."

As he spoke, he kept nervously adjusting the tilt of his hat as
if each new angle of the brim released new recollections. He explained that after his accident in Arizona he had headed north
again, this time back to Pleasanton Race Track, where he tried to
make a comeback in racing. Keeping both legs stiff, he could exercise a horse by riding high, bent only at the hips. But the very tight
crouch with which he had ridden and that had prompted compar-
isons between Kobuki and Tod Sloan was no longer possible.

So what was left for him in racing? Hot walking horses in a
monotonous circle while he only imagined the cheers of a fairground crowd was no substitute for the real uproar of a stretch
drive. And the idea of returning to mucking stalls was as demean-
ing as chauffeuring rich playboys.

By June 1948 Joe had become the "only licensed horse trainer
of Japanese ancestry in the United States." His success was immediate, and he won his first race as a trainer at Pleasanton in July
1948. A week later, he had his second win. Then Pleasanton closed,
and the fair circuit continued elsewhere. He moved to new tracks
with the horsemen and stood around the shedrows waiting for
somebody to hire him as a trainer, but no one approached him.
It was as if he were back at Hastings Park in Canada, where his
agent had called sadly, "Gentlemen! Kobuki is open!"

For the next four decades a sport that had once promised to glorify him offered him only trifles. In the fifties he exercised horses at Hollywood Park in the morning, then in the afternoons he parked cars. He bought a rust-red camper-pickup with a sink and a stove, above which he neatly arranged bottles of condiments for his cooking. He outfitted the camper's tiny windows with white curtains and parked it in a trailer park on Century Boulevard across from Hollywood Park. When the horses and trainers moved to another track, he moved with them. Parking cars, he wore a baseball cap that even with the Velcro strap cinched tight was still too big for his tiny head, and there was always an obvious fold in the back where he had safety-pinned it to fit.

He galloped horses for the celebrated trainer Reggie Cornell. In 1958 he was one of the unnamed team of grooms and stable hands and exercise boys who traveled with the famous Silky Sullivan for a disappointing performance in the Kentucky Derby. Then in August 1960 he appeared on the cover of *Turf and Sports Digest* as the outrider for the Preakness winner Royal Orbit with Willie Harmatz in the saddle. But who the outrider was and what he had done remained a mystery.

In the 1970s Hollywood Park officials made him a parking lot captain, who was entitled to wear a military officer's hat and an Ike jacket with epaulets and gold buttons. It was a return to the superficial eminence of his chauffeur's uniform, and there was no hiding the fact that he was just another tiny minion in a uniform who saluted everybody and then smiled like General Eisenhower himself. Otherwise, he was quiet and solitary and dreamy, so much so that one day he waved through and saluted the thief who was stealing his own rust-red pickup.

He had to swing his stiff leg now when he walked. His coworkers wondered how come he limped like Chester on the popular TV program *Gunsmoke*? What had happened to him? He would say only that he broke his leg in a riding accident. "They did it on purpose." Who "they" were remained a mystery.

Over time, because he remained so silent, a host of conflicting mythologies began to accumulate that explained where and when the accident had happened. Some said they heard that it had happened in '47 or '48 at Caliente where there were stories of spectacular spills involving half a dozen jockeys. After one such accident someone remembered one of the jockeys had been left unconscious in the weeds. He had not been discovered until that night after they did a head count in a San Diego hospital and found one jockey still missing. Others said they had heard that Kokomo Joe had nearly been killed in Arizona somewhere. Tucson or Phoenix. Or maybe it had happened at that camp in the desert where they kept "Japs" during the war.

Meanwhile, Jiro Kobuki, the second cousin he had quarreled with in Gardena when he had first come to California in 1938, had married and moved next door to the jockey Angel Valenzuela. When Valenzuela heard that Jiro was related to the stiff-legged Kobuki who parked cars at Hollywood Park and Santa Anita, he told Jiro and his wife Elsie, "You should go see Joe. He's pretty much alone."

They found him gaunt and nearly mute. Elsie Kobuki invited him to come visit. As soon as she started to give him directions, he insisted he could find it on his own. But he still could hardly read English, and freeway signs flashing by were especially difficult. An hour after he was scheduled to arrive at Jiro's, he called from a rest stop in San Diego.

"Where are you?" Elsie wanted to know.

"I'm lost," he admitted. It was the melancholy truth of his life, and with each month and passing year he became more and more a hermit confined to the trailer court on Century Boulevard.

One day in the summer of 1977, while Charley Brown was watching some of his horses run at Caliente racetrack, the diesel furnace in the basement of his ranch house in Chula Vista exploded and sent a tiny mushroom cloud of smoke into the air. Despite the loss of his home, on top of hard times for him in racing, Charley never lost his sense of humor or his engaging smile. Few of Charley's many friends even knew who Kokomo Joe was or what records he had set, but Charley liked to remind them anyway, "I had Kokomo Joe's contract." It was one of the proudest achievements of his life.

After his house burned, Brown moved his racing stock to a neighbor's ranch and slept in the tack room. On August 17, 1977, he arose early as usual but complained of a splitting headache. They made him return to the tack room and lie down, but in a matter of minutes he was dead. Kokomo Joe, who was parking cars that summer at Del Mar, learned the news that night in his pickup camper. Two days later, a huge crowd attended a memorial service for Charley Brown at a funeral home in Chula Vista. It would have been only a matter of an hour's drive for Kokomo Joe down the freeway. But he knew better than to risk getting lost on unfamiliar roads and winding up in Mexico or Los Angeles. Besides, what better tribute was there than his own memories of Mister Charley's broad smile and his ice-water alarms? Instead, Kokomo Joe sat alone in his trailer, grieving that the last connection to his jockey past was gone.

In the 1980s Kokomo Joe was pictured on southern California billboards and even in a TV commercial promoting racing at Del Mar. He was the pony boy in the picture, wearing an exercise rider's helmet and holding the reins of a promising thoroughbred he had led out to have its sore legs massaged in the surf. Few knew that it was Kokomo Joe. He was just an unknown pony boy whom millions of southern Californians saw on billboards or watched on TV. It made his anonymity almost cosmic.

Not long after, the trailer court where he parked his camper announced it was closing. He called Elsie Kobuki again. He had

almost no money. And arthritis had begun to spread the stiff-
ness of his one leg throughout his whole body. He could no longer even mount a horse. And Charley Brown, one of the few who
might have remembered him and been willing to take him in,
was dead.

"I don't know where to go," he told Elsie.

She hardly knew what to tell him. But then he bumped into a
trainer named T. A. Farrell, who owned a small dairy ranch in
the little town of Galt, south of Sacramento. Farrell remembered
having seen Kobuki ride at the Sacramento Fair in 1941 and win
the championship in a thrilling dead heat on the last day.

"You can come and stay on the ranch," Farrell and his wife Jan
told Kokomo Joe. He could live rent free in exchange for odd jobs
around the ranch. A small Social Security allowance would take
care of his other expenses. And even though Farrell had no race
horses at the moment, he offered Kobuki a chance to train whatever horses he acquired. It seemed like a dramatic reversal of fate
for Kokomo Joe, and in the spring of 1985 he had headed for Galt
and the Farrell ranch. Now he sat in the Sacramento Fair bleachers, once again the object of a reporter's curiosity.

"What was the highlight of your career?" the reporter continued with his questioning.

Joe didn't hesitate. "I once swept the card at the Humboldt
County Fair."

"So why did you quit racing?"

"I broke my leg exercising a horse in Arizona." There was no
reference now to the "they" who had forced him into the rail in
the predawn darkness. It would have made the end of Kokomo
Joe's career seem more like an isolated act of villainy than the
shameful World War II tragedy it was.

There was one more brief reversal of fate for Kokomo Joe. In 1988,
not long after the story on Kobuki appeared in the *Sacramento*

Bee, President Reagan signed the Civil Liberties Act, which had been introduced in Congress three years earlier. The act apologized to the Japanese American community for what it had suffered during the war. The government's apology seemed heartfelt. Francis Biddle, the wartime attorney general who had caved in reluctantly to the army's relocation plans, had written before his death that it was the "clamor of politicians" and not military necessity that had caused the suffering. Even J. Edgar Hoover, who seldom expressed regret, insisted that political pressure rather than factual data had led to the unfortunate relocation.

The government's apology was also based on testimony before a Commission on Wartime Relocation and Internment of Civilians that had been formed to investigate the issue. Among those who testified was Edward Ennis, who had nearly wept in Francis Biddle's living room when he learned that the army had plans to tighten the wartime dragnet of fear and suspicion around persons of Japanese ancestry, including American citizens. He told the commission that the internment decision was sheer folly. The commission itself concluded that the exclusion and removal of all persons of Japanese ancestry from the West Coast was done at "tremendous human cost."

Dozens of Japanese Americans appeared before the commission to give sad testimony to what that human cost had been. But the testimony left the impression that relocation had been the work mainly of racists and bigots. What was lost in the chorus of sad voices was *how* it had all gotten started. Not the *how* of construction crews that had quickly thrown up barbed-wire fences and tar-paper barracks for what some called America's concentration camps. Not the *how* of buses and railroad cars that moved tens of thousands of people. Not the *how* of feeding and bedding, of mess halls and quartermasters and "county fairs" inside the camps to help the internees forget they were behind barbed wire.

What got lost was the *how* of a fear of foreigners that was at first so general that it refused to fix itself on race. What got lost was

how that general fear led to a dragnet of suspicion about sabotage and espionage that covered five million aliens. What got lost
was an understanding of *how* that fear was then transformed by
rumors and sensational headlines and frantic radio voices into
frenzy and panic over the prospect of invasion by mysterious
enemy armadas lying hidden in the coastal fog. What got lost
was *how* a German dairy farmer in Marin County had to plead
with his panicked neighbors that his land was not a secret run-
way for airplanes from those enemy armadas. What got lost was
how a slapdash bureaucracy moved quickly and carelessly to respond to the widespread panic. What got lost, finally, was *how*
that slapdash bureaucracy had begun steadily closing the dragnet over the Japanese, one of whom was a harmless jockey no bigger than a peanut.

The Civil Liberties Act awarded a twenty thousand dollar redress payment to each Japanese victim. For many of the victims
the apology was too late and the money was meaningless. But for
Joe Kobuki, whose pickup-camper had finally broken down, the
money was a sudden lifeline, and he bought a brand-new Tudor
Honda. He also bought an old Streamline trailer and parked it
in a copse of oak trees beside Mr. Farrell's ranch house outside
the little town of Galt. His new home, as cozy as a tin cave, was as
self-contained as his rust-red pickup-camper had been but without the condiments because he drove into Galt for breakfast in
the early morning and then dinner in the evenings at a Chinese
restaurant named Polly's with Naugahyde booths and dozens of
entrees served with sweet sauces.

He got a dog and two cats who came in and out of the open
screen door of his Streamline trailer and fed on the leftovers he
brought home each night from Polly's. Then in the late 1980s he
went to Seattle to visit his brother Frank and his family, but the
pictures they all posed for showed a Kokomo Joe with a gaunt,

bony face and a fixity in his eyes that his huge glasses seemed to magnify. There was no trace of that smile that he had once thought would be the passkey to America.

He began battling arthritis, and his limp grew worse. To relieve the pain, he resorted to visits to quack doctors who subjected him to the ancient practice of cupping to suck out the pain. The cupping left keloid scars on his body and provided little relief. Then in 1993 a controlled brush fire in a ditch on the ranch had jumped the ditch and Kokomo Joe had rushed into the middle of the flames trying to stamp it out with his boots. It burned his feet so badly that his two big toes and the tips of all the others had to be amputated.

One morning in February 1997 he had awakened in his tin cave with a huge swelling in his stomach. It was an abdominal aortic aneurysm. He awarded power of attorney for his financial affairs to the Farrells, then went to a hospital in Sacramento for surgery. The doctors made a foot-long incision to get at and repair the aneurysm, but in the process they found cancer and removed half his stomach. His heart stopped four times on the operating table, and each time he had to be shocked back to life with an electric paddle. It was almost an exact rerun of his oven resurrections at birth, signifying that life was just as much a struggle for him at the end as it had been at the beginning.

After the surgery the doctors told him there was nothing more they could do to treat his cancer. Jiro and Elsie Kobuki drove from Los Angeles to visit him. They found him lying in a cranked-up bed in a convalescent hospital in Galt watching TV. He weighed seventy-two pounds. His face was bony, but his eyes were as alert as if he were maneuvering his horse for racing room in the sprint to the finish line.

"I'm gonna lie here like this and die," he told them.

"You aren't going to die," they insisted.

"Yes, I want to stay here and die." He wanted his ashes scattered in the Sacramento River, where they would somehow find their way downriver, across San Francisco Bay, out the Golden Gate, and then be carried along by the currents of the Pacific Ocean back to Japan.

It was perhaps a foolish wish inspired by the myth of ship-wrecked sailors who set bottles adrift with messages that some-how found their way across wide oceans. Furthermore, Japan had never been any more to him than a place with strange music and the smell of kelp. It had been less of a home for him than the So-noran Desert or any of the many shedrows where he had slept. But there was no arguing with him. It was what he wanted, that his ashes would somehow get back to Japan. Not because he thought of Japan as home. It was a stubborn declaration that he did *not* want to rest for eternity in a land that had forsaken him.

Jiro changed the subject. "Joe, you can't stay here in the con-valescent hospital," he said.

"I'm gonna stay here," he insisted.

"You can't do that. This is costing you plenty."

Joe seemed surprised.

"Your insurance won't cover you," Elsie told him. "You have to get up and walk."

He shook his head slowly.

"Joe," Elsie said, "you have to get up and go home."

Home? Where was home? The White River Valley, where he had already died four times? All the different racetracks from Canada to Mexico, where he had lived in the shedrows or worked parking cars? Arizona, where they had locked him up for three years? The hostile Sonoran Desert? The Gillespie Ranch, where another jockey had approached like a night rider and forced him into the rail? His tin cave now?

"Joe, you can't stay here," Elsie repeated. "You *have* to go home."

18

Stargazers

It was a rare celestial event. For two minutes that Sunday, March 9, 1997, stargazers in Russia and China watched the sun disappear behind the moon in a total solar eclipse. In the sudden cold and darkness the incoming Hale-Bopp comet then became visible as a bright globe of light with a long thin tail of stardust. Halfway around the world, in Galt, California, the occurrence of the two rare events stood as a cosmic reminder of the sad arc of Kokomo Joe's life. He had shot like a bright comet trailing stardust through the world of horse racing in 1941. Racing fans had followed his fiery path like stargazers. Then on December 7 the world had suddenly gone dark and cold.

Kokomo Joe did not come out of his trailer that Sunday morning for breakfast. Instead, he spent the morning watching his small TV from an upholstered chair in his Streamline trailer. In mid-afternoon he put out bowls of leftovers from the night before for his cats. At 5:00 p.m. he climbed into his little car and headed two miles into Galt.

He still could not read road signs as they flashed by, and when he tried to go anywhere, he frequently got lost. So he had memorized the route to Polly's restaurant in Galt like a path through the woods: out Mr. Farrell's gravel driveway, right at the mail-box, down the asphalt road, over the railroad tracks, left at the dead end, driving slowly and carefully into town now alongside the bicycle lanes, past all the familiar homes, through the busy intersection with the stoplight in the middle of Galt, and into the lot for Polly's with its red tile roof.

He found a seat in the rear of Polly's in a red Naugahyde booth beneath a ceiling fan that turned slowly. The waitress who nightly took his order for his favorite chicken chow mein noted that he seemed just as silent and stone faced as he was every night. He ate quickly and stared into the open kitchen or into space as if he was reliving his life, especially the twelve years since he had come to Galt.

He finished his dinner at Polly's at 7:00 p.m. and drove back to the ranch. The sky was dark, and there was no sign of the Hale-Bopp comet, which had been visible in the predawn sky in northern California as "an octopus trailing starry tentacles."

Once back in the trailer, he found his two cats asleep in various nooks of the trailer, and he put them outside. Then he closed the door and sat in his TV chair, leafing slowly through the scrapbook in which he had tried again and again to paste together a record of his life. But there wasn't much in it, and what few pictures and news stories there were only traced a sad arc.

There was a picture of him and his brothers and sisters dressed for their departure to Japan after their mother had died, their coats buttoned to the throat against the cold and the baby Yoshio in a knit bonnet that fit his head as tightly as a jockey's cap. There were black and white portraits of his mother and father, both of them handsome and stately in their grimness.

There he was at the apogee of his life, smiling in the saddle in the winner's circle on the runt horse Michaelmas in July 1941 at Santa Rosa and then *still* smiling four months later as he stood beside Charley Brown and weighed out at Caliente after winning four races in one day. There he was two decades later now as a groom, his riding successes all behind him, holding the reins of Silky Sullivan and limping along as he took the great horse for a morning stroll. There he was another decade later on duty at the parking lot gate of Hollywood Park in his Ike jacket and officer's hat.

Finally, there he was at his brother's house in Seattle, trying to twist the deep sad creases in his cheeks into a smile, but all those efforts were defeated by his arthritis and his cancer and his doctor's judgment that he was doomed. He was seizing up like an engine. One leg was as good as useless. He had already lost his toes. Finally, they had removed half his intestines. What else would seize up? What else would be hacked away until there was no place left on his peanut body for medical quacks to fix their glass cups onto him in a hopeless effort to suck out the pain and bad memories?

He closed the scrapbook and sat staring at the dead TV screen. A Southern Pacific freight train delivered lonely warning howls as it crawled through the intersections of Galt. Farther off, an occasional truck passing on U.S. 99 delivered an air horn blast.

He had bought a cheap metal safe in which to keep his documents, along with a long-barreled revolver he had also bought. But he had lost the combination to the safe, and now he had to bend awkwardly in order to pry it open to get the gun out along with a box of bullets. Without returning to the chair, he stood over the kitchen counter, and by the dim glow of a small sink light, he loaded the gun. When he was done, he turned out the sink light. In the dark he planted his feet on the floor of the trailer, bracing himself like a subway straphanger against the pitch and roll of the ride. Then he put the barrel tip to his head just beneath his right ear and pulled the trigger.

It wasn't until the next day when the hungry cats gathered at the door of the trailer that T. A. Farrell found Joe on the floor of his tin cave. There were no obituaries, memorials, news stories, or recollections in the world of horse racing about who he was or what he had done. He had arrived suddenly with the brightness of a comet and then disappeared into the dark.

Two weeks later, the Farrells executed his improbable last wish, which was that his ashes somehow find their way in ocean currents back to Japan. They found a secluded spot along the Sacramento River where the clear blue water slid slowly by. The ashes of Kokomo Joe made a brief milky cloud in the water before they sank and disappeared.

Sources

The source citations are arranged by chapter and page. For repeated newspaper and book citations, the initial reference contains a complete story headline or title. Subsequent references to the same source repeat only an abbreviated headline for newspapers or author and title for books. For dramatic purposes in the narrative, I have reconstructed some likely conversations based on documents, interviews, and newspaper stories. Those reconstructions appear as standard dialogue within quotation marks. The specific sources for the reconstructions are cited.

1. The Pocket Baby

1. *put him in an oven.* Telephone interview with Elsie and Jiro Kobuki, May 17, 2006; interview with Elsie and Jiro Kobuki, Mesquite NV, September 24, 2006; certificate of birth, no. 813, Yoshio Kobuki, Washington State Board of Health, October 18, 1918; Individual Record, Yoshio Kobuki, Evacuee Case Files 1942–46, War Relocation Authority, Record Group 210, National Archives and Records Administration (hereafter cited as NARA, Yoshio Kobuki).

1. *fourth oven resurrection.* Kobuki interview, May 17, 2006.

1. *carry him in the pocket.* Kobuki interview, May 17, 2006.

1. *in the White River Valley.* Stan Flewelling, *Shirakawa: Stories from a Pacific Northwest Japanese American Community* (Auburn WA: Stan Flewelling and the White River Valley Museum, 2002); Brian Niiya, ed., *More Than a Game: Sport in the Japanese American Community* (Los Angeles: Japanese American National Museum, 2000); Patricia Cosgrove and Barb Williams, eds., *White River Valley Museum Guide* (Auburn WA: n.p., n.d.); Joseph Svinth, *Getting a Grip: Judo in the Nikkei Communities of the Pacific Northwest, 1900–1959* (Guelph, Canada: Electronic Journal of Martial Arts and Science, 2003), 134–42; "Wanted: Patriots of the Soil," *Auburn Globe Republican*, March 22, 1918; interview with Mae Iseri Yamada, Auburn WA, April 26, 2006; "Noise Spoils Their Sleep," *Auburn Globe Republican*, December 19, 1934.

2. *the Spanish Flu, an invisible but vicious virus.* John M. Barry, *The Great Influenza: The Epic Story of the Deadliest Plague in History* (New York: Penguin, 2005); Kenneth Knoll, "When the Plague Hit Spokane," Historylink.org, http://www.ncbh.nlm.gov/pubmed/116/7892 (accessed July 25, 2006).

3. *Yoshino Maeda Kobuki was dead.* Certificate of death, no. 749, Yoshino Kobuki, Washington State Board of Health, December 11, 1918; e-mails from Linda Ishii, June 28 and July 5, 2006.

3. *a small cemetery in Kent, Washington.* Certificate of death, Yoshino Kobuki.

3. *Kotaro and Yoshino Kobuki.* E-mail from Linda Ishii, August 8, 2006; Kobuki interview, May 17, 2006; letter to author from Frank Kobuki, December 2, 2004; e-mail from Leslie Smith, Random Acts of Genealogical Kindness, RAOGK. org, June 15, 2006.

3. *Tacoma's Mount Fuji.* Flewelling, *Shirakawa*, 22.

3. *by 1915 hopeful Japanese were coming.* Niiya, *More Than a Game*, 16.

4. *water . . . drink.* Flewelling, *Shirakawa*, 26.

4. *When walking down the street.* Flewelling, *Shirakawa*, 19.

4. *bandy-legged, degenerate, rotten little devils.* "California Land Bill Debated," *San Francisco Chronicle*, February 3, 1909.

4. *white and brown races would never mix.* Flewelling, *Shirakawa*, 44; "Anti Japanese League of Alameda County," May 26, 1913, Thomas School Archives; Editorial, *Sacramento Bee*, July 1921, Thomas School Archives.

4. *send the four younger ones back to Japan.* Ishii e-mail, August 8, 2006; Kobuki interview, May 17, 2006; NARA, Yoshio Kobuki.

4. *Okuma and her husband Hiro.* Ishii e-mail, July 5, 2006.

5. *the couple found a Japanese wet nurse for Yoshio.* Ishii e-mail, July 5, 2006; Kobuki interview, May 17, 2006.

5. *One by one, they were buried in a terraced family graveyard.* Ishii e-mail, July 5, 2006; Kobuki interview, May 17, 2006; "At 66, Racing Still Big Part of Kobuki's Life," *Sacramento Bee*, September 1, 1985.

5. *He kept to himself.* Kobuki interviews, May 17 and September 24, 2006.

5. *often ran away.* Kobuki interviews, May 17 and September 24, 2006; NARA, Yoshio Kobuki.

5. *he was the smallest child in school.* Kobuki interview, September 24, 2006.

6. *All Japan celebrated.* Niiya, *More Than a Game*, 92–100.

6. *dragged onto the dance floor.* Niiya, *More Than a Game*, 100.

6. *In 1934 Hiro Satoh.* "PC Sports," *Pacific Citizen*, July 19, 1947.

7. *he had stopped going to school all together.* Kobuki interview, September 24, 2006.

7. *in September 1934.* NARA, Yoshio Kobuki.

2. Kokomo Joe

8. *He became a solitary figure.* Telephone interview with Junior Nicholson, March 3, 2003; telephone interview with Joe Feren, August 16, 2006; Kobuki interview, September 24, 2006.

8. *The two nearby high schools.* Auburn High School, *1935–36 Auburn Invader* (Auburn WA: Auburn High School, n.d.); Kent High School, *1935–36 Kent Kriterion* (Kent WA: Kent High School, n.d.) (both yearbooks were provided courtesy of the Greater Kent Historical Society Museum, Kent WA); Flewelling, *Shirakawa*, 126.

8. *Japanese American teenagers who were among the very best students.* Auburn High School, *Auburn Invader*; Kent High School, *Kent Kriterion*; "Japanese American Students in White River Valley High Schools—Valedictorian/Salutatorian," statistical table, Thomas School Archives; Flewelling, *Shirakawa*, 55.

9. *The flowers transfer our emotion of love, appreciation, and gratitude, when words somehow fall short.* "Cherry Tree War," Thomas School Archives; "Historic Trees Return to Thomas Academy," Thomas School Archives; Stan Flewelling, "The Thomas Japanese PTA," *Washington State PTA Magazine*, undated, Thomas School Archives.

9. *a five-dollar job to the unemployed as a Christmas gift.* "Jobs Are Scarce," *Auburn Globe Republican*, December 26, 1934.

9. *How do we "shake the depression?"* "Local and Personal News," *Auburn Globe Republican*, September 31, 1934.

10. *National Origin Acts of 1924.* Wikipedia, "Immigration Act of 1924," http://en.wikipedia.org/wiki/Immigration Act of 1924 (accessed June 4, 2006).

10. *Anti-Japanese League of the state of Washington.* Flewelling, *Shirakawa*, 70.

10. *Many times we shall be in despair.* Auburn High School, *Auburn Invader*.

10. *found work in the valley as a lettuce crate packer.* NARA, Yoshio Kobuki.

10. *Lettuce Festivals and a Lettuce Queen.* Flewelling, *Shirakawa*, 148.

10. *He then moved in with his brother Frank.* NARA, Yoshio Kobuki; Kobuki interviews, May 17 and September 24, 2006.

11. *he found temporary jobs around Seattle as a chauffeur.* NARA, Yoshio Kobuki.

11. *It came to a head one afternoon.* Kobuki interview, September 24, 2006.

12. *he showed up at his cousin's home in Los Angeles in late 1938.* NARA, Yoshio Kobuki; Kobuki interview, September 24, 2006; "At 66."

12. *selling groceries at a little store in Gardena.* Kobuki interview, September 24, 2006; Robert Paulus, "Our Gardena Neighbors," October 19, 2007, unpublished.

12. *He shared a bedroom with his cousin's son Jiro.* Kobuki interviews, May 17 and September 24, 2006.

12. *Then one night with Jiro the talk turned into an argument and shouting.* Kobuki interview, September 24, 2006.

12. *his cousin ordered him to leave.* Kobuki interview, September 24, 2006.

13. *he wanted a job "guiding the horse."* "Very Truly Yours," *Rafu Shimpo*, July 13, 1941.

13. *a scornful, singsong chant.* "At 66."

13. *Owners and trainers let him sleep in one of the empty stalls.* "At 66"; "Japanese Jockey Threat for Fair Riding Honors," *Oakland Tribune*, July 9, 1941.

14. *They finally let him exercise horses.* "At 66"; "Our Mat in Turf Classic," *Los Angeles Times*, June 19, 1939.

14. *There had even been a filly named Banzai with Japanese owners.* "Japanese Americans Discover the Horse," *San Francisco Chronicle*, June 29, 1940; "The Story of the Horse Called Banzai," *Pacific Citizen*, June 21, 1946.

15. *Kobuki watched Kayak II, a stablemate of Seabiscuit, win the Santa Anita Handicap.* Wikipedia, "Kayak II," http://en.wikipedia.org/wiki/Kayak II (accessed June 5, 2005).

15. *to Tanforan racetrack in San Bruno.* "At 66."

16. *moved to Bay Meadows racetrack.* "At 66."

16. *a sympathetic trainer told him that the place for him to break in.* "At 66"; "Speed at Golden Track," *Vancouver Daily Province*, August 23, 1947; NARA, Yoshio Kobuki; "Kobuki," *Phoenix Gazette*, January 24, 1941; Editors of the Daily Racing Form, *The American Racing Manual: Edition of 1940* (Chicago: Cecelia, 1940), 56, 599 (hereafter cited as *ARM 1940*).

16. *He rode his first mount in Phoenix on January 11, 1941.* "Arizona Stables to Make Bid for Horse Race Wins," *Arizona Republic*, January 11, 1941; "Today's Race Entries," *Arizona Republic*, January 24, 1941; Editors of the Daily Racing Form, *The American Racing Manual: Edition of 1941* (Chicago: Triangle, 1941), 97 (hereafter cited as *ARM 1941*).

16. *The following Saturday he did no better.* "At Fairgrounds Turf Meeting," *Arizona Republic*, January 18, 1941; "Race Meet Results," *Arizona Republic*, January 18, 1941; "Victory in Fairgrounds Feature," *Arizona Republic*, January 19, 1941; "Race Meet Results," *Arizona Republic*, January 19, 1941.

16. *the "only representative of the Japanese race to venture atop" a thoroughbred.* "Today's Race Entries."

16. *he sprinted to the lead and was racing along all by himself.* "Today's Race Entries."

17. *C. E. "Charley" Brown Jr.* *ARM 1941*, 481A; telephone interview with Francisco "Pancho" Rodriguez, September 4, 2007; NARA, Yoshio Kobuki; *ARM 1940*, 62; "Brown Praises Jockey Sensation," *San Francisco Chronicle*, April 6, 1940.

18. *you sit as tight as any jockey I have ever seen.* "Meadows Seeks Japanese Jockey," *San Francisco Chronicle*, April 17, 1941.

18. *forty dollars a month plus room and board.* "Speed at Golden Track."

18. *The Gillespie Land and Irrigation Company.* DesertUSA, "The Sonora Desert," http://www.DesertUSA (accessed June 16, 2007); "Sam Lindy Outsprints Favorites," *Arizona Republic*, January 13, 1941; "Jockey T. Williams in Saddle Scores," *Arizona Republic*, November 11, 1946; DeFrente.com, "History of Estero La Pinta—Part 1," http://defrente.puerto-penasco.com/editions/399/005.html (accessed May 8, 2007); Kevin Romig, "Gila Bend, Arizona: On the Road Somewhere Else," in *Yearbook of the Association of Pacific Coast Geographers*, vol. 68, 33–52 (Honolulu: University of Hawaii Press, 2006).

3. Mister Charley

19. *on the road to somewhere else.* Romig, "Gila Bend, Arizona."

19. *the heart of the Sonoran Desert.* DesertUSA, "The Sonoran Desert," http://www.DesertUSA (accessed June 16, 2007); Bureau of Land Management, Phoenix Field Office, "Planning on the Sonoran Desert National Monument," http://www.az.blm.gov (accessed July 7, 2006).

19. *As a young man Bernard Gillespie.* Earl MacPherson, *Gillespie's Gold* (Phoenix: Southland, 1973), 6, 8, 13–14, 16, 25, 27, 30; NARA, Yoshio Kobuki; *ARM 1940*, 62; "Jockey T. Williams in Saddle."

20. *they filmed The Gentleman from Arizona on the ranch.* The Gentleman From Arizona, VHS, directed by Earl Haley (1940; Baker City OR: Nostalgia Family Video, 1996).

20. *"Mister Charley," Kokomo Joe took to calling Charley Brown.* "At 66"; *ARM 1941*, 481A; *ARM 1940*, 584; Rodriguez interview, September 4, 2007; "Colorful Border Season," *San Diego Union*, August 31, 1939; taped interview with T. A. and Jan Farrell, Galt CA, March 8, 2006.

20. *He had been born in Kansas in 1905.* Certificate of death, no. 07813, Charles Edward Brown, Jr., August 19, 1977, County Clerk, County of San Diego, California; telephone interview with Jay Jackson, December 15, 2007.

20. *His legs were so bowed.* Jackson interview, December 15, 2007.

20. *a trained mule and a Brahma bull that jumped cars.* "Girl Friday Pays off Record," *San Francisco Examiner*, July 6, 1941; Jackson interview, December 15, 2007.

21. *except cash a mutuel ticket.* "Girl Friday."

21. *if he caught a groom or a jockey.* Jackson interview, December 15, 2007.

21. *Brown and Gillespie Stables, they called themselves.* *ARM 1941*, 42.

21. *he preferred . . . bush league or county fair racetracks.* "Girl Friday."

21. *In 1940 he had only ten victories.* *ARM 1941*, 598.

21. *Mister Charley was always ready to accommodate them.* "Colorful Border Season."

21. *my "Oklahoma Guarantee" on it.* "On the Nose," *San Francisco Examiner*, July 10, 1941.

22. *jockey from Idaho named Ellis Gray.* "Brown Praises Jockey"; "Tanforan Race Fix Revealed by Jockey," *San Francisco Examiner*, April 18, 1941.

22. *southern California gamblers had recruited.* "Syndicate Bet Coup Details," *San Francisco Examiner*, April 19, 1941; "Fixer Had Office in S.F. Hotel," *San Francisco Examiner*, April 22, 1941; CHRB *Records*, F3635:24, 53–67, Office of the Secretary of State, California State Archives, Sacramento.

22. *praise had only served to spoil.* "On the Nose," *San Francisco Examiner*, July 12, 1941.

22. *chance to watch "the new Japanese boy" ride in Phoenix.* "On the Nose," July 12, 1941.

22. *he kept a good seat on a horse.* "On the Nose," July 12, 1941; "Meadows Seeks Japanese Jockey."

22. *tell Kokomo Joe how bad he was.* "On the Nose," July 12, 1941.

23. *teaching the hounds to hunt coons.* NARA, Yoshio Kobuki.

23. *he wanted Mister Charley to tell him what to fix next.* "On the Nose," July 12, 1941.

23. *The nearby town of Gila Bend.* Romig, "Gila Bend, Arizona"; Gila Bend Chamber of Commerce, "From Umparsoytas to Gila Bend—Visitors Welcome!" and "Gila Bend, Arizona: Area Driving Tours," in *Gila Bend Chamber of Commerce Pamphlet* (Gila Bend: Gila Bend Chamber of Commerce, n.d.).

23. *oasis in the desert . . . where weary travelers stopped to rest.* Gila Bend Chamber of Commerce, "From Umparsoytas to Gila Bend."

23. *Brown splashed ice-cold water in Kokomo Joe's face.* "On the Nose," July 12, 1941.

23. *"For the best jockeys," Mister Charley told him.* "On the Nose," July 12, 1941.

24. *In early April 1941.* "Before and After: A Japanese Rider," *Vancouver Daily Province*, June 30, 1947; "Only One of Its Kind," *Rafu Shimpo*, June 1, 1940.

25. *He had brand-new white silks with a bright red "Sky" on the back.* "Special Turf Tilt Set Here," *Arizona Republic*, January 8, 1941.

25. *At the entrance to the Agua Caliente backstretch.* Nicholson interview, March 3, 2003.

4. Brilliant Queen

26. *When the discussion turned to blacks.* Joe Drape, *Black Maestro: The Epic Life of an American Legend* (New York: HarperCollins, 2006); William C. Rhoden, *Forty Million Dollar Slaves: The Rise, Fall, and Redemption of the Black Athlete* (New York: Crown, 2006).

27. *In the Kentucky Derby of 1875.* Rhoden, *Forty Million Dollar Slaves*, 62.

27. *some races were described as race wars.* Drape, *Black Maestro*, 61, 63, 215; Ed Hotaling, *Wink: The Incredible Life and Epic Journey of Jimmy Winkfield* (New York: McGraw-Hill, 2004), 33; Rhoden, *Forty Million Dollar Slaves*, 76; "Negro Jockeys Shut Out," *New York Times*, July 29, 1900; "War among Jockeys," *Chicago Record*, August 13, 1898.

27. *that Nigger was drunk again.* Drape, *Black Maestro,* 21.

27. *Jockey Syndrome.* Rhoden, *Forty Million Dollar Slaves,* 68.

27. *By 1910 blacks had disappeared from racing.* Drape, *Black Maestro,* 215; Rhoden, *Forty Million Dollar Slaves,* 67.

27. *If they were fit for any sport, it was only baseball.* "Japanese Is Hawaii Grid Star," *Pacific Citizen,* November 18, 1925.

27. *Nobody could remember ever having seen one.* "Meadows Seeks Japanese Jockey"; "Only One Of Its Kind"; "Kobuki To Ride at Pleasanton Race Meeting," *Rafu Shimpo,* July 6, 1941; "Very Truly Yours."

27. *the closest thing he'd ever seen to Tod Sloan.* "Meadows Seeks Japanese Jockey."

28. *Agua Caliente's clubhouse.* David J. Beltran, *The Agua Caliente Story: Remembering Mexico's Legendary Race Track* (Lexington: Eclipse, 2004); Agua Caliente Historical Society, "Agua Caliente 1929–1935," http://aguacalientehistoricalsociety.com/agua_Caliente_1929-35 (accessed September 12, 2007); "Meadows Seeks Japanese Jockey"; "Success Story of Race Bigwigs Is Interesting," *San Francisco Chronicle,* August 4, 1941.

28. *His mount would be Brilliant Queen.* "Japanese Jockey Flashes Form to 'Show' on Caliente Track," *San Francisco Chronicle,* April 14, 1941; "Very Truly Yours."

29. *Brilliant Queen broke quickly.* "Caliente Results," *San Francisco Chronicle,* April 14, 1941; "Very Truly Yours."

30. *a horse who was a stopper.* "Very Truly Yours."

30. *She had just been a little "short."* "Very Truly Yours."

30. *turf writer Oscar Otis.* "Presenting One of the Men Behind the Headlines: Oscar Otis," *San Francisco Chronicle,* April 29, 1939; "Oscar Otis Scores in Derby Broadcast," *San Francisco Chronicle,* February 23, 1940; "Will Connolly Says," *San Francisco Chronicle,* October 6, 1942; "Oscar Otis Flies East to Cover Kentucky Derby," *San Francisco Chronicle,* May 2, 1938.

31. *crouched like a monkey and was the "acme of politeness."* "Meadows Seeks Japanese Jockey."

31. *a six-year-old named Fencing Song.* "At 66"; "Before and After"; "Western Horse Racing News," *San Francisco Chronicle,* April 28, 1941; *Daily Racing Form Charts* (Chicago: Triangle, 1941), April 27, 1941 (hereafter all subsequent chart citations are DRF *Charts,* followed by the date of the race).

31. *he was a dangerous "jumper."* "At 66."

32. *Fencing Song broke slowly.* DRF *Charts,* April 27, 1941.

32. *Drifted far to the outside.* DRF *Charts,* April 27, 1941.

32. *He became the object of attention and curiosity.* "Only One of Its Kind."

32. *a four year old named Thames.* "Mexico Record: Agua Double Pays $2606," *San Francisco Chronicle,* June 2, 1941; "Sports," *Rafu Shimpo,* June 8, 1941; "Kobuki Rides in Pair of Winners," *Rafu Shimpo,* June 2, 1941.

33. *He clucks to the horses in Japanese.* "Kobuki to Ride at Meadows," *Rafu Shimpo*, April 20, 1941; "Meadows Seeks Japanese Jockey."

33. *ready for bigger game on the California major circuit.* "Meadows Seeks Japanese Jockey."

33. *would like to see the tiny laddie from Nippon in action.* "Meadows Seeks Japanese Jockey."

34. *baby-faced jockey named Robert Rousseau.* "Racing Today at Caliente," *San Diego Union*, August 13, 1939.

34. *"riding sensation" and owners were reported to be "hot on his trail."* "Youth to Stay at Border Oval," *San Diego Union*, August 18, 1939; "Rousseau's Riding Vies for Interest," *San Diego Union*, August 20, 1939.

34. *Gray admitted on the witness stand, he had pulled horses and fixed races.* "Syndicate Bet Coup Details."

5. The Yankee Doodle Boys

35. *Pleasanton in the Livermore Valley.* California Authority of Racing Fairs, "The History of Horse Racing at Northern California Fairs," http://www.cal fairs.com/about.htm (accessed December 8, 2007); "Crowds Throng Fair" and "Records Sure to Be Broke," *Oakland Tribune*, July 3, 1941; "Pleasanton Ponies Begin Racing Today," *San Francisco Chronicle*, July 3, 1941; "Pleasanton Racing Meet Ends Today," *San Francisco Chronicle*, July 12, 1941.

35. *as spic and span as a Dutch housewife's kitchen.* "Down the Stretch," *Oakland Tribune*, July 3, 1941.

35. *The joint will jump.* "It's County Fair With Slick Finish," *San Francisco Chronicle*, July 3, 1941; "Crowds Throng Fair"; "4000 Fans Set Opening Day Bet Record at Pleasanton," *Oakland Tribune*, July 4, 1941; "County Fair Opens Next Thursday at Pleasanton," *Livermore Herald*, June 27, 1941; "County Fair Underway," *Livermore Herald*, July 4, 1941.

36. *Japanese Will Ride at Pleasanton.* "Japanese Will Ride at Pleasanton," *San Francisco Chronicle*, July 1, 1941; "Kobuki to Ride at Pleasanton Meeting," *Rafu Shimpo*, July 6, 1941.

36. *a six-year-old gelding named My Mint.* "Pleasanton Harness and Running Results," *San Francisco Chronicle*, July 4, 1941.

36. *he lost his cap.* "Make Way for My Mint," *San Francisco Examiner*, July 4, 1941.

36. *sparkling ride.* "Mimosa Victory by 4 Lengths in Inaugural," *San Francisco Examiner*, July 4, 1941.

37. *he answered with an infectious smile to the nickname of Kokomo Joe.* "Very Truly Yours."

37. *Don't forget Kobuki.* "4000 Fans."

37. *The Fourth of July was proclaimed Army and Navy Day.* "12,000 People Fight Way to Buy $82,822 in Bet Tickets," *Oakland Tribune*, July 5, 1941; "County Fair Underway."

37. *blew out the tires of parked bicycles.* "Now Come Stories of the Hot Weather," *Livermore Herald*, July 11, 1941.

37. *only Japanese jockey in the United States.* "Very Truly Yours."

37. *He's no trouble at the gate at all.* "Very Truly Yours."

37. *Hank and Ben and Don and Chew Tobacco Griffin, who was as "Irish as shamrock."* "$66,000 Needed to Inaugurate Race Meeting at Pleasanton," *Oakland Tribune*, July 2, 1941.

38. *The jockey's name was Jimmy Baxter.* "On the Nose," *San Francisco Examiner*, August 19, 1941.

38. *I take care of myself.* "On the Nose," August 19, 1941.

38. *The next day, he remained in his groove.* "Japanese Jockey Rides Three Winners," *San Francisco Chronicle*, July 6, 1941.

38. *the stewards still fined Sherlock fifteen dollars.* "Japanese Jockey Threat."

38. *Japanese Boy Scores.* "Japanese Boy Scores," *San Francisco Chronicle*, July 9, 1941.

39. *Kobuki's riding was described as sensational.* "Japanese Jockey Threat"; "Handle Near Half-Million for Meeting," *San Francisco Chronicle*, July 13, 1941.

39. *fans from "among his own race."* "On the Nose," July 10, 1941.

39. *he preferred spaghetti to rice.* "On the Nose," July 10, 1941.

39. *Willie the Mouse, and he was a northern California racetrack legend.* "Japanese Jockey Threat."

40. *"What do the papers mean," the friend said.* "Japanese Jockey Threat."

40. *He's going to make it tough for the Yankee Doodle boys.* "Japanese Jockey Threat."

40. *Japanese Jockey Threat For Fair Riding Honors.* "Japanese Jockey Threat."

40. *a ten-to-one shot named Bonnie Joe.* "Pleasanton Results," *San Francisco Chronicle*, July 10, 1941; "$270,000 Bet at Pleasanton," *Oakland Tribune*, July 10, 1941.

40. *The three horses hit the finish line together.* "Pleasanton Results," *Oakland Tribune*, July 10, 1941.

41. *one of the jockeys took a swing at Kokomo Joe.* "Very Truly Yours."

41. *The next day, the stewards fined Kokomo Joe.* "Tosca Proves Pleasanton Longshot," *Oakland Tribune*, July 11, 1941; "Young Rider Scores Second Longshot," *San Francisco Examiner*, July 11, 1941.

41. *the other jockeys were jealous of his wins.* "Very Truly Yours."

42. *he hugged the rail too much.* "Very Truly Yours."

42. *a conspiracy to keep him out of the winner's circle that final day.* "Down The Stretch," *Oakland Tribune*, July 14, 1941.

42. *Mr. Big.* "Cohn-ing Tower," *Oakland Tribune*, July 12, 1941.

42. *Jerry Giesler, the chairman of the California Horse Racing Board.* "Giesler Favors Fall Pleasanton Meet," *Oakland Tribune*, July 13, 1941.

43. *The best he could do through the first seven races.* "$270,000 Bet at Pleasanton"; "10,000 to See Final Program," *Oakland Tribune*, July 12, 1941; "Running Results," *San Francisco Chronicle*, July 13, 1941.

43. *Kokomo Joe to tie Schunk came in the last race.* "Running Results."

43. *a nine-year-old gelding named Clyde.* ARM 1941, 624.

44. *The seven-horse field broke cleanly.* "Running Results"; "Down the Stretch," July 14, 1941.

44. *Kokomo Joe still had Clyde on the lead.* DRF Charts, July 12, 1941.

45. *Clyde finished fifth.* "Running Results."

45. *He publicly celebrated Kobuki's performance.* "On the Nose," July 12, 1941.

45. *The press would describe Kokomo Joe as a brilliant rider.* "Handle Near Half-Million For Meeting."

45. *there were protests of innocence with respect to the rumors.* "Down the Stretch," July 14, 1941.

45. *How could they have blocked him.* "Down the Stretch," July 14, 1941.

46. *The horses don't seem to mind who I am.* "American Nisei Jockey Races at British Columbia Track," *Pacific Citizen*, July 19, 1947.

6. Joltin' Joe

47. *stuck a feather in his cap.* Wikipedia, "Yankee Doodle," http://wikipedia.org/wiki/yankee_doodle (accessed July 7, 2007).

47. *Congress passed the Alien and Sedition Acts.* Wikipedia, "Alien Enemies Act: Component Acts," http://wikipedia.org/wiki/alien_and_sedition_acts (accessed July 8, 2007); David McCullough, *John Adams* (New York: Simon and Schuster, 2002), 467, 503–5.

47. *Chinese began pouring into the country.* *Personal Justice Denied: Report of the Commission on the Wartime Relocation and Internment of Civilians* (Washington DC: U.S. Government Printing Office, 1981), 29, 34.

47. *the problem of the hour.* Morton Grodzins, *Americans Betrayed: Politics and the Japanese Evacuation* (Chicago: University of Chicago Press, 1949), 4; *Personal Justice Denied*, 31–32; Wikipedia, "Immigration Act of 1924," http://wikipedia.org (accessed September 17, 2006).

47. *Germans were threatening America from coast to coast.* Michael Sayers and Albert Kahn, *Sabotage: The Secret War against America* (New York: Harper, 1942), 8, 142; Barry, *Great Influenza*, 124.

47. *a new government agency called the General Intelligence Division.* Sayers and Kahn, *Sabotage*, 8.

48. *Hoover and his new agency began keeping index cards.* Sayers and Kahn, *Sabotage*, 15.

48. *fear should be bred in the civilian population.* Barry, *Great Influenza*, 127.

48. *They live like beasts.* Grodzins, *Americans Betrayed*, 14.

48. *the yellowed, smoldering discarded butts in an overfilled ash tray.* Grodzins, *Americans Betrayed*, 8; *Personal Justice Denied*, 38.

48. *the Japanese government still claimed them as citizens if they were born before 1925. Personal Justice Denied*, 39–40.

48. *On the morning of August 24, 1936.* Athan Theodoris, *From the Secret Files of J. Edgar Hoover* (Chicago: Dee, 1991), 180–82.

48. *he brought Secretary of State Cordell Hull and Hoover together.* Theodoris, *From the Secret Files*, 180–82; Stephen Fox, *Fear Itself: Inside the FBI Roundup of German Americans during World War II; The Past as Prologue* (New York: iUniverse, 2005), xxxiii.

49. *He called the lists his Custodial Detention Index.* Lawrence DiStasi, ed., *Una Storia Segreta: The Secret History of Italian American Evacuation and Internment during World War II* (Berkeley: Heyday, 2001), 313; telephone interview with Edward Ennis, January 15, 1982; Edward Ennis, "A Justice Department Attorney Comments on the Japanese American Relocation," in *Japanese-American Relocation Reviewed*, vol. 1, *Decision and Exodus*, Earl Warren Oral History Project (Berkeley: University of California, 1976), 3C–23C.

49. *It was called the Special Defense Unit.* Grodzins, *Americans Betrayed*, 231.

49. *Hoover's so-called ABC lists.* Grodzins, *Americans Betrayed*, 231.

49. *she could only imagine with what satisfaction Hitler would receive the news. Congressional Record*, 77th Cong., 1st sess., May 5, 1939, H 5164.

49. *German liner the Columbus was scuttled.* James J. McBride, *Interned: Internment of the ss Columbus Crew at Ft. Stanton, New Mexico, 1941–1945*, 2nd ed. (Santa Fe: Paper Tiger, 2003), 13–23.

49. *in the mountainous wilds of New Mexico.* "A Camp for Aliens," *Time*, January 27, 1941; Stephen Fox, *The Unknown Internment: An Oral History of the Relocation of Italian-Americans during World War II* (Boston: Twayne Publishers, 1990), 42.

49. *additional camps in North Dakota and Montana.* John Christgau, *Enemies: World War II Alien Internment* (Ames: Iowa State University Press, 1985); Fox, *Unknown Internment*; Ursula Potter, *The Misplaced American* (Bloomington IN: Author House, 2006); Michael Luick-Thrams, ed., *Vanished: German-American Internment, 1941–48* (St. Paul: Traces, 2005).

50. *On May 16, 1940.* Fox, *Fear Itself*, xxxv.

50. *Congress passed the Alien Registration Act.* Spartacus Educational, "The Alien Registration Act," http://spartacus.schoolnet.co.uk/USAalien.htm (accessed July 9, 2007); Fox, *Unknown Internment*, 39; Francis Biddle, *In Brief Authority* (New York: Doubleday, 1962), 110, 151.

50. *It seems to be the fate of aliens.* "Facts Secured in Alien Registration," *Pacific Citizen*, July 1941.

50. *Heinrich Peter Fassbender sat in the spotlight.* "I Was a Gestapo Agent,"

exhibit B, submitted to Special Committee on Un-American Activities, House of Representatives, 77th Cong., 2nd sess., 1941; Edwin J. Murray, "Memo Re: Heinrich Peter Fassbender," File no. 56125/80, World War II Internment Centers, Record Group 85, NARA; "Mr. Dies Delivers," *Time*, December 2, 1940.

50. *newsletter titled* The Hour. Eclectic City, "Treason in Congress," http://www.trussel.com/HF/treason.htm (accessed July 9, 2007).

50. *Lewis Geiger and Gene Hunt.* "FBI Warns of Sabotage," *San Francisco Chronicle*, August 3, 1941.

51. *the FBI agent in charge in San Francisco warned the nation.* "FBI Warns of Sabotage."

51. *piercing terrible screams of the injured.* Sayers and Kahn, *Sabotage*, 3.

51. *the shipyard was crawling with saboteurs.* "Navy Spy Patrol," *San Francisco Chronicle*, July 23, 1941.

51. *to quickly build factories to manufacture defense material.* Reuben Levin, "Labor Beats Back Hysteria," *Machinists' Monthly Journal*, August 1941, 649–50.

51. *drew up the Model Sabotage Prevention Act.* Sam Bass Warner, "The Model Sabotage Prevention Act," *Harvard Law Review* 54, no. 4 (February 1941): 602–31; Levin, "Labor Beats Back Hysteria," 649–50.

51. *the heaven-sent instrument for local tinpot Hitlers.* Levin, "Labor Beats Back Hysteria," 649–50.

51. *Roosevelt employed his own private Sam Spade.* John A. Herzig, "Japanese Americans and MAGIC," *Amerasia Journal* 11, no. 2 (1984): 59.

51. *In mid-May 1941 "Joltin' Joe" DiMaggio.* Michael Seidel, *Streak: Joe DiMaggio and the Summer of '41* (Lincoln: University of Nebraska Press, 2002); Robert W. Creamer, *Baseball and Other Matters in 1941* (Lincoln: University of Nebraska Press, 2000), 5, 170, 185, 212, 282; "56 Game Hitting Streak by Joe Dimaggio," *Baseball Almanac*, http://www.baseball-almanac.com/feats/feats3.shtml (accessed July 4, 2007).

52. *his only flaw seemed to be his crippling heel spurs.* Ernest Hemingway, *The Old Man and the Sea* (New York: Scribner's, 1952), 75.

52. *German and Japanese spies met secretly in New York restaurants.* Department of Defense, *The "Magic" Background of Pearl Harbor*, vol. 3 (Washington DC: Department of Defense, 1978), 506.

52. *Negroes for the purpose of retarding National Defense efforts and to commit sabotage.* Department of Defense, *"Magic" Background*, 507.

52. *a secret organization called British Security Coordination.* Nigel West, *British Security Coordination: The Secret History of British Intelligence, 1940–45* (New York: Fromm International, 1999), x.

52. *to plant rumors—sometimes pure invention and sometimes half-truths.* West, *British Security Coordination*, 109.

52. *News headlines throughout the country.* "U.S. Seeks Evidence of Sabotage in Blast," *San Mateo Times*, November 18, 1940; "Sabotage Hint in Plane Crash,"

Los Angeles Times, April 8, 1948; "Attempts to Block Great Lakes Harbor Laid to Sabotage," *Los Angeles Times*, April 11, 1941; additional headlines can be found in Sayers and Kahn, *Sabotage*, 117–19.

52. *America was being overrun with "little Japs."* "Hearst's Column Turns Spotlight on Residents," *Rafu Shimpo*, February 21, 1941.

52. *the attack would come soon.* "Foreign Agent Haan Finds East Is Happy Hunting Ground, Report," *Rafu Shimpo*, April 7, 1941.

52. *Congressman Dies announced plans.* "Local Newspapers Carry First Inkling," *Rafu Shimpo*, April 10, 1941.

53. *On May 22, 1941, in a rain-interrupted game.* Creamer, *Baseball and Other Matters*, 170.

53. *a German agent met with a Japanese naval officer.* Department of Defense, *"Magic" Background*, 506; "Japan Urged To Use Nazi Tactics," *San Francisco Examiner*, August 9, 1941.

53. *something is going to happen.* "Harbor Guarded in Sabotage Plot," *San Francisco Chronicle*, May 29, 1941.

53. *the INS station in San Francisco announced plans.* "New Division to Curb Espionage," *Rafu Shimpo*, May 27, 1941.

53. *Itaru Tatibana and Toraichi Kono.* "Local: Story of the Day," *Rafu Shimpo*, June 11, 1941; "Story of the Week," *Rafu Shimpo*, June 15, 1941.

53. *Joe DiMaggio broke George Sisler's consecutive game hitting streak.* Creamer, *Baseball and Other Matters*, 188; "DiMag Hits 41-42 On Sunday," *San Francisco Chronicle*, June 30, 1941.

54. *two spy rings of unheroic Nazis.* "FBI Arrests German Spy," *Arizona Republic*, October 19, 1946; Sayers and Kahn, *Sabotage*, 24, 32, 121.

54. *The entire world was being Hitlerized.* "Hitlerizing the Japanese," *Oakland Tribune*, July 14, 1941.

54. *DiMaggio's streak hit forty-six games.* "DiMag's Mark Up to 46!" *San Francisco Examiner*, July 6, 1941; Seidel, *Streak*, 172–74.

54. *a huge fleet of innocuous looking Japanese fishing boats.* "Japan's Spies Active on Coast," *San Francisco Examiner*, July 6, 1941.

55. *it would be understandable but wrong for Japanese people to withdraw.* "Story of the Week."

55. *extended his hitting streak to an unbelievable fifty-six straight games.* Seidel, *Streak*, 193, 201–2.

55. *Fans jumped out of the bleachers to steal his bat or cap.* Creamer, *Baseball and Other Matters*, 214.

56. *Did he get one yesterday?* Creamer, *Baseball and Other Matters*, 6.

56. *Even Philip Marlowe.* Seidel, *Streak*, xii.

56. *The cabbie who drove DiMaggio to Cleveland's Municipal Stadium.* "56 Game Hitting Streak."

56. *DiMaggio went hitless and the streak was over.* Creamer, *Baseball and Other Matters*, 235.

7. The Railbird Witch

57. *in the Valley of the Moon.* Wikipedia, "Sonoma Valley," http://en.wikipedia.org/wiki/Sonoma_Valley (accessed December 10, 2007).

57. *Saturday, August 2.* "Santa Rosa Meeting Gets Away Saturday," *San Francisco Chronicle*, July 28, 1941.

57. *in the winner's circle aboard Michaelmas.* "Santa Rosa Results," *San Francisco Chronicle*, August 3, 1941; "Michaelmas and His Japanese Jockey," *Stockton Record*, August 13, 1941; "$161 Record Payoff Made at Santa Rosa," *San Francisco Examiner*, August 5, 1941.

57. *August 6, he had two more victories.* "Clipper Byrd Sets New Track Record," *San Francisco Examiner*, August 7, 1941; "Santa Rosa Racing News," *San Francisco Chronicle*, August 7, 1941.

58. *Some day you're gonna get it.* "On the Nose," *San Francisco Examiner*, August 9, 1941.

58. *it was going to be his "unlucky" day.* "Jockeys Escape Injury in Santa Rosa Fair Spill," *San Francisco Chronicle*, August 8, 1941; "Sherlock Victim in Collision: Kobuki Escapes," *San Francisco Examiner*, August 8, 1941.

58. *During the third race that afternoon.* "Spill Mars Racing at Santa Rosa Oval," *Los Angeles Times*, August 8, 1941; "On The Nose," August 9, 1941.

58. *My Mint clipped the rear heels of El Gorgorito.* "Sherlock Victim."

59. *then King Cargo, with jockey Bill Sherlock in the saddle, stumbled over My Mint.* "Sherlock Victim."

59. *The fall slammed Sherlock to the ground.* "Sherlock Victim."

59. *rush him to Sonoma County Hospital.* "Sherlock Victim."

59. *"What happened?" Charley Brown asked him.* "On the Nose," August 9, 1941.

60. *I told you it was going to happen.* "On the Nose," August 9, 1941.

60. *he was only afflicted with the "tremors of fright."* "Sherlock Victim."

61. *Japanese "stirrup boy."* "Michaelmas and His Japanese Rider."

61. *In the fifth race he was aboard Michaelmas.* "All Jammed Up," *San Francisco Examiner*, August 9, 1941; "Michaelmas and His Japanese Rider."

62. *tough time finding racing room.* "2 Stakes Top Final Sonoma Fair Card," *San Francisco Examiner*, August 9, 1941.

62. *Suddenly, he had a chance to tie Kobuki, and it came down to the last race.* "Santa Rosa Results," *San Francisco Chronicle*, August 10, 1941; "On the Nose," August 19, 1941.

63. *You gave that horse a bad ride.* "On the Nose," *San Francisco Examiner*, August 13, 1941.

8. The Oriental Invaders

64. *San Joaquin County Fair opened on Friday in Stockton.* "San Joaquin County Fair Opens," *San Francisco Chronicle*, August 15, 1941.

64. *chimps on bikes.* "Just Ethel Scores in Stockton Inaugural," *San Francisco Chronicle*, August 16, 1941.

64. *had to be able to speak English.* "New Breakage Bill," *San Francisco Chronicle*, August 19, 1941.

64. *Brown negotiated with racing officials.* "Kobuki Will Ride," *Stockton Record*, August 20, 1941.

65. *described as dangerous and "cuppy."* "Threatened Strike Forces Directors to Heed Demands," *San Francisco Examiner*, August 19, 1941.

65. *drove up the Redwood Highway.* Interview with Frank Bettendorf, San Carlos CA, August 22, 2006; Diane Hawk, *Touring the Old Redwood Highway: Humboldt County* (Piercy CA: Hawk Mountaintop Publishing, 2004), vii, 27, 44, 45, 55, 74.

65. *Ridgewood Ranch just south of Willits.* Laura Hillenbrand, *Seabiscuit: An American Legend* (New York: Random House, 2001), 336.

65. *Howard dammed one of the ranch's creeks.* Speech by Ridgewood Ranch walking-tour guide, April 28, 2006.

65. *His heart was in the bush leagues and the fair circuit.* "On the Nose," *San Francisco Examiner*, July 6, 1941.

66. *took four days to travel at the turn of the century.* Hawk, *Touring the Old Redwood Highway*, vii.

66. *Good Eats, Visitors Welcome.* Bettendorf interview, August 22, 2006.

66. *opening day of the Humboldt County Fair.* "It's Fair Week Again," *Ferndale Enterprise*, August 8, 1941; Leah Kausen, *A History of the Humboldt County Fair: An Exhibition for All Times* (Ferndale: Humboldt County Fair Association, n.d.); telephone interviews with Hugh Bower, November 19 and 30, 2007; "Program of Events," *Humboldt Times*, August 10, 1941.

67. *Twenty-five hundred soldiers headed for Washington.* "Army Ready for 'Invasion of Coast' Today," *Humboldt Times*, August 10, 1941.

67. *Troops Speed North.* "Troops Speed North to Meet Invader," *Humboldt Times*, August 19, 1941.

67. *oriental origins hovering in the fog bank.* "War Games: Armies Tense, Await Invader," *San Francisco Chronicle*, August 10, 1941.

67. *The attack had begun the previous Monday.* "War Games."

67. *an expected invasion of the entire West Coast.* "Army Ready for 'Invasion.'"

68. *The attacks could come anywhere.* "Army Ready for 'Invasion.'"

68. *an advance column of infantry was already on the way.* "10,000 Men to Pass through Arcata Next Week," *Arcata Union*, August 15, 1941.

68. *Four regiments of infantry from Ft. Ord.* "Advance Guard of Troops Camps at Park Here," *Humboldt Times*, August 17, 1941.

68. *General DeWitt . . . was already on the battlefield.* "Army Ready for 'Invasion.'"

68. *"innumerable battleships"* and *"hordes of dive bombers."* "Advance Guard."

68. *the mood of the troops was described as tense.* "Real Sendoff Is in Store at Ford Ord," *San Francisco Chronicle*, August 10, 1941.

68. *Orson Welles . . . a Martian invasion.* Wikipedia, "The War of the Worlds (radio)," http://en.wikipedia.org/wiki/The_War_of_the_Worlds_(radio) (accessed November 20, 2007).

69. *the biggest war game in the history of Western civilization.* "Enemy Makes Landing in Northwest," *Santa Rosa Independent*, August 14, 1941; "Troops Speed North."

69. *You'll never be any good.* "On the Nose," July 12, 1941.

70. *His name was Edward Heims.* "To the People of Inverness and Point Reyes," *Marin Journal*, August 14, 1941; Eddie Friede to Edward Ennis, December 29, 1941, Eddie Friede File 4290/328, World War II Internment Centers, Record Group 85, NARA; "N Ranch Dispute," *Marin Journal*, August 7, 1941; "In the Matter of the Fight between Two Detainees, Edward Herman Heims . . . , March 29, 1942," Eddie Friede File 4290/328, World War II Internment Centers, Record Group 85, NARA.

70. *to end a malicious whispering campaign against me.* "To the People"; "Marin Rancher Jailed," *San Francisco Chronicle*, December 10, 1941.

70. *I hope only to live here in peace.* "To the People."

70. *described his plea as "touching."* "German Refugee Hurls Charge of Slander," *Mill Valley Record*, August 15, 1941.

71. *invited the FBI agents to come onto his land.* "Marin Rancher Jailed."

71. *as many as five million dangerous aliens could wind up interned.* "5 Million Aliens May Be Interned," *San Francisco Chronicle*, August 11, 1941.

71. *Japan was described as arrogant, brooding, paranoid.* "Is Japanese-U.S. War Inevitable," *Humboldt Standard*, August 14, 1941.

71. *an association of Los Angeles Japanese gardeners.* "Gardeners 'Butt' of Latest 'Spy' Rumors," *Rafu Shimpo*, August 15, 1941.

71. *Japanese merchants . . . had fled after their stores were dynamited.* Grodzins, *Americans Betrayed*, 118.

71. *The four days of racing . . . with the raising of the flag.* "Good Horses Assured for Events Opening Thursday," *Humboldt Times*, August 9, 1941.

72. *Nearly a dozen jockeys were on hand.* "County Fair Races Will Begin Tomorrow," *Humboldt Times*, August 13, 1941.

72. *presented a primer on track slang.* "Horse Language to Be Heard at Ferndale Soon," *Arcata Union*, August 1, 1941.

72. *The stretch at Ferndale was less than half that length.* Editors of the Daily Racing Form, *The American Racing Manual: Edition of 1948* (Chicago: Triangle, 1948), 99A; William Leggett, "It's Been a Long Ride," *Sports Illustrated*, August 7, 1978, 26–29.

72. *Kokomo Joe rode Kriegsman.* "More Racing and Evening Program Awaited at Fair," *Humboldt Times,* August 15, 1941; "Fast Track, Good Weather Mark Opening of Race Meet," *Ferndale Enterprise,* August 15, 1941.

73. *Kobuki poked Kriegsman's head in front.* "Fast Track, Good Weather."

73. *In the third race Schunk and Kobuki again battled it out.* "Fast Track, Good Weather."

73. *Kobuki rode Michaelmas.* "Official Track Records For Co. Fair Given Out," *Ferndale Enterprise,* August 29, 1941; "Fast Track, Good Weather"; "Ferndale Race Results," *Humboldt Times,* August 15, 1941.

73. *In the winner's circle.* "Fast Track, Good Weather."

74. *Michaelmas had broken the Ferndale track record.* "Fast Track, Good Weather."

9. Lumberjacks and Truckers

75. *The bars in Eureka and off the plaza in Arcata were open.* E-mail from Frank Bettendorf, August 9, 2007.

75. *Kokomo Joe rode the favorite Cariel.* "More Racing and Evening Program"; "Today's Entries," *Humboldt Times,* August 15, 1941; "Kokomo Joe Kubuki Sets Records" and "Ferndale Race Results," *Humboldt Times,* August 16, 1941; "Ferndale Races, Opening Results," *The Humboldt Standard,* August 15, 1941.

76. *Kobuki had managed to get Cariel's nose in front at the wire.* "More Racing and Evening Program"; "Today's Entries"; "Kokomo Joe Kubuki Sets Records"; "Ferndale Race Results"; "Ferndale Races, Opening Results."

76. *Kobuki on the lead, the others trailing.* "More Racing and Evening Program"; "Today's Entries"; "Kokomo Joe Kubuki Sets Records"; "Ferndale Race Results"; "Ferndale Races, Opening Results."

76. *a small brass band.* "Grounds Scene of Activity before Opening of Fair," *Humboldt Times,* August 8, 1941.

76. *Burgoo Sal-Lea went down directly in front of the grandstand.* "More Racing and Evening Program"; "Today's Entries"; "Kokomo Joe Kubuki Sets Records"; "Ferndale Race Results"; "Ferndale Races, Opening Results."

77. *He lay lifeless on the track.* "More Racing and Evening Program"; "Today's Entries"; "Kokomo Joe Kubuki Sets Records"; "Ferndale Race Results"; "Ferndale Races, Opening Results."

77. *she began frantically biting one of her legs.* Bower interview, November 30, 2007.

77. *Suddenly, the owner pulled a pistol from his belt.* Bower interview, November 30, 2007.

77. *The crowd . . . immediately fell silent.* "More Racing and Evening Program"; "Today's Entries"; "Kokomo Joe Kubuki Sets Records"; "Ferndale Race Results"; "Ferndale Races, Opening Results"; Bower interview, November 30, 2007.

77. *an eleven-year-old relic named Clear.* "More Racing and Evening Program";

"Today's Entries"; "Kokomo Joe Kubuki Sets Records"; "Ferndale Race Results"; "Ferndale Races, Opening Results."

77. *only bruised and shaken and excused from his mounts.* "More Racing and Evening Program"; "Today's Entries"; "Kokomo Joe Kubuki Sets Records"; "Ferndale Race Results"; "Ferndale Races, Opening Results."

78. *Cold Wave, a twelve-year-old horse.* "More Racing and Evening Program"; "Today's Entries"; "Kokomo Joe Kubuki Sets Records"; "Ferndale Race Results"; "Ferndale Races, Opening Results."

78. *Cold Wave still had enough run in him.* "More Racing and Evening Program"; "Today's Entries"; "Kokomo Joe Kubuki Sets Records"; "Ferndale Race Results"; "Ferndale Races, Opening Results."

79. *some jockeys kept marbles in their cheeks.* Bower interview, November 30, 2007.

79. *a nine-year-old gelding named Beginner's Bait.* "More Racing and Evening Program"; "Today's Entries"; "Kokomo Joe Kubuki Sets Records"; "Ferndale Race Results"; "Ferndale Races, Opening Results."

79. *Kobuki took Beginner's Bait to the front.* "More Racing and Evening Program"; "Today's Entries"; "Kokomo Joe Kubuki Sets Records"; "Ferndale Race Results"; "Ferndale Races, Opening Results."

79. *Goole would not respond and finished a distant second.* "More Racing and Evening Program"; "Today's Entries"; "Kokomo Joe Kubuki Sets Records"; "Ferndale Race Results"; "Ferndale Races, Opening Results."

79. *Newspapers in Arcata, Eureka, Sacramento, Stockton, and even faraway San Francisco took notice.* "More Racing and Evening Program"; "Kokomo Joe Kubuki Sets Records"; "Ferndale Race Results"; "Ferndale Races, Opening Results"; "Kubuki Wins Five in Row!" *San Francisco Examiner*, August 16, 1941; "At 66."

80. *it had been done only twice in American thoroughbred racing.* "Remarkable Jockey Feats," *ARM 1941*, 431–32.

80. *James Lee . . . Herman Phillips.* *ARM 1941*, 432–33.

80. *Fireworks that lifted into the dark sky above the Midway Friday night.* "Program of Events"; "Grounds Scene of Activity."

80. *the largest crowd ever to attend Humboldt County racing.* "Big Crowd Sees Papini Entry Win Feature Handicap," *Humboldt Times*, August 17, 1941.

80. *Kokomo Joe had been beaten up Friday night.* Bower interview, November 30, 2007.

80. *spectators who wanted to see if Kobuki had been beaten.* Bower interview, November 30, 2007.

81. *If he had been beaten up, he showed no sign of it.* Bower interview, November 30, 2007.

81. *a six-to-one long shot named Crystal Lover.* "Ferndale Race Results"; "Big Crowd."

81. *pint-sized Japanese rider.* "Kokomo Joe Kubuki Sets Records."

81. *Despite the repeated bumping, Kobuki won the race.* "Big Crowd."

81. *disqualified Schunk for the bumping.* "Big Crowd."

81. *Aboard Zeluso.* "Big Crowd."

81. *blazing home stretch challenge.* "Big Crowd."

81. *the pup tent army was in place in Sequoia Park.* "Troops Speed North."

81. *in the grandstands there was heavy betting between fans.* Bower interview, November 30, 2007.

82. *his only victory on Sunday.* "Final Races Held at Fair Sunday," *Humboldt Times*, August 19, 1941.

82. *But that accomplishment had been in Australia or Timbuktu or someplace else remote.* ARM 1941, 431–32.

83. *Kobuki would be hailed in Stockton as an emerging star.* "Kubuki Will Ride," *Stockton Record*, August 20, 1941.

10. Joe Btfsplk

84. *Kubuki Will Ride.* "Kubuki Will Ride."

84. *a huge fire back east in Brooklyn Harbor.* "Four Dead, Many Missing," *Los Angeles Times*, August 19, 1941.

85. *home for four hundred suspected saboteurs.* "Navy Spy Patrol."

85. *a Nazi spy and his blond consort.* "Spy Trial: U.S. Charges German Agents," *San Francisco Chronicle*, February 4, 1942.

85. *the Japanese in Hawaii would "cause trouble."* "Hawaiian Japanese Will Cause No Trouble If War Comes," *Stockton Record*, August 15, 1941.

85. *on a three-year-old filly named Timber Girl.* "Stockton Races," *San Francisco Chronicle*, August 22, 1941.

85. *Scotch Straight, came flying through the stretch.* "Scotch Straight Is Surprise Winner" and "Scotch Straight Was the Thing to Buy," *Stockton Record*, August 22, 1941.

85. *Kilgore was eventually declared the winner.* "Scotch Straight Is Surprise Winner."

85. *he should have seen the horse that came "flewing" by him.* "Racing Will Start at Sacramento Today," *San Francisco Examiner*, August 29, 1941.

86. *The mother had prepared a concoction of orange juice and poison.* "Japanese Mother Kills Babe," *Stockton Record*, August 23, 1941.

86. *off his hands so that he could more easily pay his obligations.* "Japanese Mother Kills Babe."

86. *the poor comic book character Joe Btfsplk.* Wikipedia, "Joe Btfsplk," http://en.wikipedia.org/wiki/Joe_Btfsplk (accessed December 12, 2007).

86. *the greatest state fair in the nation.* "Nation's Greatest State Fair Opens," *Sacramento Bee*, August 29, 1941; "Thousands Throng State Fair," *Sacramento Bee*, August 30, 1941.

86. *golf tournament was made to fit the military theme.* "State Fair Golf Competition Will Begin Tomorrow," *Sacramento Bee*, August 29, 1941; "Defense Head Suggests Golf as Conditioner," *Sacramento Bee*, August 29, 1941.

86. *Joe Kobuki had five mounts but only a single victory.* "State Fair Chart," *Sacramento Bee*, August 30, 1941.

87. *It is our prime duty.* Flewelling, *Shirakawa*, 162–63.

87. *he found himself boxed in or trapped on the rail or having to take up.* "State Fair Chart," August 30, 1941; "State Fair Daily Racing Record," *Sacramento Bee*, September 1, 1941.

87. *zigzag riding through the stretch.* "State Fair Daily Racing Record."

87. *stewards dismissed the erratic riding.* "State Fair Daily Racing Record."

87. *Over a hundred thousand fans . . . on Labor Day.* "Labor Day Crowd of 111,604," *Sacramento Bee*, September 2, 1941; "Abbott and Costello Go Over in Big Way," *Sacramento Bee*, September 2, 1941.

87. *Kokomo Joe Kobuki, who did "some of his best riding."* "Sees Thrilling Race," *Sacramento Bee*, September 2, 1941; "Brings 'Em In," *Rafu Shimpo*, September 6, 1941.

87. *I yell at the horses in English.* "Sacramento Daily Feature Story on Jockey Joe Kabuki," *Rafu Shimpo*, August 29, 1941.

88. *Very few horses understand Japanese.* "Sacramento Daily."

88. *smiling package of Nipponese dynamite.* "Sacramento Daily."

88. *For the next three days.* "Sees Thrilling Race"; "State Fair Chart," *Sacramento Bee*, September 3, 1941; "Yesterday's Racing Chart at Fair," *Sacramento Bee*, September 4, 1941; "State Fair Chart," *Sacramento Bee*, September 5 and 6, 1941.

88. *named Isaac Bassett.* ARM 1941, 742, 756; "Yesterday's Racing Chart At Fair."

89. *"slinking" out of Iranian ports bearing opium, the "soul destroying narcotic."* "Opium Trade Is Hit," *Sacramento Bee*, September 3, 1941.

89. *Pieces of the subsequent intelligence . . . appeared in the Los Angeles Times.* Nigel West, *The Sigint Secrets: The Signals Intelligence War, 1900 to Today* (New York: Morrow, 1986), 205–6; Herzig, "Japanese Americans and MAGIC," 47–65.

89. *On Friday . . . Kobuki sprinted to an easy six-length victory.* "State Fair Chart," September 6, 1941.

89. *fairly flying down the outside.* "Many New Records Will Go into Books," *Sacramento Bee*, September 6, 1941.

89. *Saturday morning the stewards suspended Bassett.* "Many New Records."

90. *Veterans Day. Ceremonies at the Sacramento fairgrounds.* "State Fair Closes after Setting New Attendance Mark," *Sacramento Bee*, September 8, 1941; "State Fair Chart," *Sacramento Bee*, September 8, 1941.

90. *six-year-old mare named Hilda May.* "State Fair Chart," September 8, 1941.

90. *in the seventh race Kokomo Joe finished dead last.* "State Fair Chart," September 8, 1941.

91. *the eighth and final race of the day.* "State Fair Chart," September 8, 1941.

91. *aboard Brilliant Queen.* "State Fair Chart," September 8, 1941; "Sacramento Races," *San Francisco Chronicle*, September 7, 1941; "300 Nags Will Arrive," *Fresno Bee*, September 28, 1941.

91. *a four-year-old bay gelding named Wound Stripe.* "State Fair Chart," September 8, 1941; "Sacramento Races"; "300 Nags Will Arrive."

91. *Moving into the backstretch, Brilliant Queen took a one-length lead.* "State Fair Chart," September 8, 1941.

92. *Wound Stripe—from seventh to sixth, fifth.* "State Fair Chart," September 8, 1941.

92. *As the two horses flew at the wire.* "State Fair Chart," September 8, 1941.

92. *the wait for the photo-finish results.* "State Fair Chart," September 8, 1941.

92. *the decision came down from the stewards: dead heat.* "State Fair Chart," September 8, 1941.

11. Miserable Saboteurs

93. *Thursday, September 18, 1941 . . . Yosemite National Park.* "Splendors Of Yosemite," *New York Times*, May 18, 1941; "A Three-Way Attack," *San Francisco Chronicle*, September 19, 1941; National Park Service, U.S. Department of the Interior, "Yosemite," http://www.NPS.gov/archives/yosemite/nature (accessed September 13, 2007).

93. *Biddle stood at the podium in the dining room of the magnificent Ahwahnee Lodge in Yosemite Valley.* "All Individual Liberties Secure, Biddle Declares," *San Francisco Examiner*, September 19, 1941; Yosemite Park, http://www.yosemitepark.com/Accommodations_The Ahwahnee.

93. *The Power of Democracy.* "All Individual Liberties Secure"; "The War Will Not Cost Us Our Liberty," *San Francisco Chronicle*, September 19, 1941.

94. *One headline after another that spring and summer had warned of sabotage and espionage.* "Police Arrest Ex Spy of Italy," *Los Angeles Times*, April 4, 1941; "Spy Suspects Escape Traps," *Los Angeles Times*, April 14, 1941; "Senate Passes Spy Curb Bill," *Los Angeles Times*, May 5, 1941.

94. *deal firmly, yet fairly, with miserable saboteurs.* "All Individual Liberties Secure."

94. *some administrative agencies to run "hog wild."* "Biddle Justifies President's Acts," *New York Times*, September 19, 1941.

94. *U.S. census data from 1940 was being used to identify suspicious persons of "enemy ancestry."* Karen Ebel, "Timeline: 1940," German American Internee Coalition, http://www.gaic.info (accessed November 12, 2007).

94. *Those who made that claim were "timid souls."* "Biddle Justifies President's Acts."

94. *The magnitude of the threatened disaster.* "The War Will Not Cost Us."

95. *Freedom from searches and seizures . . . and trial by jury.* "All Individual Liberties Secure."

95. *individual liberties in America will be safeguarded.* "All Individual Liberties Secure."

95. *All subversive activities must be curbed.* "Biddle Warns U.S. of War Discipline," *New York Times*, June 3, 1941.

95. *The cruel stupidities of vigilantes must not take over.* "Biddle Warns U.S."

95. *Biddle had given "carte blanche" to the president.* "Biddle Justifies President's Acts."

95. *Popular resentment against Japan.* "Fair Treatment for Japanese in California Urged," *Fresno Bee*, October 5, 1941.

96. *Such animus would be un-American.* "Fair Treatment for Japanese."

96. *the four-day Del Norte County Fair.* Mary Brown racing scrapbook (courtesy of Hugh Bower); Bower interview, November 30, 2007.

96. *especially vulnerable to being swamped by a Japanese tsunami.* Wikipedia, "Natural disasters/Tsunamis," http://en.wikipedia.org/wiki/Crescent_City,_ California (accessed June 3, 2007).

97. *eight wins over four days of racing.* Bower interview, November 30, 2007; Mary Brown scrapbook; *Racing Program, Del Norte County Fair* (Crescent City CA: n.p., September 18, 19, and 20, 1941) (courtesy of Stuart Titus, general manager, Humboldt County Fair).

97. *he went to the winner's circle so many times—fourteen in all.* Race Entries, *Ninth District Agricultural Fair* (Eureka CA: n.p., September 25 and 26, 1941) (courtesy of Stuart Titus).

97. *the sensational Japanese rider who had had seven consecutive victories.* "300 Nags Will Arrive."

98. *On Saturday, October 4.* "Fair Races End with $700 Handicap Feature," *Fresno Bee*, October 4, 1941.

98. *Kobuki was on Clyde.* "Horses Avert Tragedy as Starting Gate Stalls," *Fresno Bee*, September 6, 1941.

98. *A small field of six horses broke cleanly from the gate.* "Horses Avert Tragedy."

98. *the chain cable snapped.* "Fans Shudder as Horses Dodge Starting Gate," *Fresno Bee*, October 5, 1941; "Never Blue Wins Fresno Handicap," *Fresno Bee*, October 5, 1941.

99. *dull performances under weak handling.* "Fresno Fair Chart," *Fresno Bee*, October 1, 2, 3, 1941.

99. *turf writers had faulted him for going wide.* "Fresno Fair Chart," October 3, 1941.

99. *or were simply "done early."* "Fresno Fair Chart," *Fresno Bee*, October 4, 1941.

99. *One of the gate crew, waving an arm and throwing dirt.* "Never Blue."

100. *Chiana swerved sharply just short of the gate.* "Never Blue"; "Horses Avert Tragedy."

100. *Clyde swerved even more sharply.* "Never Blue"; "Horses Avert Tragedy."

100. *a horse named Cinar came from dead last to win the race.* "Never Blue."

100. *He crossed the finish line fourth.* "Never Blue."

100. *"Refund the entire mutuel pool!" they screamed.* "Fans Shudder."

100. *one of Charles Howard's horses had crashed at full speed into a stuck gate.* "Fans Shudder."

101. *narrowly escaped a bloody disaster at Fresno.* "Fans Shudder."

101. *Germans and Italians and Japanese were being advised to get out of Mexico.* "Axis Citizens Being Told to Quit Mexico," *San Francisco Chronicle*, September 20, 1941.

12. Nipponese Dynamite

102. *the painted Zebra on the Avenida de la Revolucion.* "Tijuana: Assembly Plant to Zebra," *San Diego Union*, May 24, 1990.

102. *Went down your throat like a torchlight parade.* Beltran, *Agua Caliente Story*, 20.

102. *in the track's dormitory for jockeys and grooms.* Interview with David Beltran, Chula Vista CA, November 5, 2007; e-mail from David Beltran, November 10, 2007; Rodriguez interview, September 4, 2007.

102. *B-17 Flying Fortress bomber in flight.* Life, December 1, 1941.

103. *pull U.S. Marines out of various locations in China.* "Marines Move to Quit China Is Revealed," *Arizona Republic*, November 8, 1941.

103. *Japan was ready to move forward "by other means."* "Marines Move to Quit China."

103. *"the hour of decision" was here for America.* "Head of Navy Says Decision Hour Is Near," *Arizona Republic*, November 12, 1941.

103. *an ultimatum to the Japanese government.* United States Note to Japan, November 26, 1941, Geocities.com, http://www.geocities.com/mark_willey/hullno26.html?200712 (accessed December 13, 2007).

103. *There was no immediate response from Tokyo.* "F.D.R. Calls Navy Aide in Asia Crisis," *Los Angeles Times*, December 2, 1941.

103. *began destroying its records.* Memorandum, "Japanese Intelligence and Propaganda in the United States during 1941," Office of Naval Intelligence, December 4, 1941, *Japanese-American and Aleutian Wartime Relocation, Hearings before the Committee on Administrative Law and Governmental Relations*, 98th Cong., 2nd sess., June 20–21, 27, and September 12, 1984, 529; "F.D.R. Calls Navy Aide."

103. *America was trying to turn the Pacific Ocean into her own pond.* "Japanese Cabinet Avoids U.S. Break," *Los Angeles Times*, December 2, 1941.

103. *the United States must correct her attitude.* "Japanese Cabinet."

104. *urgent personal message to Emperor Hirohito.* "Roosevelt Sends Note to Mikado," *Los Angeles Times*, December 7, 1941.

104. *Johnny Adams, a twenty-six-year-old jockey.* "Adams Spurs Five Winners," *Los Angeles Times*, November 24, 1941.

104. *Junior Nicholson from Imperial, Nebraska.* Interview with Junior Nicholson, Pleasanton CA, November 14, 2002; Nicholson interview, March 3, 2003; "'Big Red' Ready To Fly," *San Francisco Chronicle*, April 15, 1941.

104. *young José Martin del Campo.* Beltran, *Agua Caliente Story*, 92.

104. *Seventeen-year-old Francisco "Pancho" Rodriguez.* Rodriguez interview, September 4, 2007; Beltran, *Agua Caliente Story*, 91, 177.

105. *On Sunday, October 19, he had had three winners.* "Jockey Adams Boots Abide Home" and "Race Results, Entries," *Los Angeles Times*, October 20, 1941.

105. *Japanese Pilot Steals Spotlight.* "Kabuki Rides Four Winners," *Los Angeles Times*, October 26, 1941.

105. *What in the world are you doing.* Farrell interview, March 8, 2006.

105. *Mister Charley told me . . . cut 'em off.* Farrell interview, March 8, 2006.

105. *Shortly after noon that Sunday.* "Seven Face Starter in Mile Feature" and "Agua Caliente Handicap," *San Diego Union*, December 7, 1941; "Favorites Find Going Rough" and "Agua Caliente Form Chart," *San Diego Union*, December 8, 1941.

106. *bettors and railbirds stood in small groups discussing what they had heard.* "Favorites Find Going Rough."

106. *Should all Americans head back across the border.* "Favorites Find Going Rough."

106. *There will never be a barrier between the two countries.* "Favorites Find Going Rough."

106. *"spirit of uneasiness prevailed" throughout the afternoon.* "Favorites find Going Rough."

106. *a small barn called Georgia Stables.* "Agua Caliente Form Chart."

106. *jockeys told him that he better leave the track.* Nicholson interview, March 3, 2003.

107. *The Mexican police are unpredictable.* Nicholson interview, March 3, 2003.

107. *police led him to a bullet-riddled stone wall in front of a firing squad.* "Ben Jones Defies You," *San Francisco Chronicle*, March 15, 1942.

107. *His mount was Precious Moon.* "Agua Caliente Form Chart."

107. *slid easily past Precious Moon.* "Agua Caliente Form Chart."

108. *Two track stewards appeared suddenly in the room.* Nicholson interview, March 3, 2003; Rodriguez interview, September 4, 2007.

108. *the last two races of the day had been cancelled.* DRF *Charts*, December 7, 1941.

108. *They would be sent to a camp in Sonora. Or worse.* Rodriguez interview, September 4, 2007; Stephen Fox, "The Deportation of Latin American Germans, 1941–47: Fresh Legs for Mr. Monroe's Doctrine," in *The Yearbook of German-*

American Studies, vol. 32 (Lawrence: University of Kansas, 1997), 126; Tetsuden Kashima, *Judgment without Trial: Japanese American Imprisonment during World War II* (Seattle: University of Washington Press, 2003), 97; Heidi Gurcke Donald, *We Were Not the Enemy: Remembering the United States Latin-American Civilian Internment Program of World War II* (New York: iUniverse, 2006), 30–31.

108. *You need to drive back across the border, for your safety.* Nicholson interview, March 3, 2003.

108. *named Roy "Tex" McWhorter.* Rodriguez interview, September 4, 2007.

109. *McWhorter raced to the border.* Rodriguez interview, September 4, 2007.

109. *Mexican police . . . stopped him on their side immediately.* "Border Crossing Rules Tightened," *San Diego Union*, December 8, 1941.

109. *drivers who were trying to cross back into the safety of California.* "Border Crossing Rules Tightened"; "Police, Fireman Ready to Protect City," *San Diego Union*, December 8, 1941.

110. *The border was closed to all Japanese nationals.* "Border Crossing Rules Tightened."

110. *he was stopped again.* "Border Crossing Rules Tightened"; "Japanese Held after Raids Here," *San Diego Union*, December 8, 1941; "45 Japanese Held by FBI in County Jail," *San Diego Union*, December 9, 1941.

13. Hoover's Lists

111. *the Baja Peninsula would be the staging point.* Maria Eugenia Bonifaz de Novelo, "The Hotel Riviera del Pacifico," *Journal of San Diego History* 29, no. 2 (Spring 1983).

111. *Axis spies in Mexico were using secret microdots.* West, *British Security Coordination*, 381.

111. *a "boundary outpost" for Japanese spying.* "Japanese Intelligence and Propaganda," 505.

111. *a Japanese diplomatic officer was traveling the West Coast.* "Japanese Intelligence and Propaganda," 522.

111. *in the Hotel Maria Cristina in Mexico City.* Kashima, *Judgment without Trial*, 97.

111. *San Ysidro had tightened its crossing rules.* "Border Crossing Rules Tightened."

112. *an INS immigrant inspector began grilling him.* "45 Japanese Held"; "2303 Aliens Seized since Last Sunday," *San Francisco Chronicle*, December 11, 1941.

112. *But you are also a Japanese citizen.* Department of Defense, *"Magic" Background*, 579.

113. *Persons of Japanese ancestry born anywhere in the world before 1925.* *Personal Justice Denied*, 39.

113. *It was a five-step process that took months.* "Japanese Expatriation Law,"

Pacific Citizen, August 1941; Grodzins, *Americans Betrayed*, 151; Flewelling, *Shirakawa*, 174.

114. *subject to the mandates of the Alien Enemy Control Program.* Biddle, *In Brief Authority*, 208–9; Fox, *Unknown Internment* 164.

114. *It meant that some of Kokomo Joe's belongings would be confiscated.* Biddle, *In Brief Authority*, 208–9.

114. *camps run by the Department of Justice for dangerous enemy aliens.* German American Internee Coalition, "Internment Camps," http://www.gaic.info (accessed December 12, 2007).

114. *with other Japanese aliens who are being rounded up.* "2303 Aliens Seized."

115. *a female Japanese American missionary.* Telephone interview with Don Estes, January 5, 2005.

115. *were taken to the FBI headquarters on Sixth and Broadway in San Diego.* Donald H. Estes and Matthew T. Estes, "Further and Further Away: The Relocation of San Diego's Nikkei Community, 1942," Japanese American Historical Society of San Diego, http://www.jahssd.org/cgi-bin/page2.cgi?donarticle (accessed December 15, 2007); "45 Japanese Held."

115. *joined by interrogators from the Office of Naval Intelligence.* Estes interview, January 5, 2005.

115. *moved to the Department of Justice detention facility for enemy aliens at Big Tujunga Canyon.* Estes interview, January 5, 2005.

115. *Missoula, Montana, and Bismarck, North Dakota.* Fox, *Unknown Internment*, 168, 176–77; DiStasi, *Una Storia Segreta*, 240; Christgau, *Enemies*, 1–85; Fox, *Fear Itself*, 85–105, 108–10; Potter, *Misplaced American*, 46, 117–19.

115. *they were being held on "open charges."* "45 Japanese Held."

115. *teams of FBI agents, joined by local police, swung into action.* "The Alien Roundup," *San Francisco Chronicle*, December 9, 1941.

116. *the authority of the Alien Enemies Act and presidential proclamations focused on enemy aliens.* Biddle, *In Brief Authority*, 206–8.

116. *German Bundists, Italian fascists, and Japanese organizational leaders.* Fox, *Unknown Internment*, 165; DiStasi, *Una Storia Segreta*, 12; *Personal Justice Denied*, 54; "400 German and Italian Agents Arrested as Enemy Aliens," *San Mateo Times*, December 8, 1941; "FBI Rounds Up Alien Enemies," *Los Angeles Times*, December 10, 1941.

116. *more hearsay, rumor, and ethnic gossip than hard evidence.* Christgau, *Enemies*, 50–85; Dr. Arthur Sonnenberg File 4290/391, Wolfgang Thomas File 4290/395, and Edgar Friede File 4290/328, World War II Internment Centers, Ft. Lincoln, Record Group 85, NARA; FBI Alien Enemy Case Files: Dr. Arthur Sonnenberg, Wolfgang Thomas, and Edgar Friede, FBI Records Management Division, Washington DC; "Marin Rancher Jailed."

116. *the arrest of over two thousand enemy aliens in the days immediately following Pearl Harbor.* "2303 Aliens Seized."

116. *around shipyards, coastal gun batteries, power plants, or munitions factories would be cause for arrest.* Personal Justice Denied, 72.

116. *No Jap should be permitted to remain in America.* Grodzins, *Americans Betrayed,* 419.

116. FBI *teams had swept into Terminal Island.* Personal Justice Denied, 108.

117. *they were continuing to pick off German and Italian enemy aliens, among them Edward Heims.* "FBI Rounds Up Marked Japanese, Italians, Germans," *San Diego Union,* December 10, 1941; "Alien Roundup"; "Marin Rancher Jailed."

117. *It would be, newspapers warned, another sneak attack.* "Coast on Alert for Sneak Blow," *San Diego Union,* December 8, 1941.

117. *Hardware stores sold out their supplies of long-handled shovels.* "S.F. People Move to Peninsula for Crisis," *San Mateo Times,* December 11, 1941.

117. *Sentries shot a woman.* "Sentry Shoots S.F. Woman," *San Mateo Times,* December 8, 1941.

117. *be calm, stay home.* "Air Raid Rules," *San Francisco Chronicle,* December 10, 1941.

117. *on December 10 an unusual thunderstorm struck southern California.* "S.D. Blacked Out for Three Hours" and "L.A. Excited; Many Accidents," *San Diego Union,* December 11, 1941.

117. *a great pall of darkness spread.* "S.D. Blacked Out."

118. *Mein Gott! Mein Gott! We're raided.* Tom Clark, "Comments on the Japanese-American Relocation," in *Japanese-American Relocation Reviewed,* vol. 1, *Decision and Exodus,* Earl Warren Oral History Project (Berkeley: University of California, 1976), 16B.

118. *Citizens shot out streetlights.* "L.A. Excited."

118. *dragged from his car and severely beaten.* "S.D. Blacked Out."

118. *Los Angeles hospitals were swamped with calls.* "L.A. Excited."

118. *Decided then to head north for Seattle.* "At 66."

118. *Alien Japanese, Germans, and Italians were being rounded up.* "Alien Roundup"; "FBI Rounds Up"; Grodzins, *Americans Betrayed,* 232.

119. *refused to talk to him.* "Before and After"; "At 66."

119. *there were calls to ship all Japanese back to Japan.* Grodzins, *Americans Betrayed,* 21.

119. *"This is total war," an admiral declared.* "Navy Warns: Think before You Talk," *San Francisco Chronicle,* December 14, 1941.

119. *The recruiters politely escorted him out of the enlistment office.* "Before and After"; "At 66."

119. *loaded with Japanese enemy aliens from Seattle who were being trained to the prison in Missoula.* Flewelling, *Shirakawa,* 181, 189.

119. *which even included family radios, BB guns, and toy telegraph keys.* Flewelling, *Shirakawa,* 185.

119. *railroad workers threatened to strike.* Flewelling, *Shirakawa*, 187.

120. *the racing seasons at various California racetracks had been cancelled.* Biff Lowry, *Hollywood Park: From Seabiscuit to Pincay* (Los Angeles: Hollywood Park, 2003), 35; Herb Phipps, *Bill Kyne of Bay Meadows* (Cranbury NJ: Barnes, 1978), 85.

120. *a wing assembly plant for fighter planes.* John Christgau, *Sierra Sue II: The Story of a P-51 Mustang* (Minneapolis: Great Planes Press, 1993), 14; Lowry, *Hollywood Park*, 35.

120. *thoroughbred owners were shipping their stock back east.* Lowry, *Hollywood Park*, 35.

121. *American troops abandoned Manila to the Japanese.* "Army Quits Manila," *San Francisco Chronicle*, January 3, 1942.

121. *battle kits to a militia bracing itself for a Japanese invasion.* "Australian Isle Taken," *San Francisco Chronicle*, January 23, 1942.

121. *within sixty miles of Moscow.* "Russ in Mozhaisk," *San Francisco Chronicle*, January 19, 1942.

121. *kitchen fat . . . the tin foil from gum wrappers.* Interview with Borel Book Club, December 12, 2007.

121. *headed for Arizona.* "At 66."

14. Fibber McGee

122. *"Mr. President," a young reporter asked, "there are rumors in Washington."* "Washington a Rumor Factory," *Washington Post*, February 18, 1942.

122. *Herbert Hoover had complained.* Suite101, "FDR's Press Conferences," http://suite101.com (accessed October 18, 2007).

122. *a heroic GI who had killed 116 Japanese soldiers.* "One Man Army Kills 116 Japs," *Washington Post*, February 16, 1942.

123. *The enemy could come in and shell New York tomorrow night.* "Washington a Rumor Factory."

123. *Roosevelt took advantage of the silence to lift a piece of paper.* "Washington a Rumor Factory."

123. *in the home of Attorney General Francis Biddle.* Grodzins, *Americans Betrayed*, 266; Biddle, *In Brief Authority*, 126; Walter Isaacson and Evan Thomas, *The Wise Men: Six Friends and the World They Made* (New York: Simon and Schuster, 1986), 197.

123. *The seven men sat in a circle in Biddle's living room.* Grodzins, *Americans Betrayed*, 265–66; Biddle, *In Brief Authority*, 126; James H. Rowe, "The Japanese Evacuation Decision," in *Japanese-American Relocation Reviewed*, vol. 1, *Decision and Exodus*, Earl Warren Oral History Project (Berkeley: University of California, 1976), 29.

123. *For months, under a shaky agreement.* Grodzins, *Americans Betrayed*, 239, 265; Stephen Fox, "General John DeWitt and the Proposed Internment of German

and Italian Aliens during World War II," *Pacific Historical Review*, November 1988, 411; Fox, *Unknown Internment*, 56; "Facts Force America to Stop Pussyfooting," *San Francisco Chronicle*, February 21, 1942; Grodzins, *Americans Betrayed*, 42; Ennis, "A Justice Department Attorney," 19C.

123. *Riding point for the War Department was sixty-two-year-old General John DeWitt.* John DeWitt, *Final Report: Japanese Evacuation from the West Coast, 1942* (Washington DC: U.S. Government Printing Office, 1943), 1–6, 19, 294; Fox, "General DeWitt and the Proposed Internment," 410.

124. *Justice had focused on the removal of only what it considered "dangerous" German, Italian, and Japanese enemy aliens.* Christgau, *Enemies*, 65.

124. *There was no time to separate the sheep from the goats.* Fox, *Unknown Internment*, 46; Herbert Wenig, "The California Attorney General's Office," in *Japanese-American Relocation Reviewed*, vol. 1, *Decision and Exodus*, Earl Warren Oral History Project (Berkeley: University of California, 1976), 11D.

124. *there were "known subversives" among them.* Estes and Estes, "Further and Further Away."

124. *Governor Olson of California warned.* Fox, *Unknown Internment*, 46; "New Army Alien 'Laws' in 48 Hours," *San Francisco Chronicle*, February 26, 1942.

124. *columnist Walter Lippman.* Grodzins, *Americans Betrayed*, 387; DeWitt, *Final Report*, 33–38.

124. *dismissed as "jackasses."* Grodzins, *Americans Betrayed*, 73.

124. *two small prohibited zones—the San Francisco waterfront and the Los Angeles airport.* Grodzins, *Americans Betrayed*, 241.

124. *enemy aliens would have until February 24 to clear out.* Grodzins, *Americans Betrayed*, 241.

125. *The San Francisco Examiner charged that the evacuation timetable was too slow.* Grodzins, *Americans Betrayed*, 265.

125. *third assistant dog catcher.* Grodzins, *Americans Betrayed*, 265.

125. *General DeWitt, who promptly announced he was ready to take charge of the entire program.* Fox, "General John DeWitt," 413.

125. *Ten thousand German, Italian, and Japanese enemy aliens.* Grodzins, *Americans Betrayed*, 249.

125. *necessary and proper acts of national defense.* "Leave It to Washington," *San Francisco Chronicle*, February 1, 1942.

126. *Six vigilantes—the very vigilantes.* DeWitt, *Final Report*, 6; "More about Army Being Ordered to 'Take Over,'" *San Francisco Chronicle*, February 21, 1942; *Personal Justice Denied*, 79; Grodzins, *Americans Betrayed*, 140.

126. *The Japanese race is an enemy race.* DeWitt, *Final Report*, 33–38.

126. *"Do what you think best," the president told Stimson.* Jean Edward Smith, *FDR* (New York: Random House, 2007), 552; Biddle, *In Brief Authority*, 218; Rowe, "The Japanese Evacuation Decision," 34.

126. *Evacuation must be a military decision.* Biddle, *In Brief Authority*, 219.

126. *the San Francisco Chronicle had reported a "tidal wave of demands."* "S.F.

Aliens: Forbidden Zones Virtually Clear," *San Francisco Chronicle*, February 16, 1942; DeWitt, *Final Report*, 33–38; Biddle, *In Brief Authority*, 215; Grodzins, *Americans Betrayed*, 265.

126. *the "insuperable" problem.* Fox, "General John DeWitt," 416.

126. *If there were to be mass evacuations.* Rowe, "The Japanese Evacuation Decision," 10.

127. *Evacuation . . . will create misery and hardship.* Grodzins, *Americans Betrayed*, 266.

127. *Edward Ennis sat in a straight back chair.* Grodzins, *Americans Betrayed*, 266; Ennis, "A Justice Department Attorney," 2C.

127. *suppose you and Rowe are wrong.* Rowe, "The Japanese Evacuation Decision," 12E.

127. *Justice is unequipped to handle mass evacuations for military necessity.* Rowe, "The Japanese Evacuation Decision," 34.

127. *You have to do it. It's military necessity.* Rowe, "The Japanese Evacuation Decision," 34.

127. *Biddle considered it a "mystic cliché."* Biddle, *In Brief Authority*, 226.

127. *Jack McCloy joined.* Isaacson and Thomas, *Wise Men*, 65–68; Ennis, "A Justice Department Attorney," 19C.

127. *the Constitution is just a scrap of paper to me.* Smith, *FDR*, 551.

128. *How can I tell these fellows.* Rowe, "The Japanese Evacuation Decision," 31.

128. *It is all pretty thin stuff.* Rowe, "The Japanese Evacuation Decision," 34.

128. *"cool" the fear.* Ennis, "A Justice Department Attorney," 2C.

128. *Gullion . . . retrieved a folded paper.* Grodzins, *Americans Betrayed*, 266; Biddle, *In Brief Authority*, 217; Ennis interview, January 15, 1982.

128. *"We have a war to fight!" he reminded Gullion.* Ennis, "A Justice Department Attorney," 19C.

128. *He had in his hands . . . General DeWitt's recommendations.* Grodzins, *Americans Betrayed*, 266, 189.

129. *That the Secretary of War receive authority from the president.* DeWitt, *Final Report*, 25, 33–38; Grodzins, *Americans Betrayed*, 266.

129. *The Secretary of War may exclude from those combat zones all Japanese.* DeWitt, *Final Report*, 33–38.

129. *Ennis and Rowe broke out laughing.* Grodzins, *Americans Betrayed*, 266.

129. *Ridiculous.* Grodzins, *Americans Betrayed*, 266.

130. *Citizens cannot be taken from their homes.* Ennis interview, January 15, 1982.

130. *that all enemy aliens be evacuated and interned immediately.* DeWitt, *Final Report*, 33–38.

130. *Mass internment is largely a temporary expedient.* DeWitt, *Final Report*, 33–38.

130. *But then he had said no more.* Rowe, "The Japanese Evacuation Decision," 33; Ennis, "A Justice Department Attorney," 19C.

130. *whose deep, resonant voice put Biddle in a state of respect and awe.* Biddle, *In Brief Authority*, 80.

131. *If the president himself said it was a "military matter," then that was the end of it.* Biddle, *In Brief Authority*, 219.

131. *Ennis had to struggle not to cry.* Ennis interview, January 15, 1982; Grodzins, *Americans Betrayed*, 266.

15. The Whiz Kid with the Jive Drive

132. *in the Block 15 mess hall.* NARA, Yoshio Kobuki; *Personal Justice Denied*, 151–52.

133. *But two days after the meeting in Biddle's living room.* Personal Justice Denied, 85; Grodzins, *Americans Betrayed*, 267; DeWitt, *Final Report*, 25–26; "FDR Orders Army Rule for All Strategic Areas," *San Francisco Chronicle*, February 21, 1942.

133. *remove "any or all persons" from them.* Grodzins, *Americans Betrayed*, 90; Fox, *Unknown Internment*, 61.

133. *a Japanese submarine had surfaced.* "Army and Navy Hunt Attacker by Sea and Air," *San Francisco Chronicle*, February 25, 1942; Rowe, "The Japanese Evacuation Decision," 35.

133. *California especially needed to be preserved as a "white man's paradise."* Grodzins, *Americans Betrayed*, 49.

133. *General DeWitt had explained that he would "probably take the Japs first."* Fox, "General John DeWitt," 421; DeWitt, *Final Report*, 28.

133. *DeWitt's first move on March 3.* Personal Justice Denied, 100–101; "Western Half of Washington, Oregon, California, Southern Arizona," *Pacific Citizen*, March 1, 1942; Fox, *Unknown Internment*, 137; Grodzins, *Americans Betrayed*, 303; DeWitt, *Final Report*, 32, 297; Flewelling, *Shirakawa*, 211–12; "Pacific Coast—a Military Zone," *San Francisco Chronicle*, March 4, 1942.

133. *DeWitt's voluntary plan had flopped.* Personal Justice Denied, 93, 103.

133. *Interior states protested against becoming "dumping grounds" for dangerous spies.* "Enemy Aliens: 200,000 Face Internment," *San Francisco Chronicle*, February 28, 1942; *Personal Justice Denied*, 103.

133. *kill their own snakes.* "The Fifth Column Danger," *San Francisco Chronicle*, February 22, 1942; Grodzins, *Americans Betrayed*, 34.

134. *hasty construction was begun on ten sites in six states.* Personal Justice Denied, 106.

134. *facilities called assembly centers.* Personal Justice Denied, 107, 135–37.

134. *On March 24, DeWitt had begun issuing a series of Exclusion Orders.* Personal Justice Denied, 109; DeWitt, *Final Report*, 49, 53.

134. *Throughout March and April DeWitt had continued issuing Exclusion Orders.*

DeWitt, *Final Report*, 53; Fox, "General John DeWitt," 425; *Personal Justice Denied*, 135.

135. *series of intermediate decisions.* DeWitt, *Final Report*, 1.

135. *a fifty dollar fee paid to FBI or Secret Service agents.* "Private Investigator Convicted of Swindling Arizona Japanese," *Pacific Citizen*, June 4, 1942.

135. *the FBI agents were in fact two swindlers.* "Private Investigator."

135. *On May 8, 1942, lugging his small cardboard suitcase.* NARA, Yoshio Kobuki; "Racing Suspension," *San Francisco Chronicle*, February 22, 1942.

135. *hardly had time to plant flowers and vegetable gardens.* Jeffrey Burton, Mary Farrel, Florence Lord, and Richard Lord, "Mayer Assembly Center," in *Confinement and Ethnicity: An Overview of World War II Japanese American Relocation Sites*, National Park Service, http://www.cr.nps.gov/history/online_books/anthropology74/ce16c.htm (accessed September 16, 2006); *Personal Justice Denied*, 106, 138.

136. *Five thousand workers from the Del Webb construction company.* Burton, Farrel, Lord, and Lord, "Poston Relocation Center," in *Confinement and Ethnicity*; Matthew T. Estes and Donald H. Estes, "Hot Enough to Melt," Japanese American Society of San Diego, http://www.jahssd.org (accessed September 6, 2007); "Nisei in Arizona," *Pacific Citizen*, June 26, 1948.

136. *a Devil's Island in the Desert.* Burton, Farrel, Lord, and Lord, "Poston Relocation Center."

136. *Roastin, Toastin, and Dustin.* Burton, Farrel, Lord, and Lord, "Poston Relocation Center."

136. *the center had put ice water and salt tablets on the table.* *Personal Justice Denied*, 151; Estes and Estes, "Hot Enough to Melt."

136. *Kotaro Kobuki had died just three weeks earlier in Washington.* "Vital Statistics," *Camp Harmony Newsletter*, July 10, 1942, University of Washington Libraries, http://www.lib.washing.edu/exhibits/harmony/exhibit/cycle.html (accessed October 27, 2007).

138. *The head chef was demanding but very dignified.* "Statistics, Profile, Summary," Poston Series no. 5, Block no. 15 (Ithaca NY: Cornell University, Carl Kroch Library, 1942).

138. *barracks 13, one of the bachelor barracks in Block 15.* Burton, Farrel, Lord, and Lord, "Poston Relocation Center."

138. *kitchen helper, washing dishes for twelve dollars a month.* *Personal Justice Denied*, 166; "Burdick in Move to Clarify Status of Kitchen Workers," *Poston Press Bulletin*, September 26, 1942; "Statistics, Profile, Summary."

139. *what they called the Yuma County Fair.* "Programs," *Poston Official Daily Bulletin*, August 16, 1942; "Flash," *Poston Press Bulletin*, October 3, 1942.

139. *All roads lead to the County Fair.* "Flash."

139. *Join the Fair Crowd.* "Poston Fair to be Held as Scheduled," *Poston Press Bulletin*, October 16, 1942.

139. *shrunk the redwood barracks siding.* Burton, Farrel, Lord, and Lord, "Poston Relocation Center."

139. *some internees soaked their mattresses in water.* "How to Keep Cool in Poston," *Poston Official Daily Bulletin,* July 5, 1942.

139. *Japanese mite nicknamed Stump somewhere in Poston.* Wimp Hiroto, "Jockey: George Taniguchi," *Scene Magazine,* June 1954, 6–9.

139. *Calls came for young Japanese Americans. Personal Justice Denied,* 253–54; "Memorial Services," *Poston Daily Bulletin,* November 8, 1944; Morton Grodzins, *The Loyal and the Disloyal* (Chicago: University of Chicago Press, 1956), 110.

140. *a small riot against stooges in the camp. Personal Justice Denied,* 178–79; Burton, Farrel, Lord, and Lord, "Poston Relocation Center."

140. *beginning to come back in military caskets.* "Memorial Services."

140. *There was nothing to do but come back.* "Statistics, Profile, Summary."

140. *His name was Wat Misaka.* "Wat Misaka Will Return to Utah," *Pacific Citizen,* August 31, 1946; "Misaka Leaves for Exhibitions in Honolulu," *Pacific Citizen,* April 12, 1947.

141. *Whiz Kids with the Jive Drive.* "Cinderella Kids," *Pacific Citizen,* October 11, 1948.

141. *the darling of fifteen thousand wild fans at Madison Square Garden.* Douglas Stark, "Wat Misaka: An Asian Basketball Pioneer," *Basketball Digest,* February 2002, HighBeam Research, http://www.highbeam.com/doc/1G1-82258798.html (accessed August 22, 2007); "Utah Whips Dartmouth," *San Francisco Chronicle,* March 29, 1944.

141. *a Hollywood short film that highlighted their basketball heroics.* "Cinderella Kids."

142. *released from Poston in late March 1945.* NARA, Yoshio Kobuki.

142. *in the White River Valley residents were slapping up posters saying "Remember Pearl Harbor" and "We want no Japs here."* Svinth, *Getting a Grip,* 134–42.

142. *Even a brief Charities Day Meet at Hollywood Park.* Lowry, *Hollywood Park,* 36.

142. *Mister Charley . . . had disappeared from his life.* Jackson interview, December 15, 2007.

16. The Canadian Mounties

143. *his right leg fixed to pulleys and weights.* Final Coroner's Report of Investigation—Joe Kobuki, Sacramento County Coroner, March 24, 1997; telephone interview with Dr. Roger Christgau, July 18, 2007; Kobuki interview, May 17, 2006; Farrell interview, March 8, 2006; "At 66."

143. *in the tiny towns of Waitsburg and Dayton.* "Three Day Race Meet Gets Underway Friday, Waitsburg," *Walla Walla Union-Bulletin,* March 25, 1946; "Crowds See Second Big Day of Races," *Walla Walla Union-Bulletin,* March 26, 1946.

144. *In June he moved to Longacres.* DRF *Charts*, June 23, 28, 29, and 30 and July 7, 8, 11, 12, 13, and 18, 1946.

144. *he moved to Gresham Park outside Portland.* DRF *Charts*, August 20, 1946.

144. *In the spring of 1947.* "Waitsburg Talks Racing," *Walla Walla Union-Bulletin*, May 20, 1947; "Three Day Race Meet Gets Underway," *Walla Walla Union-Bulletin*, May 24, 1947; "Racing Program in Waitsburg" and "Saturday Race Results," *Walla Walla Union-Bulletin*, May 25, 1947.

144. *glowing fluorescence.* "Northern Lights Observed Here," *Walla Walla Union-Bulletin*, May 24, 1947.

144. *ding dong affair.* "Dayton Days Program Ends," *Walla Walla Union-Bulletin*, June 2, 1947.

144. *at Longacres where swarms of riders fought to be assigned mounts.* "1947 Turf Opener Today," *Seattle Post-Intelligencer*, June 28, 1947.

144. *a drunken brawl in which a hundred jockeys.* Interview with Dion Dubois, South San Francisco, October 22, 2002; Nicholson interview, March 3, 2003.

145. *"Jap man eaters" on Mindanao.* "Jap Man Eaters Bare Jungle Horrors," *Vancouver Daily Province*, June 9, 1947.

145. *bedded down in one of the shedrow stalls at Hastings Park.* "Before and After"; "American Nisei Jockey."

145. *No Japs from the Rockies to the Sea.* "Rising Wind in British Columbia," *Pacific Citizen*, August 2, 1947; Biddle, *In Brief Authority*, 217.

145. *Vancouver newspapers described Kobuki's presence as a "bombshell."* "American Nisei Jockey."

145. *The horses don't mind who I am.* "Before and After"; "American Nisei Jockey."

145. *The Canadian Mounties arrived.* "American Nisei Jockey."

145. *The horse might have won but for its Japanese rider.* "Runs Different Race" and "The Form Chart," *Vancouver Daily Province*, July 8, 1947.

146. *Gentlemen! Kobuki is open.* "Ken Coppernoll Rides Shasta Sue," *Vancouver Daily Province*, July 29, 1947.

146. *But he is hoping that one day he'll be accepted by society.* "Before and After."

146. *Ocean Moon in the fourth race.* "The Form Chart," *Vancouver Daily Province*, September 2, 1947.

146. *Charley had settled permanently on his ranch in San Ysidro.* Jackson interview, December 15, 2007.

147. *Why don't you go back to camp, you yellow Jap.* "Race Prejudice Forced Shundo from Pro Baseball," *Pacific Citizen*, July 23, 1949.

147. *On the Gillespie Ranch the new hot rider.* "Jockey T. Williams in Saddle."

148. *began to force him steadily toward the rail.* Kobuki interview, May 17, 2006; Farrell interview, March 8, 2006.

148. *right thigh had fractured cleanly.* Final Coroner's Report; Kobuki interview, May 17, 2006; Farrell interview, March 8, 2006.

148. *they surgically widened the break site along the outside of his thigh to nearly a foot.* Final Coroner's Report; Dr. Christgau interview, July 18, 2007.

148. *his kneecap had shattered.* Final Coroner's Report; Kobuki interview, May 17, 2006; Farrell interview, March 8, 2006; telephone interview with Greg Dubois, July 8, 2006; telephone interview with Joe Feren, August 16, 2006.

149. *He wound up hospitalized for almost a year.* "At 66."

149. *Misaka was described as a "ball hawk" and "a sensational defensive player."* "Expect Misaka to Aid Pro Cagers at Gate," *Pacific Citizen,* September 20, 1947.

149. *what competition he could find in bowling leagues in Salt Lake City.* "New York Team Seeks Waivers on Nisei Star," *Pacific Citizen,* November 29, 1947; "Wat Misaka Sprains Ankle in Basketball," *Pacific Citizen,* February 3, 1951.

149. *They rode me into the rail.* Kobuki interview, May 17, 2006; Farrell interview, March 8, 2006.

150. *his knee had frozen and he walked with a stiff leg.* Kobuki interview, May 17, 2006; Farrell interview, March 8, 2006; Greg Dubois interview, July 8, 2006; Feren interview, August 16, 2006.

17. Chester from *Gunsmoke*

151. *high up in the bleachers of the Sacramento State Fair.* "At 66."

151. *"It was a nickname," he explained.* "At 66."

151. *Norman Mineta . . . had introduced the Civil Liberties Act.* "The Civil Liberties Act of 1985," 99th Cong., 1st sess., *Congressional Record—Extension of Remarks* (January 3, 1985), College of Behavioral and Social Sciences, San Francisco State University, http://bss.sfsu.edu/internment/Congressional%20Records/19850103b.html (accessed November 17, 2007).

152. *foreign spies carrying briefcases bulging with secrets.* "The Civil Liberties Act of 1985."

152. *I was riding in Tijuana.* "At 66."

152. *Pleasanton Race Track, where he tried to make a comeback in racing.* "New Nisei Horse Trainer," *Pacific Citizen,* July 24, 1948; "Sports," *Pacific Citizen,* July 2, 1949.

152. *only licensed horse trainer of Japanese ancestry.* "New Nisei Horse Trainer."

152. *won his first race as a trainer at Pleasanton.* "Japanese and Cuban in Spotlight," *San Francisco Chronicle,* July 14, 1948; DRF Charts, July 13, 1948.

153. *in the afternoons he parked cars.* Greg Dubois interview, July 8, 2006; Feren interview, August 16, 2006.

153. *a rust-red camper-pickup with a sink and a stove.* Greg Dubois interview, July 8, 2006; Feren interview, August 16, 2006; Joe Kobuki scrapbook (courtesy of Elsie and Jiro Kobuki).

153. *in a trailer park on Century Boulevard.* Greg Dubois interview, July 8, 2006; Feren interview, August 16, 2006; Kobuki interview, September 24, 2006; Farrell interview, March 8, 2006.

153. *a baseball cap that even with the Velcro strap cinched tight was still too big.* Greg Dubois interview, July 8, 2006.

153. *who traveled with the famous Silky Sullivan.* Kobuki interview, September 24, 2006; Joe Kobuki scrapbook.

153. *on the cover of Turf and Sports Digest. Turf and Sport Digest,* August 1960; e-mail from Dan Smith, July 10, 2000.

153. *a military officer's hat and an Ike jacket.* Joe Kobuki scrapbook.

153. *he was quiet and solitary.* Feren interview, August 16, 2006; Greg Dubois interview, July 8, 2006; Nicholson interview, November 14, 2002; Farrell interview, March 8, 2006.

153. *the thief who was stealing his own rust-red pickup.* Feren interview, August 16, 2006.

153. *he limped like Chester on the popular TV program Gunsmoke.* Feren interview, August 16, 2006.

154. *one of the jockeys had been left unconscious in the weeds.* Beltran interview, November 5, 2007.

154. *Tucson or Phoenix.* Kobuki interview, September 24, 2006; Farrell interview, March 8, 2006.

154. *You should go see Joe. He's pretty much alone.* Kobuki interview, September 24, 2006.

154. *"I'm lost," he admitted.* Kobuki interview, September 24, 2006.

154. *the diesel furnace in the basement of his ranch house.* Jackson interview, December 15, 2007.

155. *I had Kokomo Joe's contract.* Jackson interview, December 15, 2007.

155. *slept in the tack room.* Jackson interview, December 15, 2007.

155. *complained of a splitting headache.* Jackson interview, December 15, 2007; certificate of death, no. 07813, Charles Edward Brown, Jr., August 19, 1977, County Clerk, County of San Diego, California.

155. *in a matter of minutes he was dead.* Jackson interview, December 15, 2007.

155. *a memorial service for Charley Brown.* Jackson interview, December 15, 2007; certificate of death, Charles Brown.

155. *Kokomo Joe was pictured on southern California billboards.* Greg Dubois interview, July 8, 2006; e-mail from Gary Meads, July 12, 2006.

155. *He was the pony boy in the picture.* Greg Dubois interview, July 8, 2006.

156. *I don't know where to go.* Kobuki interview, September 24, 2006.

156. *T. A. Farrell, who owned a small dairy ranch.* Farrell interview, March 8, 2006.

156. *You can come and stay on the ranch.* Farrell interview, March 8, 2006.

156. *in the spring of 1985 he had headed for Galt.* "At 66"; Farrell interview, March 8, 2006.

156. *I broke my leg exercising a horse in Arizona.* "At 66."

157. *President Reagan signed the Civil Liberties Act.* Fox, *Unknown Internment*, 198.

157. *clamor of politicians.* Biddle, *In Brief Authority*, 223.

157. *Hoover . . . insisted that political pressure.* Biddle, *In Brief Authority*, 224.

157. *Among those who testified was Edward Ennis.* *Personal Justice Denied*, vii.

157. *the internment decision was sheer folly.* Ennis interview, January 15, 1982.

157. *tremendous human cost.* *Personal Justice Denied*, 3.

157. *America's concentration camps.* Roger Daniels, *Concentration Camps, USA: Japanese Americans and World War II* (New York: Holt, Rinehart and Winston, 1978).

158. *Civil Liberties Act awarded a twenty thousand dollar redress payment.* Fox, *Unknown Internment*, 198.

158. *a brand-new Tudor Honda . . . an old Streamline trailer.* Kobuki interview, September 24, 2006.

158. *he drove into Galt for breakfast in the early morning.* Farrell interview, March 8, 2006.

158. *Chinese restaurant named Polly's.* Farrell interview, March 8, 2006.

158. *fed on the leftovers he brought home each night from Polly's.* Farrell interview, March 8, 2006.

158. *he went to Seattle to visit his brother Frank and his family.* Kobuki interview, September 24, 2006.

159. *the ancient practice of cupping.* Final Coroner's Report; Dr. Christgau interview, July 18, 2007.

159. *Kokomo Joe had rushed into the middle of the flames.* Farrell interview, March 8, 2006.

159. *his two big toes and the tips of all the others.* Final Coroner's Report.

159. *It was an abdominal aortic aneurysm.* Final Coroner's Report.

159. *went to a hospital in Sacramento for surgery.* Kobuki interview, September 24, 2006.

159. *they found cancer and removed half his stomach.* Kobuki interview, September 24, 2006.

159. *His heart stopped four times on the operating table.* Kobuki interview, September 24, 2006.

159. *"I'm gonna lie here like this and die," he told them.* Kobuki interview, September 24, 2006.

159. *he wanted his ashes scattered in the Sacramento River.* Kobuki interview, September 24, 2006; Farrell interview, March 8, 2006.

160. *Joe, you can't stay here.* Kobuki interview, September 24, 2006.

160. *You have to go home.* Kobuki interview, September 24, 2006.

18. Stargazers

161. *stargazers in Russia and China.* "Double Delight," *Stockton Record*, March 10, 1997.

161. *the incoming Hale-Bopp comet.* "Double Delight"; "Train Accident," *Galt Herald*, March 19, 1997.

161. *Kokomo Joe did not come out of his trailer.* Farrell interview, March 8, 2006.

161. *climbed into his little car and headed two miles into Galt.* Final Coroner's Report; Farrell interview, March 8, 2006.

162. *his favorite chicken chow mein.* Final Coroner's Report; Farrell interview, March 8, 2006.

162. *an octopus trailing starry tentacles.* "Double Delight."

162. *the scrapbook in which he had tried again and again to paste together a record of his life.* Joe Kobuki scrapbook.

163. *a cheap metal safe . . . a long-barreled revolver.* Kobuki interview, September 24, 2006.

163. *he had lost the combination.* Kobuki interview, September 24, 2006.

163. *the barrel tip to his head just beneath his right ear.* Final Coroner's Report.

163. *Farrell found Joe on the floor of his tin cave.* Final Coroner's Report; Farrell interview, March 8, 2006.

164. *the Farrells executed his improbable last wish.* Farrell interview, March 8, 2006; Kobuki interview, September 24, 2006.

www.ingramcontent.com/pod-product-compliance
Ingram Content Group UK Ltd.
Pitfield, Milton Keynes, MK11 3LW, UK
UKHW030630150325
456285UK00001B/10